STARRY SKY ADVENTURES ARIZONA

HIKE, PADDLE, AND EXPLORE UNDER NIGHT SKIES

Isaiah Ortiz

FALCONGUIDES

ESSEX, CONNECTICUT

FALCONGUIDES®

An imprint of Globe Pequot, the trade division of
The Rowman & Littlefield Publishing Group, Inc.
4501 Forbes Blvd., Ste. 200
Lanham, MD 20706
Falcon.com

Falcon and FalconGuides are registered trademarks and Make Adventure Your Story is a
trademark of The Rowman & Littlefield Publishing Group, Inc.

Distributed by NATIONAL BOOK NETWORK

Photos by Isaiah Ortiz

Maps by Melissa Baker and The Rowman & Littlefield Publishing Group, Inc.

British Library Cataloguing in Publication Information available

Library of Congress Cataloging-in-Publication Data

Names: Ortiz, Isaiah, 1995- author.
Title: Starry sky adventures Arizona : hike, paddle, and explore under night skies / Isaiah Ortiz.
Description: Essex, Connecticut : Falcon Guides, [2023] | Includes bibliographical references. |
    Summary: "Starry Sky Adventures Arizona guides readers to 50 outdoor adventures to
    take under the darkest skies around. Guided adventures, including camping, backpacking,
    paddling, and hiking, show readers the way to safely experience the best of the night sky in
    astrotourism destinations, designated Dark Sky Places, and locations with outstanding natural
    darkness"—Provided by publisher.
Identifiers: LCCN 2022050034 (print) | LCCN 2022050035 (ebook) | ISBN 9781493069019
    (paperback) | ISBN 9781493069026 (epub)
Subjects: LCSH: Outdoor recreation—Arizona—Guidebooks. | Astronomy—Arizona—Observers'
    manuals. | Camp sites, facilities, etc.—Arizona—Guidebooks. | Hiking—Arizona—Guidebooks. |
    Trails—Arizona—Guidebooks. | Kayaking—Arizona—Guidebooks. | Arizona—Guidebooks.
Classification: LCC GV191.42.A7 O77 2023 (print) | LCC GV191.42.A7 (ebook) |
    DDC 796.509791—dc23/eng/20221212
LC record available at https://lccn.loc.gov/2022050034
LC ebook record available at https://lccn.loc.gov/2022050035

♾️[TM] The paper used in this publication meets the minimum requirements of American National
Standard for Information Sciences—Permanence of Paper for Printed Library Materials, ANSI/
NISO Z39.48-1992.

The Desert View Watchtower stands guard over the Grand Canyon's southeastern rim.

CONTENTS

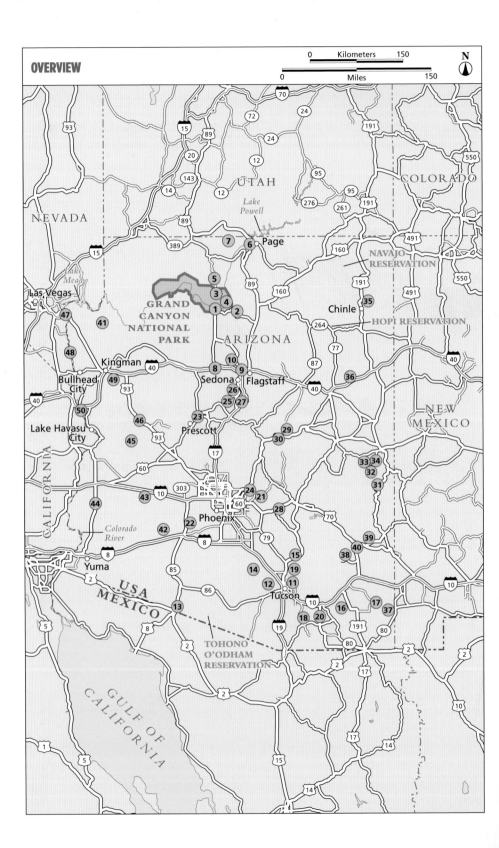

MAP LEGEND

Municipal

- Freeway/Interstate Highway (40)
- US Highway (191)
- State Road (85)
- County/Paved/Improved Road (64)
- Railroad
- International Border
- State Border
- County Border

Trails

- Featured Trail
- Trail or Fire Road

Water Features

- Body of Water
- Marsh/Swamp
- River/Creek
- Intermittent Stream
- Spring
- Waterfall

Land Management

- National Park/Forest
- National Monument/Wilderness Area
- State/County Park
- Reservation
- Private Land

Symbols

- Boat Ramp
- Bridge
- Building/Point of Interest
- Campground
- Cave
- Cemetery
- Elevation
- Gate
- Inn/Lodging
- Mountain/Peak
- Parking
- Picnic Area
- Ranger Station
- Restroom
- Scenic View/Overlook
- Steps/Boardwalk
- Tower
- Trailhead
- Tunnel
- Visitor/Information Center
- Water

MEET YOUR GUIDE

My name is **ISAIAH ORTIZ**, and I have a confession as your guide, photographer, and author—I am afraid of the dark. You see, growing up in Las Vegas, Nevada, I got used to light everywhere I looked. In Las Vegas the casinos are lit from the outside, nearly every street is lined with bright streetlights, and the sky itself is lit by the massive Luxor light. To make it short and sweet, I grew up seeing more streetlights than starlight. When it came to darkness, I grew up feeling that it was dangerous and harbored unknown nightmares.

When it came to stars, planets, and the darkness of space, I was ironically in love with all of it. Movies like *Star Wars* and characters like Buzz Lightyear filled my imagination of what it would be like to be in space. I pored over books about the planets in my

elementary school library and my dad's college astronomy textbook. If there was a documentary about space on TV, I was hooked on it, and I'll never forget piloting starfighters in *Star Wars* games on my Game Cube. In fifth grade I got my first taste of a real starry sky in 2006 at my science camp field trip on Mount Charleston, just northwest of Las Vegas.

The huge number of stars in the skies over the forest blew my mind, and I couldn't believe how I had never seen stars like that before. That first glimpse of a dark sky made me feel like I was going to float up into space. My love for astronomy and space has stayed with me for years, but I didn't regularly connect with dark skies until one summer night in 2014. A friend showed me how to photograph the night sky on their camera at Red Rock Canyon National Conservation Area just west of Las Vegas. I could not believe that I could take pictures of the stars like that, and soon after I bought my first Canon DSLR camera to photograph the night skies around Southern Nevada.

Since the hot Las Vegas summer of 2014, I have been photographing the night sky around the Southwest for fun. My first time seeing the Milky Way galaxy's core was in May 2015 with two of my closest friends at Pahranagat National Wildlife Refuge north of Las Vegas. The stars were incredible, and I knew I wanted to see more dark skies and capture their awesome beauty. Although my passion for the night sky has grown significantly since I started photographing it, the kid from Las Vegas who's afraid of the dark still has something to say. Almost every time I go out for astrophotography, I have that voice in my head that says, "Hey, it's dark; it's not safe!" or "You're going to get jumped by a mountain lion!"

Through lots of starry sky therapy, I can see that voice for what it is, a scared Vegas kid who just wants some comfort. When I'm feeling afraid on an astrophotography shoot—by myself, in the middle of the dark woods—I simply remind myself of a few things. I say to myself: "Right now, I am okay; there is no danger, this is beautiful, and I'm so grateful to be here." When I reassure myself this way, I feel at peace and can truly soak in all the wonders of the night sky. Nowadays, I live in Tucson, which has been an incredible access point for the starry skies around the state.

My mission with writing this book was to create an experience of cosmic wonder by guiding you through adventures under Arizona's dark skies. It has been my honor to serve you by embarking on all of these adventures and capturing the insane beauty of Arizona's night skies. Creating this book was a labor of love, and there were many times that I did not want to crawl out of my warm tent for a picture. I did it anyway—for my love of the stars and so that you will know how great they are in Arizona. Thank you to everyone who has supported me on this journey, I appreciate you deep in my heart.

See more of my work on Instagram (@isaiah.ortiz_) and on my website (Isaiahortiz .squarespace.com).

INTRODUCTION

DEEP IN THE SPRAWLING DESERTS, rocky canyons, and green forests of Arizona, the stars shine like diamonds in the sky. Known globally as the Grand Canyon State, Arizona sports a unique geography like no other place in the world. Abundant dark skies in a variety of unique environments such as the Sonoran Desert and the ponderosa pine forests of the Mogollon Rim make Arizona one of the best places to have a starry sky adventure. The state's rich cultural history of Native Americans, Spanish missions, and cowboys represents the epitome of the Wild West and a great place to learn lessons from the past. Arizona's awe-inspiring geography, rich cultural history, and magical dark skies make it a premier place to stargaze.

The Grand Canyon best summarizes the geographical diversity of Arizona, from the lush alpine forest of the North Rim to the parched deserts on the banks of the Colorado River. Arizona is widely known as a hot desert state, but did you know it's the only state to have all four of the Southwest's major deserts? The Mojave, Great Basin, Sonoran, and Chihuahuan Deserts all call Arizona home and bring a variety of wildlife, like the Sonoran Desert's iconic saguaro cactus. The state has a surprising abundance of high-desert grasslands and mountain meadows that fill with wildflowers during the summer monsoon season. Rolling grasslands give way to mystical red rock canyons in mystical places like Sedona and the Navajo Lands to the northeast. A significant part of the state is covered in forest that gets buried with winter snows and occasionally ignites in summer wildfires. Winter snows feed rivers such as the Salt River, Gila River, and the almighty Colorado River, a major lifeline for Arizonans and people across the Southwest. Arizona also contains part of the largest continuous ponderosa pine forests in the world on the Mogollon Rim. Sky islands rise out of the desert seas of Arizona, harboring unparalleled biodiversity on their forested mountaintops. Millions of acres of public lands are available to explore all of Arizona's wonderful terrain under a dark sky.

Arizona offers the magical experience of seeing the Milky Way stretching from horizon to horizon over a saguaro or a cool mountain forest. Astronomers love Arizona's dark skies and have created large observatory complexes including Kitt Peak National Observatory and Lowell Observatory to study the stars with some of the largest telescopes on the planet. Starry sky adventurers can marvel at the stunning night skies in a dozen International Dark Sky Parks, like Grand Canyon National Park or Chiricahua National Monument. With more International Dark Sky Parks yet to come, you don't have to go to a certified park to have an amazing experience under the night sky. Plentiful public lands and wilderness areas across the state possess pure dark skies that are just as dark as any International Dark Sky Park. Although massive light domes from big cities like Phoenix and Tucson can be seen from hundreds of miles away, some communities in Arizona are working to coexist with the night sky. Headquartered in Tucson, the International Dark-Sky Association certified Flagstaff as the world's first International Dark Sky Community in 2001 for its efforts to protect the night. Citizens and visitors to

Flagstaff and Arizona's four other Dark Sky Communities can see hundreds of stars and the shadow of the Milky Way in the night sky from downtown. Generations of ancient native tribes and astronomers have interacted with the cosmos over Arizona.

It's important to honor the heritage of Native American cultures that cared for Arizona's wild and beautiful lands for generations before the first modern cities laid a foot of concrete. Ancestors of the modern-day Tohono O'odham tribe, known as the Hohokam, were masters of the Sonoran Desert who created sophisticated irrigation canal networks in the present-day Phoenix and Tucson areas. The resilient Navajo have the largest Native American reservation in the United States in their traditional homelands around the Four Corners in northeastern Arizona. Puebloan peoples have left petroglyphs and great stone cliff dwellings across Arizona that have stood for thousands of years. Native Americans were in touch with astronomical cycles for agricultural activities and to foster spiritual connection through star stories. The arrival of European Americans dramatically changed Native Americans' way of life in Arizona and introduced numerous armed conflicts that decimated their populations.

Tragic events such as the Long Walk of the Navajo in 1864 led to countless deaths and widespread trauma. The sacrifice of Native Americans cannot be ignored and should be remembered with compassion. The influx of European Americans into Arizona eventually led to its creation as the nation's forty-eighth state in 1912. In the past one hundred years, Arizona's population has exploded to more than 7 million. Big cities like Phoenix and Tucson attract transplants from all over the United States and serve as the engines of Arizona's economic development with manufacturing, defense, and technology leading new growth. Arizona's small to medium-size towns like Willcox and Sedona rely on industries such as copper mining, agriculture, and tourism for their growth.

Arizona is prime for adventuring under a starry night sky due to diverse and plentiful public lands, vibrant night skies, and the important lessons to be learned from its cultural history. From the Grand Canyon and beyond, Arizona has millions of acres of public land to explore forests, deserts, and rivers, under a clear night sky. Dazzling night skies can be

enjoyed throughout the state's many International Dark Sky Parks and Communities. Here you can learn the history of what has happened in the state's past to enrich your understanding of Arizona today. This book invites people of all skill levels to connect with Arizona's dark skies on fifty guided adventures across the state.

MEET THE DARK SKY

What is a dark sky? For me, the definition of a dark sky changed over time. As a child, it started with staring at the stars with wonder in my backyard in suburban North Las Vegas, Nevada. Everything changed when I saw my first sky full of stars in the ponderosa pines of Mount Charleston. Through my astrophotography adventures, I've seen raw night skies with collections of stars so bright they cast faint shadows on the ground. The truth is, a dark sky is subject to light pollution, both artificial from cities and natural from the moon.

A dark sky can best be described through the senses and emotions that come up when immersed under the stars. In a place far from light pollution, you'll see hundreds to thousands of stars slowly drifting across the night sky. Bright stars organized by chance into familiar shapes like triangles, crosses, hooks, and dippers will bring you a sense of order. The coalescence of stars and dust along the Milky Way shows that we are living inside a disk of dust and stars of unimaginable magnitude. Perhaps feelings of gratitude, peace, and insignificance will fill you when you experience a dark night sky.

The night sky is also a place of constant movement and action. Shooting stars blaze through the night sky every night, and comets occasionally grace the night skies with their dramatic ion tails. As the Earth rotates, seasonal constellations like Orion and Scorpius rise and fall over the horizon, while Polaris stays still in the north. The giant moon rises in the east and washes the sky with a blue-gray glow that is simply magical. Deep sky nebulae and galaxies far, far away shine more than millions of light-years from Earth so we can see a picture of their past. These are the wonders of our natural night sky, one thing that connects the whole world.

IMPORTANCE OF NATURAL DARKNESS

It's estimated that 80 percent of people in the United States can no longer see the Milky Way due to light pollution. This sad fact means that dark skies free of light pollution are inaccessible to four out of five people living in the United States. As someone who grew up in heavily light-polluted Las Vegas, I had to travel for at least 30 minutes out of the city to catch a glimpse of the Milky Way. Not only is it inconvenient to have to travel so far to see the stars, it is inaccessible for some, and unhealthy for everyone. Natural darkness is important for human health and for igniting our innate sense of wonder and excitement for the world around us.

Humans evolved with the natural diurnal cycles of day and night, which means the dark is as much a part of our existence as the light. Research suggests that artificial lights at night affect human health through loss of sleep and increased risk of depression, sleep disorders, and other health problems. One reason camping trips are restorative is that they put us in touch with our natural circadian rhythm of going to bed soon after the sun goes down. Safety is another drawback of intense light pollution. Despite the common belief that strong lighting can promote safety around homes, the intense glare of undirected lighting can create shadows that thieves can use to hide.

DARK SKY DEFINITIONS, THREATS, AND PROTECTIONS

DEFINITIONS

ARTIFICIAL LIGHT: Light that is created, directed, or used by humans for any purpose.

DARK SKIES: Night skies free, or at least relatively free, of light pollution.

INTERNATIONAL DARK-SKY ASSOCIATION (IDA): Headquartered in Tucson, the International-Dark Sky Association advocates for dark skies by certifying International Dark Sky Parks and Communities. The IDA also provides tools and guidance to the world on how to limit or eliminate harmful light pollution.

INTERNATIONAL DARK SKY COMMUNITIES: Legally organized cities and towns that adopt quality outdoor lighting ordinances and engage in public outreach programs to teach citizens about the night sky.

INTERNATIONAL DARK SKY PARKS: Publicly or privately owned spaces protected for natural conservation that implement good outdoor lighting and provide visitors with dark sky programs.

INTERNATIONAL DARK SKY PLACES CONSERVATION PROGRAM (IDSP): An IDA program founded in 2001 that recognizes and promotes excellent stewardship of the night sky.

INTERNATIONAL DARK SKY RESERVES: Dark Sky Reserves are made up of a dark "core" zone surrounded by populated areas that have enacted policy controls to protect the darkness of the core region.

INTERNATIONAL DARK SKY SANCTUARIES: The darkest and most remote places in the world that have a fragile conservation state.

LIGHT POLLUTION: Any adverse effect or impact attributable to artificial light at night.

URBAN NIGHT SKY PLACES: Sites near, or surrounded by, large urban areas whose planning and design promote authentic nighttime experiences despite significant light pollution and that otherwise do not qualify for designation within any other IDSP category.

THREATS

The biggest threat to dark skies is uncontrolled light pollution from growing cities, towns, and industrial operations. Another threat to a dark night sky is massive satellite launches that create trains of bright satellites across the sky at night, disrupting astronomy and stargazing activities.

PROTECTIONS

Preservation of public lands in their natural state is one of the best ways to protect the night sky. Organizations like the International Dark-Sky Association help protect the night sky by educating the public on responsible artificial lighting practices and officially recognizing dark sky areas and communities. Everyone can protect the night sky by updating outdoor light fixtures to shine lower intensity light downward or only where it is needed.

ARIZONA DARK SKY AREAS AND EFFORTS

Arizona has five International Dark Sky Communities: Flagstaff, Cottonwood, Sedona, Big Park/Village of Oak Creek, and Fountain Hills. Arizona also has twelve International Dark Sky Parks certified by the IDA as of the time of this writing: Chiricahua National Monument, Grand Canyon National Park, Grand Canyon–Parashant National Monument, Kartchner Caverns State Park, Oracle State Park, Pipe Spring National Monument, Petrified Forest National Park, Sunset Crater Volcano National Monument, Tumacácori National Historical Park, Tonto National Monument, Walnut Canyon National Monument, and Wupatki National Monument. More International Dark Sky Communities and Parks, Urban Night Sky Places, Sanctuaries, and Reserves may be designated in the future. Lake Havasu City and Tucson have intentionally designed streets without streetlights or with lower-power lights in an effort to preserve night sky quality in and around the city. State tourism magazines and organizations actively promote the dark sky assets Arizona has to offer. The International Dark Sky Parks selected for this guide are open for stargazing on a nightly basis. At the time of this writing, some of the dark sky parks not covered in this guide have limited daytime hours and are only open for stargazing during special events.

CONSTELLATIONS

Constellations are ancient patterns of stars in the night sky that are often associated with a story relating to gods, family, nature, and agricultural practices. An asterism such as the Big Dipper is not a constellation but instead a familiar part of a larger constellation like Ursa Major. Different cultures see the stars in different ways and therefore have different constellation shapes and stories. For example, in Greek mythology, Orion's familiar "belt-stars" asterism is seen as the belt of a warrior, while in Apache astronomical lore, the three stars represent the "Three Vertebrae." Constellations also differ depending on where you are positioned on the Earth. The night sky in Arizona is very different from that of Australia because observers are looking at the universe from different vantage points.

SEASONS OF CONSTELLATIONS

Constellations come in four "seasons": winter, spring, summer, and fall. There are "seasons" of constellations due to Earth's rotation and position around the sun in its orbit. Examples of seasonal constellations include Scorpius in summer, Orion in winter, and Leo in spring.

HOW TO FIND MAJOR CONSTELLATIONS

Learning the sky takes time, practice, and patience. Star maps and smartphone apps like Stellarium with augmented reality features can help significantly with locating major constellations by comparing what you see on the map to what you see in the sky. Attending star parties, watching constellation guide videos, or listening to stargazing podcasts can also be very helpful for learning major constellations.

EQUIPMENT

All you need for stargazing are your eyes . . . and a pair of glasses if you're nearsighted. For optimal night vision, let your eyes adjust to the night sky with no artificial lights for 30 minutes to an hour. Red flashlights can preserve your night vision while you go on starry sky adventures. Equipment that enhances stargazing experiences include telescopes, binoculars, and star maps. DSLRs, mirrorless cameras, and some capable smartphone cameras paired with a tripod can help you capture the night sky through photo and video.

STARGAZING RESOURCES

There is a wealth of knowledge online and in literature about stargazing and learning the night sky. Some great resources include: books, online stargazing guides, videos, and astronomy courses from a college. A YouTube channel that has helped me and thousands of others learn how to identify constellations is Learn the Sky by Janine Bonham: youtube.com/c/Learnthesky. Other great video channels and literature exist, such as National Geographic's handy Pocket Guide *Night Sky of North America* by Catherine Herbert Howell (2017).

PLANNING YOUR TRIP

TWO OF THE MOST IMPORTANT PARTS OF HAVING A FUN EXPERIENCE under the night sky are planning and safety. For the best stargazing conditions, plan your trip far from light pollution and for a time that the moon will not interfere with the darkness of the sky. Avoid the moon's natural light pollution by stargazing during a new moon, before moonrise, and after moonset. The moon is certainly an important part of the night sky experience; however, it is so bright that it will prevent you from seeing full constellations and faint meteors, even in dark sky regions. In addition, check the weather forecast before you stargaze to ensure that there are little to no clouds blocking the view.

In this guidebook, there are many adventures rated easy, moderate, or hard. Know your own abilities, and choose adventures that are appropriate for you. Help can be miles and hours away if you are in an exhausting and dangerous situation at night. Awareness of weather is crucial to safety, as temperatures in Arizona can fall below freezing overnight in winter and blazingly hot during summer, even at night! Dress appropriately for the conditions, and never risk your safety for any reason. Stargazing is best with a friend, but it's also okay to enjoy it alone as well. Be sure to let someone know exactly where you are going, when you plan to return, and whom to call if you don't return/reach out by your designated time. Learning navigation at night is critical because less landmarks are visible in the dark. Study your route, and always carry a map and GPS device and have the necessary skills to use them. Learn how to locate the north star by using the big dipper and Cassiopeia to orient yourself to north no matter where you are. Planning and executing your trips safely will ensure that you know where you are at all times on your adventures and that you have a great time.

EQUIPMENT

Equipment requirements vary significantly by trip description in this guidebook. All trips require that you bring water to stay hydrated and extra food when you need nutrition, especially if you get lost. A water filter and a gallon of water per person per day will ensure adequate hydration for every day of your trip. A map, GPS unit, compass, flashlight with extra batteries, and navigation skills will help you on all of these trips as well. First-aid kits and basic first-aid knowledge are important to have in case of injury. Hygiene toiletries such as hand sanitizer, a toothbrush, and sunscreen are important for maintaining health. Dressing in layers with appropriate clothing and footwear will ensure you are dressed for whatever the weather throws at you. A red-bulb flashlight will help preserve your night vision better than a white-light flashlight. Red cellophane or clear red tape can help convert a white light into a red light.

Every trip in this book requires different equipment to get the job done.

- Night hiking and single-night stargazing trips: Bring a backpack for supplies and a flashlight.

- Astrophotography trips: You will need a camera or smartphone camera with manual controls and a tripod.
- Car camping trips: You will need a vehicle or trailer, a tent or shelter if you're not sleeping in your trailer/vehicle, sleeping bag/quilt, sleeping pad, camp pillow, cookware, flashlight, and warm sleeping clothes.
- Backpacking trips: You will need a sturdy framed backpack, cookware, trowel and toilet paper for human waste disposal, food storage devices/paracord and bag to hang food, portable tent, sleeping bag, sleeping pad, and warm sleeping clothes.
- Mountain biking trips: You will need a mountain bike with aggressive tire tread, bike flashlight, air pump or air cartridges, backpack or frame bags, extra inner tube and materials to fix a flat, and tools to fix the bike.
- Mountain bikepacking trips: You will need a mountain bike with aggressive tire tread, bike flashlight, backpack or frame bags, extra inner tube and materials to fix a flat, air pump or air cartridges, tools to fix the bike, cookware, food storage devices/paracord and bag to hang food, portable tent, sleeping bag, sleeping pad, and warm sleeping clothes.
- Kayaking trips: You will need a kayak or paddleboard with storage space, dry bags, life vest, boat lights, and tools to fix a leak.
- Kayak camping trips: You will need a kayak or paddleboard with storage space, dry bags, life vest, boat lights, tools to fix a leak, food storage devices/paracord and bag to hang food, cookware, portable tent, sleeping bag, sleeping pad, and warm sleeping clothes.
- Four-wheel-drive off-road camping: You will need a four-wheel-drive vehicle with high clearance (all-wheel drive is not the same as four-wheel drive), spare tire, shovel, tools to change a tire, sleeping bag/quilt, tent or shelter if not sleeping in your trailer/vehicle, sleeping pad, camp pillow, warm sleeping clothes, cookware, and flashlight.

CAMPING

Camping offers a great way to reset your natural circadian rhythm and get back to nature. Half the trips in this book require an overnight camping component. Be sure to know your skill level, especially when it comes to the strenuous activities of backpacking, kayak camping, and bikepacking. Important camping gear includes a tent, sleeping pad, sleeping bag, a pillow, warm sleeping clothes, cookware, food, water filtration, trowel and toilet paper for human waste disposal, water, food storage system, hygiene toiletries, and first-aid gear. Water is scarce throughout much of Arizona, so be sure to bring enough water for your entire trip or a water filtration system to pull water from the environment and disinfect it. A cloth strainer and iodine tablets can be a great way to filter and clean water in an emergency situation.

TIPS FOR HIKING IN ARIZONA

Arizona is a beautiful place, but its landscape can be dangerous for the unprepared. Water is scarce, so be sure to carry more than you think you need at all times to ensure that you have enough. As a general rule, explore the deserts in fall, winter, and spring and the high-altitude forests in spring, summer, and fall. Opportunities for summer swimming in the desert and snowshoeing the high country in winter are featured in this book. Most of these trips have been designed with the best season/weather noted. Mountain lions, snakes, bears, and other wildlife dangers are present throughout the state and should be treated with respect. When hiking in bear country, make sounds to make your presence known and carry bear spray for protection. In the deserts, keep your eyes on the trail for snakes, scorpions, and other wildlife. None of the wildlife in Arizona is actively out to get you, but keep your guard up and keep a respectable distance between you and any wildlife.

LOCATING DARK SKY AREAS

Dark skies on public lands are easy to find in Arizona. In general, the state's darkest regions are in the north around the Grand Canyon and in the east around the White Mountains. Federally designated wilderness areas, national parks, national forests, BLM land, wildlife refuges, and state parks are also great places to find dark skies across the state. You can easily find dark sky areas in the state by browsing interactive dark sky maps online on websites like darksitefinder.com/maps/world and lightpollutionmap.info

ASTRONOMICAL EVENTS

Calendars of astronomical events such as lunar eclipses and meteor showers can be found in literature or online at timeanddate.com/astronomy/sights-to-see.html. The Milky Way can be seen at all times of the year, however its core cannot be seen at all times. The Milky Way core season starts in February and lasts until November. Comets, rocket launches, and rare meteor storms can be seen occasionally and stargazers may get short notice of these events from astronomical news sources. Local radio stations, TV news channels, astronomy-focused websites, podcasts, and YouTube channels produce content notifying people of astronomical events.

LEAVE NO TRACE

The Leave No Trace principles are essential for keeping nature wild and reducing our impact on the environment while recreating. The principles are:

- Plan ahead and prepare.
- Travel and camp on durable surfaces.
- Dispose of waste properly.
- Leave what you find.
- Minimize campfire impacts.
- Respect wildlife.
- Be considerate of other visitors.

Practice these principles whenever you recreate to protect the recreational resources that we all share.

HOW TO USE THIS GUIDE

THIS GUIDE HAS BEEN DESIGNED TO BE SIMPLE YET THOROUGH to take you on some of the best adventures you can have under a dark sky. Adventure types include night hiking, single-night stargazing, astrophotography, car camping in established campgrounds, backpacking into wilderness areas, four-wheel-drive/off-road dispersed camping, night mountain biking, snowshoeing, bikepacking, night kayaking, and kayak camping. All of these adventures require different skill levels and significant preparation before embarking on your trip.

ADVENTURE RATINGS

The rating system for this book has three categories: easy, moderate, and hard. Easy trips require little to no prior experience in the activity, are a relatively short distance, require a relatively short amount of time, and have routes that are easy to navigate. Moderate trips are more involved in terms of navigational skills, physical exertion, and usually involve longer miles. Hard trips involve significant navigation skills, strenuous physical exertion, special equipment needs, and gritty determination.

CONSIDERATIONS

The season, weather, wildlife, and safety are all critical to the proper planning of a starry sky adventure in Arizona.

SEASON

Summers are notoriously hot in Arizona's deserts but cool and temperate in Arizona's high country. Winters are cold and snowy in Arizona's high country, making travel in these areas dangerous if not impossible. Winter is the best season to explore Arizona's deserts. Fall and spring are great seasons to explore all of Arizona's regions, with mid-fall and late spring being the most accessible times of year. The summer monsoon and winter rains/snow send water to the creeks and streams across the state. Fire season can produce large wildfires in Arizona's high deserts and forests, creating a significant threat for both recreators and citizens. Smoke from wildfires and clouds from widespread storms can prevent stargazing activities.

WEATHER

Arizona experiences biannual seasons of precipitation. Gentle, soaking winter rains drench the deserts and lay blankets of snow across the forests. In summer, powerful monsoon storms flow into the state. Widespread flooding, including flash floods, can occur at any time of year due to the inability of the dry soils to retain much moisture. Storms can produce lightning, strong winds, hail, torrential rain, and blizzards that are life threatening. In spring and summer, wildfires can be sparked by lightning strikes.

WILDLIFE

Arizona's wildlife is beautiful and needs to be respected. Mountain lions, black bears, rattlesnakes, Gila monsters, elk, coyotes, bobcats, and javelinas are just some of the wildlife species that inhabit Arizona. Insects such as bees, flies, and mosquitoes can be an annoyance in almost any environment across the state. Rodents like squirrel and skunks are present throughout the state and are more likely to steal your food and become a nuisance than other animals. Much of Arizona's wildlife is nocturnal and may be seen at night. Creatures like owls, bats, and tarantulas are a common nocturnal sight around Arizona. Store food properly and make noise while exploring at night to keep animals alert of your presence. Keep your distance from wildlife and carry bear spray to protect yourself from large animals.

SAFETY AT NIGHT

Safety is of greatest importance while exploring at night. Many of the adventures in this guidebook are intended to be completed by arriving in the daytime and staying until it gets dark. Some trips require you to arrive and leave the location at night. Regardless of circumstances, if you do not feel safe, either change the trip so that you feel safer or simply do not engage in it. As a suggestion, do a trip in the daytime to become familiar with the terrain and then repeat the trip at night. One of the risks of night hiking and stargazing in remote places is that help may be hours and miles away. Another risk is the cold, as many places have freezing overnight temperatures in late fall, winter, and early spring. Be sure to let someone know where you are going and when you expect to be back, especially if traveling alone.

The West Fork of the Little Colorado River meanders through a meadow in the moonlit Mount Baldy Wilderness.

ASTROPHOTOGRAPHY BASICS

ASTROPHOTOGRAPHY IS ONE OF THE BEST WAYS TO EXPERIENCE the night sky and create art. This art form was one of my primary motivations for working on this book project. The right cameras and lenses and a variety of creative and technical skills are required for successful astrophotography sessions. Weather conditions are just as important, and luckily Arizona is chock-full of hundreds of nights with clear skies every year.

EQUIPMENT

At a basic level, a camera with manual controls and a tripod are all that you need for astrophotography. Major camera manufacturers such as Canon, Sony, and Nikon produce DSLR and mirrorless cameras capable of capturing the night skies. More important than the camera bodies are the lenses you attach to your camera. Invest in quality lenses with "fast" apertures of f/2.8 or lower to allow the maximum amount of light into the camera. Some smartphone cameras can also capture the night skies in their night modes, manual "pro" modes, or with special photography apps. Tripods can be purchased at camera, electronics, or online stores.

CAMERA SETTINGS AND TECHNIQUES

The three most important settings for successful astrophotography are ISO, aperture, and shutter speed. ISO is the camera's sensitivity to light, and it should be placed at a high number: ISO 1600 to 3200. Aperture is a dilating opening in the camera's lens that controls how much light comes into the camera and is denoted by an f-stop number, such as f/2.8. Set your aperture to a low number, such as f/2.8 or f/1.8, to achieve a wide aperture and maximize the amount of light coming into the camera. Lastly, shutter speed is the amount of time light is allowed to expose the camera sensor and should be set to a long exposure time of 15 to 30 seconds. Multiple exposures or a single, extremely long exposure of 5 minutes or more can be taken to create star trail images.

Other important settings include a remote-shutter or timed-shutter release of 2 seconds or more to ensure that the camera is not vibrating when the image is being taken. Let your tripod hold your camera; do not touch it while it is taking a picture of the night sky. Focus must be set manually on a distant light source, like a star or the moon, prior to pressing the shutter. For lenses with zoom functions, be sure to reset the focus after every change in zoom for sharp photos. Finally, white-balance settings can be adjusted in the camera or during editing to make your photos of the night sky look true to life.

PLANNING

Proper planning will allow you to capture unforgettable images of Arizona's night skies and unique environments. Planning for photography under clear, moonless night skies is ideal for capturing tons of stars in your photos. Factor in astronomical conditions such as meteor showers, setting/rising moons, and the position of the Milky Way to raise the bar on your photos and make them great. Composition, proper photo editing, and luck can all come together to create your photo of the year.

ENVIRONMENTAL CONDITIONS

I often have to remind myself that I cannot control the sky when clouds, smoke, and the moon affect my astrophotography. To maximize the number of stars you capture in your photos, check the forecast and do your best to shoot under a clear sky with no moon. Clouds and the moon are not the enemy; they simply demand that you be more creative—or patient. Also, make sure that areas are not closed due to heavy snow, flooding, or wildfires. The moon rises at a different time every night of the year. To determine accurate moonrise times, I recommend using a website like timeanddate.com to find the moonrise times and phase of the moon for the particular area in which you are going to be taking pictures. The phase of the moon is also an important consideration. In general, the moon is brightest through these phases: first quarter (waxing half-moon) to full moon to third quarter (waning half-moon). The moon can provide natural landscape lighting and add a cool blue glow to the sky that adds unique effects to your astrophotography. Remember, astrophotography is an art form, so work with the environmental conditions to create dramatic and memorable scenes.

The flower stalk of a century plant shares the sky with a dagger of zodiacal light over the Red Rock–Secret Mountain Wilderness.

PHOTO COMPOSITION

Composition can make or break a photo. Principles such as the rule of thirds and leading lines are great starting points for creating great astrophotography images. Lighting can be accomplished with natural lighting such as twilight and the moon. Artificial lighting such as a campfire, flashlight, or camera flash can also help light the scene. When using artificial lighting, be careful not to ruin your own night vision and be courteous to others who may be stargazing or photographing the night sky in your area. The most important rule for photography is to shoot what interests you in the way that gets you most excited. Seek what impassions you, not what draws the most likes on social media, and you will create your best work.

PHOTO EDITING

The photo editing process can bring the best out of your photos by boosting colors, contrast, and clarity of the night sky. Post-processing of night sky photos can be challenging due to constraints on "acceptable" image noise, composition, and color saturation. If you are seeking clean, low-noise images of the night sky, do as much work as possible in-camera on location. This will reduce the amount of noise added in editing and sharpen your field skills to create solid photos. When it comes to editing, be creative. Create something you adore; it will bring you more joy than any editing preset currently floating around the internet.

NORTHERN ARIZONA

HOME OF THE MIGHTY COLORADO RIVER, the vast Grand Canyon, and abundant dark skies, Northern Arizona is a must-see for stargazing adventurers. The Colorado Plateau geographically defines the region bound by the remote Arizona Strip to the northwest, Navajo and Hopi Country to the northeast, and the Mogollon Rim to the south. International Dark Sky Parks, such as the Grand Canyon, and Dark Sky Communities like Flagstaff help create a dark sky corridor throughout Northern Arizona. People have long called this place home, from generations of Navajo to newly minted Arizonans. Awe-inspiring landscapes, gorgeous night skies, and a rich history make Northern Arizona a top destination for everyone seeking an adventure under the stars.

Forces of earth, wind, water, and fire have shaped Northern Arizona's dramatic landscapes. The combination of the Colorado Plateau's uplift and the downcutting of the Colorado River shaped Arizona's most distinct feature, the Grand Canyon. At an average 4,000 feet deep and 27 miles long, the canyon is regarded as a "wonder of the world" and one of the finest examples of arid-land erosion on Earth. Higher precipitation levels and wind have sculpted sandstone into rock spires and mesmerizing shapes at places like Vermillion Cliffs National Monument west of Page. Winter snows often cover Arizona's tallest mountains, the San Francisco Peaks north of Flagstaff, earning the range the Navajo name Dook'o'oslííd, which means "the summit that never melts." Spectacular monsoons bring torrential rain to the vast Coconino and Kaibab National Forests every summer, helping sustain part of the largest ponderosa pine forest in North America. Volcanism has also shaped much of the region, with more than 600 extinct cinder cones present in the San Francisco Volcanic Field around Flagstaff. Wildfire has certainly left its mark throughout the region but has also made way for the rebirth of new forests from the ashes. Just as earthly elements have shaped Northern Arizona's landscape, the heavenly elements of starry skies have also left their impression.

Generations of astronomers have cherished the truly dark skies of Northern Arizona. Navajo astronomers told unique stories about the stars that represented the family and natural phenomena found in their homeland. The Navajo's star stories were often shared by an elder in a family setting. Major scientific observatories in the region include the historic Lowell Observatory and the US Naval Observatory west of Flagstaff. Credited with the 1930 discovery of dwarf planet Pluto, Lowell Observatory still performs astronomical research today. In an effort to preserve the night sky in Northern Arizona, the City of Flagstaff became the world's first International Dark Sky Community in 2001. This region has the most International Dark Sky Parks in the state, including: Grand Canyon National Park and Sunset Crater Volcano, Walnut Canyon, Wupatki, Grand Canyon–Parashant, and Pipe Spring National Monuments. Like its dark skies, Northern Arizona's long history and diverse cultures have been preserved.

The outer reaches of the galaxy set over a lone pine tree at White Pocket in Vermillion Cliffs National Monument.

The cultural history of Northern Arizona begins with the Native peoples who called the area home for thousands of years before Arizona was even a territory. Puebloan peoples built places like the Wupatki pueblo northeast of Flagstaff, thought to be a trading hub between Native communities. The Hopi and Navajo people have inhabited the area for hundreds of years, with the Hopi village of Oraibi consistently inhabited since at least 1150 CE, making it the oldest community in the United States. Native religions emphasized connections to the natural landscape, and the Hopi see the San Francisco Peaks as the home of the Kachina spirits, ancestors who became clouds following their death. Spanish expeditions introduced Christianity and competing pressures on the Native Americans who lived in the area. Some of the greatest conflicts were with the US government, which forced thousands of Navajo from their homelands in tragic events like the Long Walk. The resilient Navajo still exist today on the largest reservation in the United States, with a population close to 400,000 strong. Today, tourism drives the economy of modern-day towns like Flagstaff, Williams, and Page, which offer gateways to Northern Arizona's great outdoors.

Come visit Northern Arizona to learn about its deep history and enjoy dark skies you can almost touch. Whether night hiking at the North Rim or peering deep into the cosmos at Lowell Observatory, you'll find plenty of ways to enjoy a dark sky. When taking a journey to Northern Arizona, prepare yourself for a safe adventure, during which you can experience any kind of weather at any time. Be respectful of Native American lands, artifacts, and tribal law, keeping in mind that they have called this place home longer than anyone else. You'll never forget a starry sky adventure in Northern Arizona, guaranteed.

1 GRAND CANYON—SOUTH RIM STARGAZING

Take an easy stroll under the stars along the South Rim of the Grand Canyon and witness a truly dark sky in one of the best places to stargaze in the world.

Activity: Stargazing and walking
Location: Grand Canyon National Park South Rim; GPS: N36 03.568' / W112 06.419'
Start: Grand Canyon National Park South Rim Visitor Center parking lot; GPS: N36 03.568' / W112 06.419'
Elevation gain: 90 feet
Distance: 1.8 miles out and back
Difficulty: Easy
Hiking time: About 30 minutes
Seasons/schedule: Open year-round; great all seasons
Dark sky designation: International Dark Sky Park
Timing: No moon to a quarter moon
Fees and permits: National park entrance fees apply; see nps.gov/grca/planyourvisit/fees.htm for current fees.
Trail contacts: Grand Canyon National Park, PO Box 129, Grand Canyon 86023; (928) 638-7888; nps.gov/grca/index.htm
Dog-friendly: Yes, leashed up to 6 feet in length on trails above the rim

Trail surface: Mostly paved; rocky at some viewpoints
Land status: National park
Nearest town: Tusayan, Arizona
Other trail users: Runners, backpackers, photographers, those in wheelchairs
Maps: Grand Canyon National Park maps available online at nps.gov/grca/planyourvisit/maps.htm
Water availability: Yes; available at the visitor center and other popular areas in the park
Special considerations: Some areas of the Rim Trail are located near unfenced edges of the canyon with sharp drop-offs. Ice can form on walkways, rocks, and stairs during winter months. Overnight temperatures in winter are normally below freezing.
Other: Grand Canyon National Park normally hosts a large annual star party in June; check the official website for details.

FINDING THE TRAILHEAD

From Tusayan, drive north on AZ 64 for 6.1 miles, including the stop at the park entrance station. As the entrance road curves northwest, make a right turn to the north for the large Mather Point parking lots, about 300 feet ahead. Park in one of the Mather Point parking lots and take one of the paths north from the lot to the Rim Trail to begin hiking west along the South Rim. Trailhead GPS: N36 03.568' / W112 06.419'

THE ADVENTURE

At 277 miles long, 18 miles wide, and 1 mile deep, the massive depth and scale of the Grand Canyon is truly astonishing. The canyon was carved by the mighty Colorado River over millions of years, and every year millions of people come to view one of the Seven Wonders of the Natural World. Although millions visit annually, not nearly as many people stay after dark to see another part of what makes the Grand Canyon

> The Grand Canyon has been carved over 6 million years as a result of geologic uplift of the Colorado Plateau and downcutting from the Colorado River.

A quarter moon illuminates the depths of the Grand Canyon from the South Rim.

special: its incredibly dark skies. Designated an International Dark Sky Park in 2016 by the International Dark-Sky Association, the park is far from any major sources of light pollution. A fun and easy way to experience the Grand Canyon at night is to take a walk along the Rim Trail of the South Rim.

Start your stargazing adventure from the South Rim Visitor Center and the Mather Point parking lots. Walk toward the north side of the parking lot and take one of the paved access paths north for about 300 feet to the Rim Trail. Once you reach the Rim Trail, turn left (west) and start walking 0.15 mile toward Mather Point, a developed viewpoint with wheelchair access. Arrive

The oldest human-artifacts found in the Grand Canyon date back 12,000 years.

at sunset or with a quarter moon in the sky for incredible views of the Grand Canyon. The scale of the canyon and its many side canyons is truly immense, matched only by the grandeur of the dark skies above.

From Mather Point, "hear" the awesome quiet of the Grand Canyon and look up to see tens of thousands of stars. Look to the northern part of the sky to see the Big Dipper and the Little Dipper asterisms dancing around Polaris above the canyon. When you're ready to see more, head south back to the Rim Trail and continue 0.08 mile west along the path toward a quiet and spectacular viewpoint just down some stairs. If you are visiting when there's no moon in the sky, notice how the glow of starlight alone allows you to see in surprising detail. Climb back up the stairs and continue west on the Rim Trail through the trees for a little over 0.55 mile to reach an amphitheater and Yavapai Point.

As the Rim Trail curves north, find a break in the trees and the Yavapai Point Amphi-theater on the rim of the canyon. The amphitheater area allows you to sit on one of the benches and absorb the dark skies in a more relaxed way. Finish the walk along the rim by

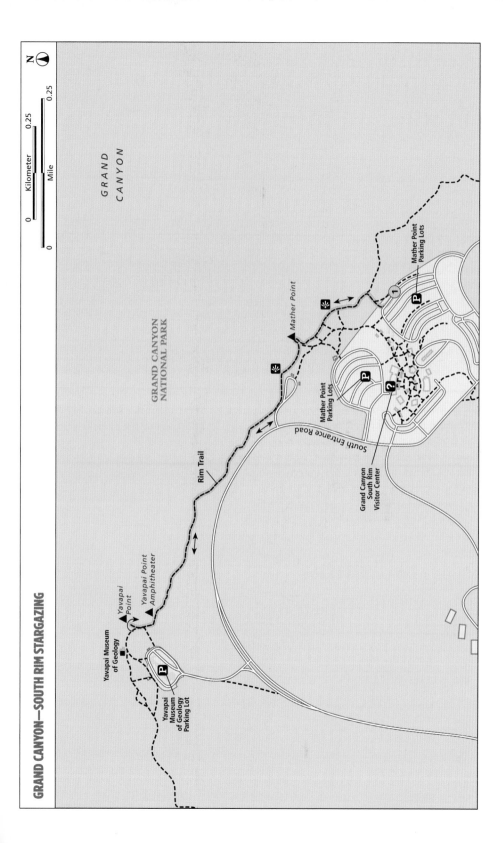

GRAND CANYON—SOUTH RIM STARGAZING

N

0   Kilometer   0.25

0   0.25
                    Mile

GRAND CANYON

GRAND CANYON NATIONAL PARK

Yavapai Museum of Geology

▲ Yavapai Point

▲ Yavapai Point Amphitheater

Yavapai Museum of Geology Parking Lot

Rim Trail

▲ Mather Point

Mather Point Parking Lots

Grand Canyon South Rim Visitor Center

Mather Point Parking Lots

South Entrance Road

Zodiacal light and the outer bands of the Milky Way hover above the dark abyss of the Grand Canyon shortly after twilight.

going just 250 feet north to Yavapai Point for another look inside this incredible canyon and an open view of the sky. Once you're ready to head back to your car, simply walk eastward along the Rim Trail for 0.9 mile until you reach the pathway to the Mather Point parking lots. From views miles across the Grand Canyon to millions of light-years into space, seeing the Grand Canyon at night is simply an opportunity you can't pass up.

LOOK UP
Stars survive the crushing force of gravity by creating enough heat and pressure in their cores to counterbalance gravity.

MILES AND DIRECTIONS

0.0   Start from the Mather Point parking lot and walk 300 feet north to the Rim Trail.

0.06   Turn left (west) on the Rim Trail and walk 0.15 mile to Mather Point.

0.21   Arrive at Mather Point. Return to the Rim Trail and walk west 0.09 mile to another viewpoint down a set of stairs to the north.

0.3   Arrive at the viewpoint. Return to the Rim Trail and walk west 0.55 mile until you reach the Yavapai Point Amphitheater, on the north side of the trail.

0.85   Arrive at the Yavapai Point Amphitheater. Continue west on the Rim Trail for 250 feet to Yavapai Point.

0.9   Arrive at Yavapai Point. Head east on the Rim Trail for 0.9 mile to get back to the Mather Point parking lots.

1.8   Arrive back at the trailhead.

2 GRAND CANYON—DESERT VIEW WATCHTOWER STARGAZING AND ASTROPHOTOGRAPHY

Take a short walk on the South Rim of the Grand Canyon to photograph the historic Desert View Watchtower against a backdrop of stars.

Activity: Astrophotography
Location: Grand Canyon Desert View Watchtower; GPS: N36 02.634' / W111 49.577'
Start: Desert View parking lot; GPS: N36 02.480' / W111 49.606'
Elevation gain: 45 feet
Distance: 0.4 mile out and back
Difficulty: Easy
Hiking time: About 10 minutes
Seasons/schedule: Open year-round; great any season
Dark sky designation: International Dark Sky Park
Timing: No moon to a quarter moon; arrive at sunset or any time of the night.
Fees and permits: National park entrance fees apply; see nps.gov/grca/planyourvisit/fees.htm for current fees.
Trail contacts: Grand Canyon National Park, PO Box 129, Grand Canyon 86023; (928) 638-7888; nps.gov/grca/index.htm

Dog-friendly: Yes, leashed up to 6 feet in length on trails above the rim
Trail surface: Mostly paved; rocky at some viewpoints
Land status: National park and National Historic Landmark
Nearest town: Cameron, Arizona
Other trail users: Walkers, those in wheelchairs
Maps: Grand Canyon National Park maps available online at nps.gov/grca/planyourvisit/maps.htm
Water availability: Yes
Special considerations: Some areas around the Desert View Watchtower are located near unfenced edges of the canyon with sharp drop-offs. Ice can form on walkways, rocks, and stairs during winter months. Overnight temperatures in winter are normally below freezing.
Other: Grand Canyon National Park normally hosts a large annual star party in June; check the official website for details.

FINDING THE TRAILHEAD

From the Grand Canyon South Rim Visitor Center, take the south entrance road south for 0.6 mile to AZ 64 and turn left (east). Continue on AZ 64 East for 21.4 miles; then turn left (north) onto Desert View Road. Park in the Desert View parking lot and begin the trail to the Desert View Watchtower by walking north to one of the paved paths leading to the tower. Trailhead GPS: N36 02.480' / W111 49.606'

THE ADVENTURE

Built in 1932 on the southeastern rim of the Grand Canyon, the Desert View Watchtower was the creation of Mary Colter, also known as the "architect of the Southwest." Mary Colter drew inspiration from the watchtowers of Puebloan cultures such as the Hopi to create the Desert View Watchtower. The structure is regarded as a work of art, with interior paintings by Hopi artist Fred Kabotie and an exterior stone structure that seamlessly blends into the surrounding landscape of the Grand Canyon. The beauty of the Desert View Watchtower and the massive dark skies above the Grand Canyon

The Desert View Watchtower stands firm on the edge of the Grand Canyon under a sky full of stars.

combine to create wonderful astrophotography opportunities. To capture the skies above the Desert View Watchtower, start your journey from the Desert View parking lot.

Look Up
Up to one hundred satellites can be seen in a single night when observing in dark skies.

The show begins when you arrive at the Desert View parking lot after dark and see thousands of stars shining overhead. Walk to the northern side of the lot and find one of the paved pathways to the Desert View Watchtower, which should be lit in the distance. Follow one of the pathways north for about 0.2 mile and feel the excitement build as you approach the mysterious tower at the edge of the Grand Canyon. As you near the watchtower, admire the beauty of individually placed stones encircling the tower all the way to the top. Get creative and set up your camera for astrophotography with long-exposure settings.

With a wide-open aperture, high ISO, and long shutter speed, find a star in the sky or use the lights of the Desert View Watchtower to manually set your focus. Take aim at the historic structure and look for compositions that reflect your unique vision of the Grand Canyon. Astronomical structures like the Milky Way core or large constellations like Ursa Major make excellent starry backdrops for this location. As your camera is exposing the photographs, take some time to just enjoy the night sky and all it has to offer your

Mary Colter was known for being detail oriented, and on one occasion during construction, she directed the workers to replace two whole layers of stones from the tower because one stone was not placed the way she envisioned.

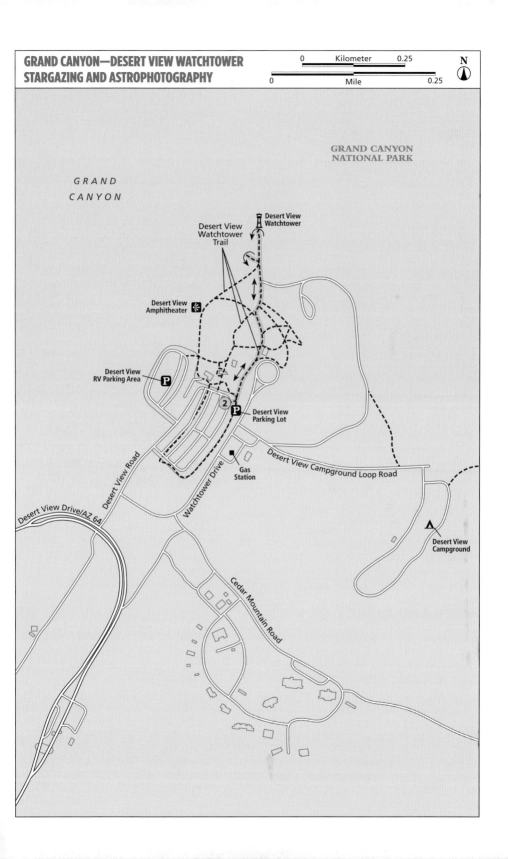

GRAND CANYON—DESERT VIEW WATCHTOWER STARGAZING AND ASTROPHOTOGRAPHY

0 — Kilometer — 0.25

0 — Mile — 0.25

N

GRAND CANYON NATIONAL PARK

GRAND CANYON

Desert View Watchtower

Desert View Watchtower Trail

Desert View Amphitheater

Desert View RV Parking Area

Desert View Parking Lot

Gas Station

Desert View Road

Desert View Campground Loop Road

Watchtower Drive

Desert View Drive/AZ 64

Desert View Campground

Cedar Mountain Road

Lit from the inside like a jack-o'-lantern, the Desert View Watchtower looms under the dark skies over the Grand Canyon.

naked eyes. Keep a sharp eye out for meteors streaking across the sky; they may make an unexpected appearance in your images as well!

Different vantages and compositions can be found in the area around the Desert View Watchtower; however, be cautious of the canyon's edge. Astrophotography can be very rewarding and fun for its creativity, but it is not worth risking your life unnecessarily to improve image composition. Also, be sure to respect any closed areas at the Watchtower, since you are likely visiting after-hours. When ready to depart, simply find the paved path to the parking lot and walk 0.2 mile south to your vehicle. Astrophotography at the Desert View Watchtower will leave you with great memories and photos you can share with your friends and family.

MILES AND DIRECTIONS

0.0   Start from the Desert View Visitor Area parking lot and walk north for 0.2 mile on a paved path to the Desert View Watchtower.

0.2   Arrive at the Desert View Watchtower. To return to the parking lot, walk back on the paved path south for 0.2 mile.

0.4   Arrive back at the trailhead.

 To photograph the starry sky and the details in the Grand Canyon simultaneously, time your visit for a quarter moon or wait until the last 30 minutes of twilight to light the landscape.

3 GRAND CANYON—NORTH RIM VISITOR CENTER STARGAZING

Answer the call to the Grand Canyon's North Rim, the one that everyone says they want to see "one day." For this adventure, enjoy a short hike under pure night skies to Bright Angel Point and around the historic Grand Canyon Lodge.

Activity: Night hiking
Location: Grand Canyon North Rim Visitor Center; GPS: N36 11.964' / W112 03.130'
Start: Bright Angel Point Trailhead; GPS: N36 11.906' / W112 03.133'
Elevation gain: 83 feet
Distance: 1.15-mile lollipop
Difficulty: Easy
Hiking time: About 15 minutes
Seasons/schedule: Open May 15 to Dec 1; best spring through fall
Dark sky designation: International Dark Sky Park
Timing: No moon to a quarter moon
Fees and permits: National park entrance fees apply; see nps.gov/grca/planyourvisit/fees.htm for current fees.
Trail contacts: Grand Canyon National Park, PO Box 129, Grand Canyon 86023; (928) 638-7888; nps.gov/grca/index.htm
Dog-friendly: No
Trail surface: Paved and dirt

Land status: National park
Nearest town: Fredonia, Arizona
Other trail users: Walkers, photographers
Maps: Grand Canyon National Park maps available online at nps.gov/grca/planyourvisit/maps.htm
Water availability: Yes; drinking water available at the visitor center
Special considerations: Be careful at the edge of the canyon rim. Dress for low nighttime temperatures at the canyon's North Rim due to high elevation. Watch your step on uneven surfaces at the viewpoints. The North Rim is closed winter through mid-spring. Be alert for monsoon storms, which can produce damaging wind, hail, lightning, and torrential rain at any time during the summer. Monsoon season can create clouds that limit visibility of the night sky. Wildfires and smoke are a threat throughout the fire season.

FINDING THE TRAILHEAD
From Jacob Lake, take AZ 67 south for 43.5 miles. Park in the Grand Canyon North Rim Visitor Center parking lot, on the left. The Bright Angel Point Trailhead is located at the southeastern corner of the parking lot, near the bathrooms. Trailhead GPS: N36 11.906' / W112 03.133'

THE ADVENTURE
Arizona's darkest skies can be found at the North Rim of the Grand Canyon. Located hundreds of miles from cities, light pollution is essentially nonexistent at the North Rim. Low light pollution combined with a high elevation of 8,200 feet makes this part of the Grand Canyon a prime Arizona stargazing location. On this adventure, enjoy an easy 1.0-mile night hike on a small network of trails around the North Rim Visitor Center. Start your adventure from the Bright Angel Point Trailhead at night.

The hike starts as a dirt trail heading south and then changes to a paved path once you break out of the trees around 0.16 mile south of the trailhead. Get your first taste

The Bright Angel Point Trail climbs past a pine tree under a sky full of stars at the North Rim.

of the stars once you break out of the trees and continue hiking south on the paved trail for 0.3 mile until you reach Bright Angel Point. At Bright Angel Point you'll be amazed at the sheer number of stars in the sky shining over the dark maw of the Grand Canyon. Next, turn around and hike 0.25 mile north toward the trailhead; then turn left at the first fork from the Bright Angel Point Trail onto a dirt path. Head northwest on the dirt path to access a few more viewpoints to enjoy the stars.

Look Up
The Milky Way appears at an angle in the night sky because the solar system plane is 60 degrees off the plane of the Milky Way.

About 0.13 mile up the dirt path, you'll come across a set of stairs leading to another viewpoint overlooking the canyon. Once you have enjoyed this viewpoint, continue northwest on the dirt path for another 0.1 mile to a second point for more stargazing. Afterward, climb a set of stairs on the south side of the visitor center lodge to a deck lit by yellow lights. The decks flanking the Grand Canyon Lodge feature wooden lounge chairs that face south over the canyon, giving you a relaxing way to sit and enjoy the stars. After lounging on the deck, return to the visitor center parking lot by making your way north on the paths weaving between the historic cabins of the Grand Canyon Lodge for 0.11 mile.

MILES AND DIRECTIONS

0.0 Start from the Bright Angel Point Trailhead and head south on the Bright Angel Point Trail for 0.46 mile.

0.46 Arrive at Bright Angel Point. Turn around and head north on the Bright Angel Point Trail for 0.25 mile to a fork in the trail.

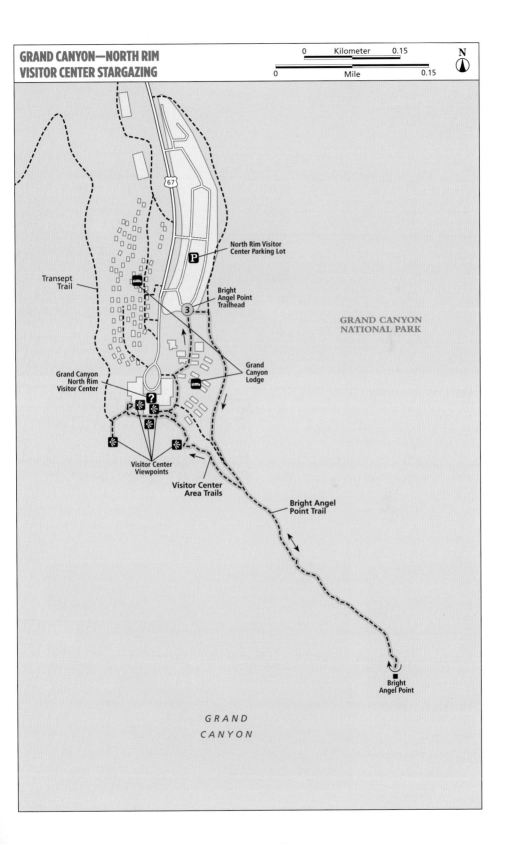

GRAND CANYON—NORTH RIM
VISITOR CENTER STARGAZING

0   Kilometer   0.15
0   Mile   0.15

N

67

North Rim Visitor
Center Parking Lot

P

Transept
Trail

Bright
Angel Point
Trailhead

3

GRAND CANYON
NATIONAL PARK

Grand
Canyon
Lodge

Grand Canyon
North Rim
Visitor Center

?

Visitor Center
Viewpoints

Visitor Center
Area Trails

Bright Angel
Point Trail

Bright
Angel Point

GRAND
CANYON

The Grand Canyon Lodge sits atop the North Rim of the Grand Canyon as the Milky Way sets in the west.

0.71   Turn left at the fork and head northwest on a dirt trail for 0.23 mile, stopping at the viewpoints along the way.

0.94   At the second viewpoint, turn around and travel east 0.1 mile back down the dirt trail to a set of stairs leading up to the Grand Canyon Lodge.

1.04   Arrive at the Grand Canyon Lodge and enjoy the chairs on the deck. To return to the Bright Angel Point Trailhead, head north on the paved trails between the Grand Canyon Lodge cabins for 0.11 mile.

1.15   Arrive back at the trailhead.

> There has been continuous human use and occupation of the Grand Canyon for nearly 12,000 years.

Look Up
Jupiter is the largest planet in the solar system, containing twice the mass of all the other planets combined.

The Milky Way shines bright over wooden lounge chairs at the North Rim's Grand Canyon Lodge.

4 GRAND CANYON—CAPE ROYAL STARGAZING AND ASTROPHOTOGRAPHY

Stargaze and photograph the night sky at Cape Royal, one of the most beautiful, accessible, and dark locations in Grand Canyon National Park. A quick 0.7-mile sunset-to-night hike will lead you to dramatic views of Wotan's Throne, Vishnu Temple, and the vastness of the Grand Canyon.

Activity: Stargazing and astrophotography
Location: Grand Canyon National Park, Cape Royal; GPS: N36 07.033' / W111 56.929'
Start: Cape Royal Trailhead; GPS: N36 07.334' / W111 56.965'
Elevation gain: 60 feet
Distance: 1.1 miles out and back
Difficulty: Easy
Hiking time: About 30 minutes
Seasons/schedule: Open May 15 to Dec 1; best in spring, summer, and fall
Dark sky designation: International Dark Sky Park
Timing: No moon to a quarter moon. Arrive at sunset for the best lighting.
Fees and permits: National park entrance fees apply; see nps.gov/grca/planyourvisit/fees.htm for current fees.
Trail contacts: Grand Canyon National Park, PO Box 129, Grand Canyon 86023; (928) 638-7888; nps.gov/grca/index.htm

Dog-friendly: No
Trail surface: Paved, dirt, rock
Land status: National park
Nearest town: Fredonia, Arizona
Other trail users: Walkers, photographers
Maps: Grand Canyon National Park maps available online at nps.gov/grca/planyourvisit/maps.htm
Water availability: None
Special considerations: Be careful at the edge of the canyon rim. Dress for low nighttime temperatures at the canyon's North Rim due to high elevation. Watch your step on uneven surfaces at the viewpoints. The North Rim is closed winter through mid-spring. Be alert for monsoon storms, which can produce damaging wind, hail, lightning, and torrential rain at any time during the summer. Monsoon season can create clouds that limit visibility of the night sky. Wildfires and smoke are a threat throughout the fire season.

FINDING THE TRAILHEAD

From the Grand Canyon North Rim entrance, take AZ 67 south for 9.6 miles; turn left onto Cape Royal Road and continue for 5.4 miles to the Y junction. Turn right at the Y and continue on Cape Royal Road for 10 miles to the Cape Royal parking lot. The Cape Royal Trailhead is located at the southeastern corner of the lot. Trailhead GPS: N36 07.334' / W111 56.965'

THE ADVENTURE

The long, winding road to Cape Royal is a real joy, featuring beautiful alpine trees and numerous viewpoints of the Grand Canyon. Upon reaching the Cape Royal parking lot, the area appears unassuming, with a scrubby forest of piñon and juniper trees blocking views of the canyon. However, looks can be deceiving, as these little trees hide one of the

As twilight fades to night over the Grand Canyon, the core of the Milky Way makes its appearance over Wotan's Throne at Cape Royal.

most spectacular views of the Grand Canyon. What's more, Cape Royal also features one of the darkest night skies in the park, making it ideal for stargazing and astrophotography. Begin this adventure an hour before sunset and take the paved Cape Royal Trail south into the woods.

Heading south on the Cape Royal Trail, you'll first find educational signs and then jaw-dropping views of the Grand Canyon. Interpretive signs along this 0.7-mile route to the main Cape Royal vista will teach you about hardy plants, animals, and how Native peoples utilized plants for generations. At

> **LOOK UP**
> The night sky looks like a dome due to the curvature of the Earth and the atmosphere.

0.13 mile from the trailhead you'll have your first view of Angel's Window, a hole in a large cliff that looks directly at the Colorado River. Slightly farther down the trail, by 0.12 mile you'll approach a turnoff for a quick 0.2-mile side trip to the top of Angel's Window featuring dizzying heights above the Grand Canyon. Return to the Cape Royal Trail and hike the remaining 0.25 mile to incredible views of Wotan's Throne and Vishnu Temple at Cape Royal.

The sunset view from Cape Royal cannot be underestimated; it is one of the best in the park and easy to access. Use your camera to capture the sun's final rays on the west side of Wotan's Throne and the massive Grand Canyon below. As twilight begins, you'll have to exercise some patience for about 45 minutes to an hour as the night slowly begins to arrive. Astrophotographers should take long-exposure images in the deep nautical twilight to astronomical twilight of both the stars and the landscape features. When the night settles in for good, you'll see why the Grand Canyon is an International Dark Sky Park.

> As the crow flies, the North Rim and South Rim Visitor Centers are only 10 miles apart, but to get to both visitor centers by road, you must drive 215 miles.

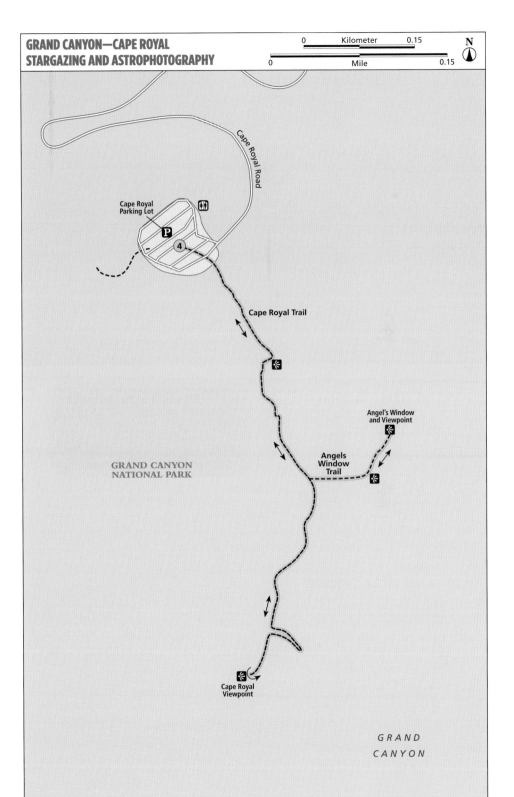

Kilometer

0   0.15

0   Mile   0.15

N

Cape Royal Road

Cape Royal
Parking Lot

P

4

Cape Royal Trail

Angel's Window
and Viewpoint

Angels
Window
Trail

GRAND CANYON
NATIONAL PARK

Cape Royal
Viewpoint

GRAND
CANYON

The Milky Way hangs over the Grand Canyon from Cape Royal, dwarfing the San Francisco Peaks, to the bottom left of the frame.

The Milky Way bridges horizons, glowing so bright you can see everything by starlight. Night skies like this are special and rare throughout much of Arizona and the United States. Use a stargazing app on your phone to learn new constellations and facts about stars in the constellations you already love. For photographers, the stars are going

LOOK UP
Altair, in the constellation Aquila, is the twelfth-brightest star in the night sky and is only 16.6 light-years away.

to appear thick like snow in your images, with details in the night sky that you just can't achieve in light-polluted skies. Once you have stargazed and taken the last shot, simply head north on the Cape Royal Trail back to the parking lot for 0.4 mile.

MILES AND DIRECTIONS

0.0 Start from the Cape Royal Trailhead and head south for 0.13 mile to the first viewpoint.

0.13 Reach the first viewpoint; continue south on the Cape Royal Trail for 0.12 mile to the Angel's Window view trail.

0.25 Turn left and head 0.1 mile east to the Angel's Window viewpoint.

0.35 Arrive at the Angel's Window viewpoint. Return to the Cape Royal Trail the same way you came; continue south on the trail for 0.25 mile.

0.7 Arrive at the Cape Royal Vista. Return to the Cape Royal parking lot by heading north on the Cape Royal Trail for 0.4 mile.

1.1 Arrive back at the trailhead.

5 DEMOTTE CAMPGROUND CAR CAMPING

Camp out on the Kaibab Plateau at Demotte Campground, a wonderful campground 30 minutes from the Grand Canyon's North Rim. Enjoy one of the darkest night skies in Arizona from Demotte Park, a large open grassy meadow located just outside the campground.

Activity: Car camping
Location: Demotte Campground; GPS: N36 24.642′ / W112 08.060′
Difficulty: Easy
Seasons/schedule: Open mid-May to mid-Oct; best in late spring, summer, and fall
Timing: New moon to a crescent moon
Fees and permits: Nightly campsite fees required. Reservations are accepted for some sites; others are first come, first served; see recreation.gov/camping/campgrounds/234722?tab=seasons for current fees.
Campground contacts: North Kaibab Ranger District, 430 South Main St., PO Box 248, Fredonia 86022; (928) 660-3913; fs.usda.gov/recarea/kaibab/recarea/?recid=11697
Dog-friendly: Yes, leashed and under control
Land status: National forest
Nearest town: Fredonia, Arizona
Suitable camp setups: RVs, trailers, tents, cars, trucks, SUVs, vans

Facilities: Campground hosts, self-pay station, drinking water spigots, pit toilets, fire rings, food hanger, picnic tables, trash services
Maps: Forest Service map available online at fs.usda.gov/recarea/kaibab/recarea/?recid=11699
Water availability: Yes; drinking water spigots
Special considerations: Bears, squirrels, elk, mountain lions, coyotes, and other animals inhabit the area; use caution. Store food properly in bear-proof containers, vehicles, or hung in a tree to avoid attracting wildlife to your campsite. Located at more than 9,000 feet elevation, overnight temperatures can be very cold, even in summer. Monsoon season can create heavy rain, damaging winds, and lightning. Wildfires and smoke are a threat throughout the fire season. Fire restrictions including campfire bans may be in place; be sure to check current fire restrictions.

FINDING THE CAMPGROUND
From Jacob Lake, take AZ 67 South for 25.6 miles. Turn right onto FR 616 and head west for 0.2 mile to Demotte Campground. Campground GPS: N36 24.642′ / W112 08.060′

THE ADVENTURE
Demotte Campground is a sleepy campground located at the edge of a large meadow called Demotte Park on the Kaibab Plateau. A campsite is almost always available at this

Meadows along AZ 67 leading to the North Rim like Demotte Park were created by a variety of natural factors, including exclusive competition from grasses, water drainage patterns, and soil chemistry.

The Cygnus region of the Milky Way floats over the Kaibab National Forest at Demotte Campground.

A thunderstorm moves in over Demotte Campground, obscuring the Milky Way.

DEMOTTE CAMPGROUND CAR CAMPING

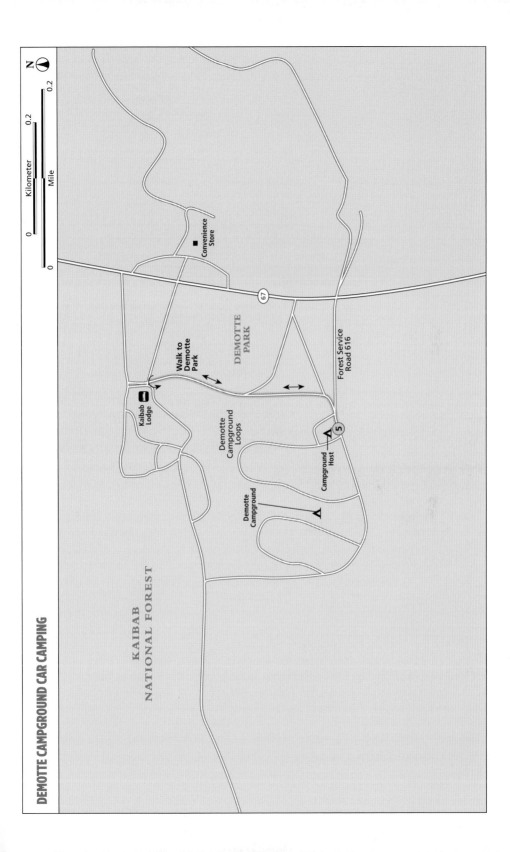

The Pleaides and Taurus rise in the eastern sky over Demotte Park on the Kaibab Plateau.

forested campground next to Demotte Park, which is part of a series of long meadows along AZ 67 between Jacob Lake and the Grand Canyon's North Rim. Deer, elk, and even bison roam these scenic subalpine meadows both day and night. At night, the universe shines with brilliant clarity in one of the darkest skies available in Arizona. Demotte Campground makes a perfect base camp for adventures just 30 minutes away from the North Rim and a destination of its own with its dark skies, flowery meadows, and fresh air.

LOOK UP

The sun and the solar system move through the Milky Way in the direction of the bright star Vega in the constellation Lyra.

The sun and the solar system are traveling away from Sirius, the brightest star in the sky, as we move through the Milky Way.

Check in to your campsite and feel the cool breeze at this campground located at an elevation of more than 9,000 feet. Tall trees tower over the thirty-plus campsites at Demotte Campground, providing shade and a place for birds to caw and chirp in the forest. After setting up your campsite, enjoy some daytime activities, like taking a walk to Demotte Park or driving to the North Rim. Wildflowers and plenty of space to picnic on the grass make Demotte Park a great place to relax in nature. As clouds drift by and the sun sets behind the trees, watch the night show come together with the glow of tens of thousands of stars.

Take a short walk from your campsite to Demotte Park after dark to see an immense night sky. Timing your visit for a moonless night will maximize your view of the cosmos at Demotte Park, including full constellations and dozens of shooting stars. For the best night vision, walk to a place where the lights from the Kaibab Lodge and other buildings won't interfere, and make sure not to look at any passing cars on AZ 67. It's so dark here that you can see the landscape by starlight and even faint shadows cast by the light of the Milky Way. After a night of stargazing, return to your campsite and enjoy a good night's rest and many more nights on the Kaibab Plateau.

6 GLEN CANYON KAYAK CAMPING

Kayak and camp on the Colorado River's world-famous Horseshoe Bend under the starry skies of Glen Canyon. Enjoy an easy paddle through this spectacular canyon to discover its ancient petroglyphs, sandy beaches, soaring cliffs, and clear waters.

Activity: Kayak camping
Location: Glen Canyon, downstream of Glen Canyon Dam; GPS: N36 54.128' / W111 30.193'
Put-in: Beach downstream of Glen Canyon Dam; GPS: N36 55.514' / W111 28.902'
Takeout: Lees Ferry; GPS: N36 51.945' / W111 35.188'
Distance: 15.15 miles point to point
Paddling time: About 8 hours
Difficulty: Easy due to an upstream shuttle and a calm steady current
Rapids: Class I, easy; smooth water, light riffles, clear passages
Waterway type: River
Current: Slow to medium slow
River gradient: ~2.44 feet per minute
River gauge: Average 10,900 cubic feet per second at Lees Ferry
Land status: National recreation area

Park contact: Glen Canyon National Recreation Area, PO Box 1507, Page 86040; (928) 608-6200; nps.gov/glca/index.htm
Nearest town: Page, Arizona
Seasons/schedule: Open year-round; best in summer and fall
Timing: Any time and any phase of the moon. Start the paddle from morning to early afternoon at the latest.
Fees and permits: National park entrance fees apply; see nps.gov/grca/planyourvisit/fees.htm for current fees.
Boats used: Kayaks, paddleboards, canoes
Maps: NPS map available online at nps.gov/glca/planyourvisit/camping.htm

PUT-IN/TAKEOUT INFORMATION

For the put-in, reserve a backhauling service from Lees Ferry to Glen Canyon Dam and go to Lees Ferry, 43 miles southwest of Page, Arizona. To get to Lees Ferry, take US 89 South for 23 miles; turn right onto US 89A and head north for 14.3 miles. Turn right on Lees Ferry Road and head north for 5.8 miles to the Lees Ferry boat launch. Unload your kayak and camping gear at the boat ramp with your backhaul service provider and then park your vehicle in the overnight parking area south of the boat ramp (GPS: N36 51.960' / W111 35.499'). The river shuttle will use a motorized boat to backhaul you and your boat 15 miles upstream to a beach, where you will put in your kayak and start your adventure downstream. You will take out your boat once you return to Lees Ferry. Several backhauling services are available, including Wilderness River Adventures, Kayak Horseshoe Bend, and Kayak the Colorado.

THE ADVENTURE

The Colorado River cuts a spectacular path through Glen Canyon, characterized by the meander of ice-cold water between massive sandstone cliffs. On this 15-mile kayaking camping adventure, see the picturesque Horseshoe Bend and historic Lees Ferry, two of the more famous landmarks on the Colorado River's entire length. Adventurers of all skill levels can enjoy

Archaeologists believe that the descending sheep petroglyph panel in Glen Canyon is 3,000 to 6,000 years old.

Horseshoe Bend glows in a brilliant red sunset from the rim of Glen Canyon.

a quick backhaul upriver followed by an easy overnight paddle downstream of the Glen Canyon Dam to one of five campgrounds on the water's edge. As night settles in, you can count satellites and the hundreds of stars over the campfire with friends and family. To begin this adventure, meet up with your backhauling service at Lees Ferry and take a scenic cruise up to a beach downstream of Glen Canyon Dam.

Feel the wind in your hair and the spray of water as the backhaul makes its way up the Colorado. Dramatic red cliffs surround you in every direction as you journey deeper into this riparian wilderness. Hear the engine wind down and feel your excitement build as you approach your put-in point, a sandy beach just downstream of Glen Canyon Dam. Set up your kayak/paddleboard on the shore and take your first strokes into the calm current running through super-clear waters. As you kayak down the Colorado River, you'll see hanging gardens on the canyon walls, forests of plants, and fish beneath the river's surface.

> **SIDETRIP:** Drive to a spectacular view of Horseshoe Bend at an overlook located just off US 89, 2.6 miles south of Page, Arizona.

Kayak downstream for 4.75 miles to reach a beach and trailhead leading to one of the highlights of this trip, a wall of ancient petroglyphs. Take the short 0.2-mile hike west of the river to see a panel of bighorn sheep petroglyphs and other figures etched into the desert varnish. Return to your kayak and continue downstream for up to 1.8 miles around iconic Horseshoe Bend, where a swift current will quietly carry you around the bend. Choose Nine-Mile or Eight-Mile Campground, located on the inner shores of Horseshoe Bend, for a unique camping experience with one of the widest sky views. Many campsites are available for your enjoyment and include fire rings, and there's a pit toilet for your convenience. Once camp is set up, take some time to enjoy the sandy shores and cold water of the river by fishing, hiking, or simply standing around in the river with a snack.

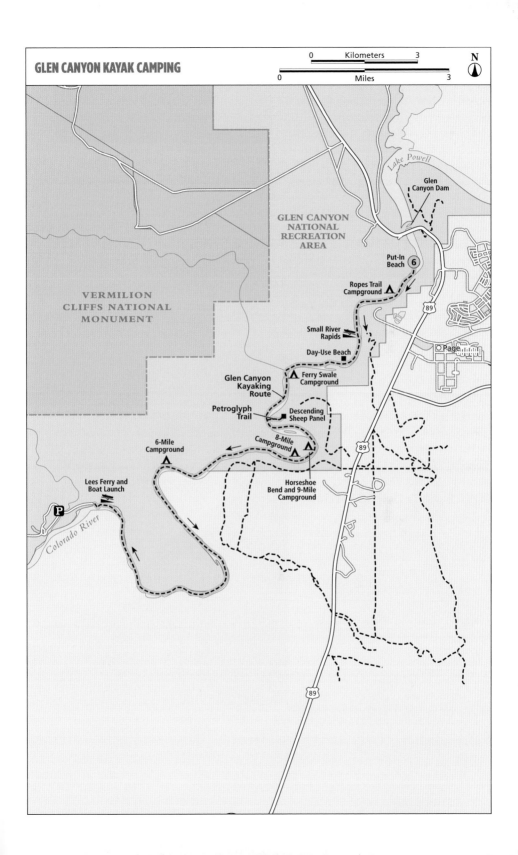

GLEN CANYON KAYAK CAMPING

0 Kilometers 3

0 Miles 3

N

Glen
Canyon Dam

Lake Powell

GLEN CANYON
NATIONAL
RECREATION
AREA

Put-In
Beach 6

Ropes Trail
Campground

89

VERMILION
CLIFFS NATIONAL
MONUMENT

Small River
Rapids

Day-Use Beach

Page

Glen Canyon
Kayaking
Route

Ferry Swale
Campground

Petroglyph
Trail

Descending
Sheep Panel

89

6-Mile
Campground

8-Mile
Campground

Lees Ferry and
Boat Launch

P

Horseshoe
Bend and 9-Mile
Campground

Colorado River

89

Watch a pretty sunset over the canyon and note how the red canyon walls reflect the warm colors of the sky. Enjoy a band of hundreds of stars shining in the dark skies between canyon rims as night settles over Glen Canyon. Listen to the sounds of this riparian area at night—bats chirping overhead, crickets singing,

LOOK UP
The constellation Coma Berenices, located between Leo and Boötes, contains the Coma open star cluster, about 280 light-years away.

the constant flow of water. After a good night's rest, pack up camp in the morning and continue your paddle downriver for 8.6 miles back to Lees Ferry. Several sandy beaches along the way make great spots for taking a break and enjoying the canyon for a while longer before your eventual takeout. In the last couple miles of paddling down the river, you may see wild horses grazing on the water's edge, adding another touch of the Wild West to your adventure. When you reach Lees Ferry, simply land your boat on the boat ramp and fetch your vehicle for the journey home.

THE PADDLING

The current throughout Glen Canyon is slow with some areas of moderate current that will swiftly carry you downstream. Small riffles and few obstacles such as boulders make it easy to navigate while in the river. Beaches and day-use areas with restrooms throughout the paddle allow for convenient breaks.

MILES AND DIRECTIONS

0.0 Start from the put-in point at a beach just downstream of Glen Canyon Dam. Paddle south with the current on the Colorado River.

0.64 Reach the Ropes Trail Campground.

3.77 Reach the Ferry Swale Campground.

5.95 Reach the 9-Mile Campground.

6.58 Reach the 8-Mile Campground.

8.85 Reach the 6-Mile Campground.

15.15 Arrive at Lees Ferry.

The Colorado River bends to the south as moonlight lights up the striking red cliffs of Glen Canyon.

7 WHITE POCKET ASTROPHOTOGRAPHY AND 4X4 CAMPING

Take an adventurous four-wheeling trip across Vermillion Cliffs National Monument to the sandstone wonderland of White Pocket. Camp under unforgettable night skies and photograph the stars over White Pocket's iconic sandstone landscape.

Activity: 4×4 driving, astrophotography, camping

Location: White Pocket; GPS: N36 57.363' / W111 53.756'

Campground: White Pocket dispersed camping area; GPS: N36 57.360' / W111 53.539'

Start: White Pocket Trailhead; GPS: N36 57.311' / W111 53.623'

Elevation gain: 0 feet

Distance: 0.3 mile out and back

Difficulty: Moderate due to required route-finding and map-reading skills

Hiking time: About 1 hour

Seasons/schedule: Open year-round; best in fall and spring

Timing: No moon to a quarter moon

Fees and permits: None

Trail and campground contacts: Vermillion Cliffs National Monument, Arizona Strip Field Office, 345 East Riverside Dr., St. George, UT 84790-6714; (435) 688-3200; blm.gov/national-conservation-lands/arizona/vermilion-cliffs

Dog-friendly: Yes, under control

Trail surface: Rock, dirt, sand

Land status: National monument managed by the Bureau of Land Management

Nearest town: Kanab, Utah

Other trail users: Photographers, hikers

Suitable camp setups: Tents; 4×4 trucks, SUVs, vans, UTVs/ATVs, dirt bikes

Maps: Map for the route to White Pocket available online at blm.gov/sites/blm.gov/files/documents/files/AZ%20White_Pocket_PDF.pdf

Facilities: None

Water availability: None

Special considerations: Four-wheel-drive vehicles only on the roads to White Pocket due to deep sand and rocky obstacles. Off-road four-wheel-driving skills are required to navigate the narrow sandy roads to White Pocket. Four-wheel-drive rental services are available in Page, Arizona, and Kanab, Utah. Tour companies that offer astrophotography workshops and camping are available. All-wheel-drive and two-wheel-drive vehicles will get stuck on the way to White Pocket. Do not attempt to bring a trailer; it could get stuck in the deep sand. Cell phone signal is limited throughout the area. A tow/rescue from Vermillion Cliffs National Monument is very expensive. Be sure to close all gates on the dirt roads after you pass through. Roads may become impassible when wet during rain- or snowstorms. Be cautious while driving around blind corners and driving through mud. Overnight temperatures can be freezing in winter, and daytime temperatures in the summer can exceed 100°F. Snakes and scorpions inhabit the area; be cautious. Respect delicate rock formations—walk around them, not on them.

FINDING THE CAMPGROUND AND TRAILHEAD

From House Rock Valley Road (BLM 1065), 23.5 miles south of US 89 or 9.3 miles north of US 89A, turn east on BLM 1017. Drive east on BLM 1017 for 6.2 miles; at the junction with BLM 1087, put your vehicle in four-wheel-drive "high" and proceed northeast on BLM 1087 for 3.94 miles. At the fork with BLM 1086, go left and continue north for 5.42 miles to the White Pocket parking/camping area. Campground GPS: N36 57.360' / W111 53.539'; trailhead GPS: N36 57.311' / W111 53.623'

THE ADVENTURE

Vermillion Cliffs National Monument exhibits the rugged and wild beauty of the Arizona Strip. Dark skies reign over White Pocket, an area of swirling sandstone and quilt-like erosional patterns deep within the national monument. White Pocket's elegantly eroded sandstone punctuated by water-filled tinajas make it a photographer's paradise. The area doesn't require a permit for access, and you are allowed to camp at the trailhead; however, it's impossible to reach without a four-wheel-drive vehicle. Take the thrilling offroad adventure across Vermillion Cliffs National Monument to White Pocket with your 4×4, a rented 4×4, or a tour company.

The drive to White Pocket feels like a roller coaster through the desert as your tires track through deep, sandy grooves in the road. Arrive at White Pocket during the day so you can see the landscape and set up a campsite near the trailhead. Go to the White Pocket Trailhead on the west side of the parking lot and take the short 0.15-mile walk west to White Pocket. Hike around the otherworldly red, white, and yellow sandstone formations and scope out compositions for astrophotography later in the night. As the sun drops toward the horizon, take some final golden-hour images and prepare for a spectacular night of stargazing and astrophotography.

There are unlimited compositions for a stunning photo of White Pocket under a clear night sky. Starting from 45 minutes after sunset, stars will begin to shine in the sky through

The Milky Way shines over a crescent-shaped pool in the smooth sandstone landscape of White Pocket.

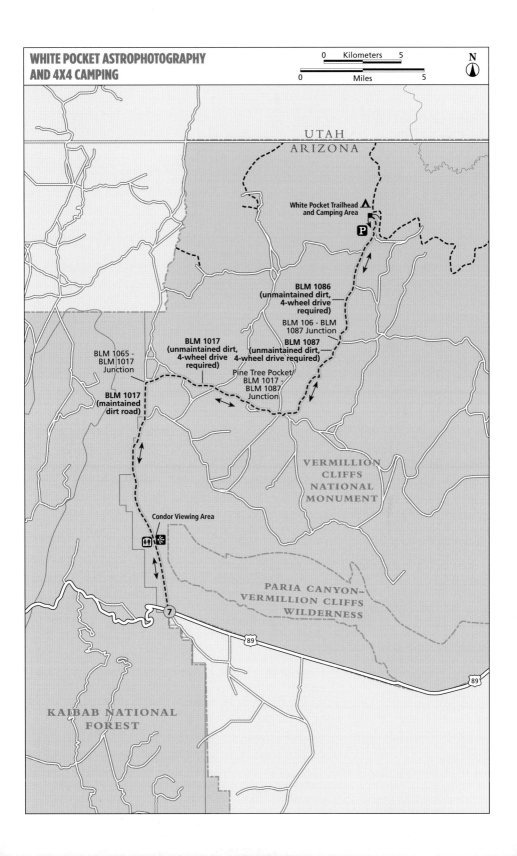

The moon rises in the eastern skies as early twilight casts a blue glow over the white sandstone of White Pocket.

the twilight. Photographers can rely on natural twilight or moonlight to capture images of the textured sandstone under the cosmos. Those with powerful low-light cameras can crank up their ISO sensitivity to image sandstone patterns lit by starlight. Capture tinaja reflections of the stars, rock formations, or a pine tree to spice up your photography.

Between exposures, be sure to lie down on the pillow-like rocks and enjoy your view of our beautiful universe. Staring up into the sky while lying down is an immersive experience that can make you feel like you're floating in space. You may meet other astro-photographers on the hunt for the perfect shot at White Pocket, so be mindful of their work before using light sources in yours. Stay up as long as you want to image the night skies; when you need the rest, head east to the White Pocket Trailhead. When it's time to head home, drive the same dirt roads you came in on and hit the smooth pavement with shots that will make you proud.

MILES AND DIRECTIONS

0.0 Start from the White Pocket Trailhead and head west into White Pocket for at least 0.15 mile.

0.15 Reach White Pocket and explore freely in the sandstone landscape. To return to the White Pocket Trailhead, come back to where you first entered White Pocket and head east to the trailhead for 0.15 mile.

0.3 Arrive back at the trailhead.

8 DOGTOWN LAKE CAMPGROUND CAR CAMPING

Car camp at Dogtown Lake, a forested reservoir in the Kaibab National Forest just south of the small town of Williams. Take a short walk to the shore of the lake and watch the stars rise over the trees and set over Bill Williams Mountain.

Activity: Car camping

Location: Dogtown Lake Campground; GPS: N35 12.704' / W112 07.435'

Difficulty: Easy

Seasons/schedule: Generally open May through Sept, depending on the weather; best in late spring to early fall

Timing: No moon to a quarter moon

Fees and permits: Nightly campsite fees required; see recreation.gov/camping/campgrounds/233956?tab=seasons for current fees. Campsites are offered on a first-come, first-served basis at the end of spring and beginning of fall or when not reserved.

Campground contacts: Kaibab National Forest, Williams Ranger District, 742 South Clover Rd., Williams 86046; (928) 635-5600; fs.usda.gov/recarea/kaibab/recarea/?recid=11653

Dog-friendly: Yes, leashed and under control.

Land status: USDA Forest Service campground

Nearest town: Williams, Arizona

Suitable camp setups: Cars, trucks, SUVs, vans, RVs, trailers, tents

Maps: Campground map available online at recreation.gov/camping/campgrounds/233956

Facilities: Pit toilets, trash services; picnic tables, fire rings, grills; wheelchair-accessible campsites; sometimes drinking water; no RV/trailer hookups available

Water availability: Yes; however, the drinking water system is sometimes shut down. Check for drinking water availability, and prepare to pack in your own water.

Special considerations: Respect the elk, deer, skunk, squirrels, and black bears that inhabit the forest. Store food properly in hard-sided containers like bear cans, or store food inside vehicles. Fire restrictions may be in place; check before you have a fire. Wildfires and smoke are a danger throughout fire season. Monsoon storms can produce lightning, damaging winds, torrential rain, and flooding that can wash out the dirt roads leading to Dogtown Lake.

FINDING THE CAMPGROUND

From Williams, take 4th Street/Perkinsville Road south for 3.7 miles; turn left onto Dogtown Road, a maintained dirt road. Head east on Dogtown Road for 2.7 miles; at a fork in the road, go left and continue north on Dogtown Road for 0.9 mile. At a second fork, go right and continue northeast on Dogtown Road to Dogtown Lake Campground, 0.4 mile ahead. Campground GPS: N35 12.704' / W112 07.435'

THE ADVENTURE

"Dogtown" refers to the extensive prairie dog families that were found in the fields around Dogtown Lake. This reservoir south of Williams is surrounded by an extensive forest of ponderosa pine. Ravens, elk, and squirrels call the forests home, while trout,

DOGTOWN LAKE CAMPGROUND CAR CAMPING

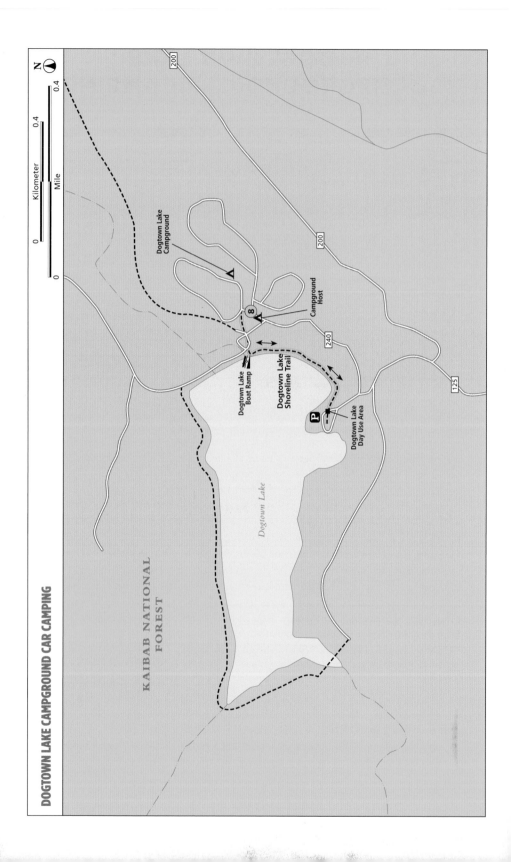

N

Kilometer
0   0.4   0.4

Mile
0   0.4

200

Dogtown Lake
Campground

Campground
Host

8

200

240

Dogtown Lake
Boat Ramp

Dogtown Lake
Shoreline Trail

P

Dogtown Lake
Day Use Area

125

KAIBAB NATIONAL
FOREST

Dogtown Lake

The Small Sagittarius Star Cloud sets over the Kaibab National Forest west of Dogtown Lake.

crappie, and catfish inhabit Dogtown Lake. Located miles from light-pollution sources, the lake is a great place to stargaze and enjoy spectacular views of the Milky Way setting behind Bill Williams Mountain across the lake. Claim your space at one of the dozens of campsites at Dogtown Lake Campground and enjoy a wonderful night sky.

Although the drive to Dogtown Lake is only 25 minutes from Williams, the bumpy dirt roads make just getting to the lake feel like an adventure. Suitable for passenger cars, Dogtown Road will get you to where you need to go deep in the Kaibab National Forest. After checking in to your campsite and getting camp set up, take some time to see the lake during the day; it's located immediately southwest of the campground. Here you'll find wildflowers bursting around the lake during the summer monsoon season and fish breaking the surface all over the lake. Anglers can enjoy a day of fishing around the lake from the shoreline or from a small boat.

As the sun sets behind Bill Williams Mountain, prepare for a magical night of stargazing from the lakeshore. Get out of the forest and go to any spot on the shore for an open view of the night sky. Thousands of stars shining over the lake make an incredible view and a great photo opportunity for astrophotographers. Use your telescope or binoculars to see astronomical objects deeper in the cosmos, like star clusters or nebulae. Anglers may also enjoy night fishing, and hikers have the option to circle the entire lake by walking along the shore. Those looking for a simple night can just head back to camp after your stargazing session to enjoy a warm fire or the comfort of your sleeping bag.

9 LOWELL OBSERVATORY— STARGAZING WITH THE EXPERTS

Tour Lowell Observatory, the historic place where Pluto was discovered and home of the legendary Clark Telescope. After your tour, join the nightly star party hosted by passionate and knowledgeable astronomers at the Giovale Open Deck Observatory. At the Open Deck, take a look at our planetary neighbors and peer deep into the universe through six modern telescopes.

Activity: Stargazing, history, astronomy education
Location: Lowell Observatory, 1400 West Mars Hill Rd., Flagstaff
Start: Lowell Observatory Visitor Center
Difficulty: Easy
Adventure time: About 3 hours
Seasons/schedule: Open year-round; best in spring, early summer, early winter, and fall for clear skies
Timing: Any time, any phase of the moon
Fees and permits: Admission fee; see ticket options at lowell.edu/visit/experiences/.
Contacts: Lowell Observatory, 1400 West Mars Hill Rd., Flagstaff 86001; (928) 774-3358; Lowell.edu
Dog-friendly: Service dogs only
Trail surface: Concrete sidewalks

Land status: Privately owned by Lowell Observatory
Nearest town: Flagstaff, Arizona
Maps: Maps provided at the visitor center; campus map available online at lowell.edu/visit/campus-map/.
Water availability: Yes; at the visitor center
Special considerations: Overnight temperatures in winter can be below freezing, and ice may form on some surfaces. Telescope viewing at the Giovale Open Deck Observatory and through the Clark Telescope is limited by weather. Summer monsoon season and winter storms will produce clouds that prevent stargazing. On Tues, Lowell Observatory closes at 5 p.m. Flash photography is not permitted around the telescopes.

FINDING THE OBSERVATORY

From Flagstaff, drive west on Route 66 for 0.2 mile and turn right onto Santa Fe Avenue. Continue west on Santa Fe Avenue, which becomes Mars Hill Road, for 1 mile up to the Lowell Observatory parking lot. Park and walk to the visitor center, located immediately north of the parking lot. Observatory GPS: N35 12.204' / W111 39.945'

THE ADVENTURE

Founded atop Mars Hill on Flagstaff's west side by Percival Lowell in 1894, Lowell Observatory still plays an important role in astronomical research and educational outreach. Known as the "Home of Pluto," Lowell Observatory is credited with the discovery of Pluto in 1930 by astronomer Clyde Tombaugh. Visitors to this historic observatory can take educational tours of

The Lowell Observatory assisted in the mapping of the moon in 1961 for the Apollo missions.

the campus, stargaze with professional astronomers, and look at the cosmos through the legendary Clark Telescope, built in 1896. The Giovale Open Deck Observatory

The 8-inch Moonraker and 5.5-inch TEC wide-field refractor telescopes peer into the night skies over the Giovale Open Deck Observatory.

(GODO) was opened at Lowell in 2019 to give visitors a nightly star party, featuring state-of-the-art telescopes designed to see planets and galaxies far, far away. For this adventure, take a tour of the observatory by day and then enjoy a fascinating night of stargazing at the GODO.

Pluto's largest moon, Charon, was discovered by the US Naval Observatory, just west of Flagstaff, in 1978.

Taking one of the daytime tours of Lowell Observatory is a great way to learn its history and to see the same telescope that discovered Pluto. The Lowell Tour begins with a brief presentation covering the history of the observatory and how the institution continues research to this day with modern technology. After getting a sense of place, you'll step outside and walk through the campus to see its historic buildings and the impressive 24-inch Clark Telescope. For the Story of Pluto Tour, you'll learn about Pluto's discovery and its controversial reclassification from planet to dwarf planet in 2006. You'll also visit the Pluto Discovery Telescope, which Clyde Tombaugh used to painstakingly study images of the night sky, leading to his discovery of Pluto. At the end of your daytime tours, take some time to see more of the observatory's exhibits, talks, and demonstrations, or take a break and grab dinner before nightfall.

When the sun dips below the horizon at sunset, the roof of the Giovale Open Deck Observatory will slide back for a night of stargazing. Take a short walk northwest of the

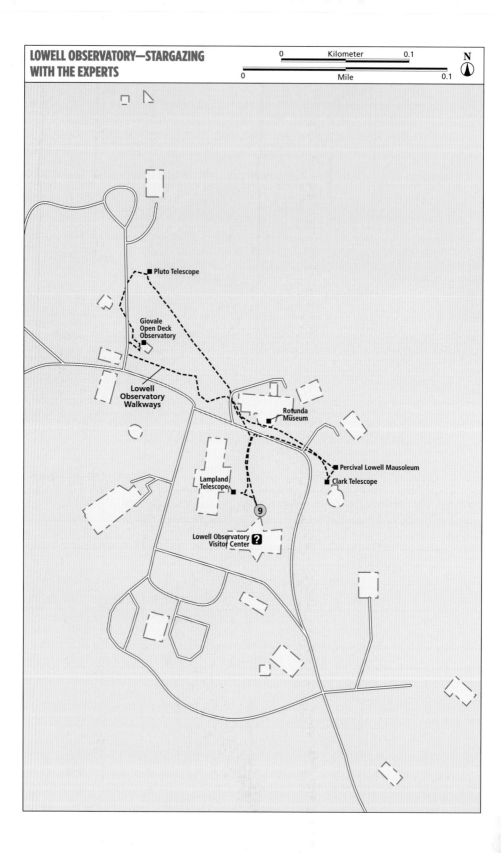

0   Kilometer   0.1

0   Mile   0.1

N

Pluto Telescope

Giovale
Open Deck
Observatory

Lowell
Observatory
Walkways

Rotunda
Museum

Percival Lowell Mausoleum

Lampland
Telescope

Clark Telescope

9

Lowell Observatory
Visitor Center

Left: A 32-inch Dobsonian reflector telescope stares at the star clusters of the Milky Way at the Giovale Open Deck Observatory.
Right: A 16-inch Meade reflector telescope points at the dark skies over Lowell Observatory.

visitor center to the GODO, where you'll find six large telescopes fixed on the stars and staff ready to answer your questions about the cosmos. See the rings of Saturn or elegant nebulae thousands of light-years away in delightful detail through the telescopes. Thousands of stars shine over Lowell Observatory thanks to the lighting ordinances of Flagstaff, an International Dark Sky Community east of the observatory. Constellation tours are also provided so that you can revisit asterisms you know, like the Big Dipper, and constellations you've never seen before.

LOOK UP
Olympus Mons on Mars is the largest volcano in the solar system, with a base as large as the state of New Mexico.

Make a worthwhile side trip to the Clark Telescope at night so you can look at the stars through this legendary telescope used by Percival Lowell himself. Viewing the deepest reaches of space from the telescopes at Lowell may give you a sense of awe and wonder. Enjoy the "ooo" and "ahh" moments with the cosmos at the GODO and Clark Telescope for as long as you want until closing time at 10 p.m. By the end of the night, hopefully you'll leave Lowell feeling like an astronomer with a deeper connection to the night sky.

10 KENDRICK MOUNTAIN BIKEPACKING ADVENTURE

Bikepack through the tall trees and grassy fields of the Coconino and Kaibab National Forests west of Flagstaff. Here you can camp under dark, star-filled skies and explore even darker lava tubes. Dig your tires into challenging mountain climbs then feel the rush of speeding down wide-open forest roads.

Activity: Bikepacking

Location: Coconino and Kaibab National Forests, west of Flagstaff

Start: City of Flagstaff Thorpe Park; GPS: N35 12.184' / W111 39.513'

Elevation gain: 4,449 feet

Distance: 77.7-mile loop

Difficulty: Hard due to high elevation, long miles, steep climbs, heavy weight, and necessary route-finding abilities

Riding time: 24–30 hours

Seasons/schedule: Open year-round; best in late spring, summer, and fall

Timing: New moon to a quarter moon

Fees and permits: None

Trail contacts: Coconino National Forest, Flagstaff Ranger District, 5075 North Hwy. 89, Flagstaff 86004; (928) 526-0866; fs .usda.gov/recarea/coconino/ recarea/?recid=70983

Kaibab National Forest, Williams Ranger District, 742 South Clover Rd., Williams 86046; (928) 635-5600; fs.usda.gov/recarea/kaibab/ recarea/?recid=11653

Dog-friendly: Yes, under control; dogs not allowed in the Lava River Cave

Trail surface: Dirt, maintained gravel, paved roads

Land status: National forest

Nearest town: Flagstaff and Bellemont, Arizona

Other trail users: Cars, trucks, RVs, SUVs, UTVs/ATVs, equestrians, pedestrians, heavy roadwork machinery

Maps: Coconino National Forest Maps available online at fs.usda.gov/ main/coconino/maps-pubs

Water availability: Water is unreliable at stock tanks. It's highly recommended that you carry as much water as possible and stage water jugs along the route, such as the US 180 and FR 164H junction.

Special considerations: Riding along US 180 is hazardous due to road traffic, so use extra caution while riding on the shoulders of US 180. High winds can greatly reduce riding speed, especially in open valleys. Stock tanks may harbor pathogens; be sure to purify any water taken from a stock tank. Bears, mountain lions, venomous snakes, cattle, and elk inhabit the area; be cautious. Hang food from a tree or use bear cans for food storage. Be prepared for flash flooding, monsoon storms, hail, and snowstorms, which can occur at any time of year in this area. Do not cross flooded roads or washes. Be prepared to fix a flat tire at any time during your trip. Do not leave your vehicle in Thorpe Park overnight; you risk having your vehicle towed. Try to park your vehicle on the streets of the neighborhood just east of Thorpe Park and ride to the trailhead. Bring at least two flashlights for the Lava River Cave. Always wear a helmet.

The San Francisco Volcanic Field surrounding Flagstaff contains more than 600 extinct cinder cone volcanoes.

FINDING THE TRAILHEAD

From Flagstaff, take historic Route 66 west for 0.3 mile; continue west on West Santa Fe Avenue for 0.4 mile. Turn right and head north on North Thorpe Road/North Toltec Street for 0.1 mile. The trailhead is just west of the Coconino County Community Services Center and the Thorpe Park tennis courts. Overnight street parking can be found in the residential neighborhood just east of Thorpe Park. Trailhead GPS: N35 12.184' / W111 39.513'

THE ADVENTURE

One big advantage of bikepacking is that it allows you to explore a lot of terrain in shorter amounts of time than backpacking. The Coconino and Kaibab National Forests west of Flagstaff offer incredible forested landscapes featuring open grasslands, old cinder cone volcanoes, and even a lava tube! In the big picture, you'll start from the west side of Flagstaff, circle Kendrick Mountain, and then return to Flagstaff via miles of dirt and paved forest roads. Some roads on this route present significant uphill challenges; however, most of the roads have gentle grades with a significant portion of exciting downhill runs. Begin the journey in the morning on some dirt trails at Thorpe Park on Flagstaff's west side.

A gravel track just west of the Coconino County Community Services Center at Thorpe Park will begin your first day in the forest. A steady climb westward up the Mars Hill Trail will lead you to USDA Forest Service roads for a gentle descent westward. As you alternate through shady forests and sunny fields, you'll have fantastic views of old cinder cone volcanoes covered in trees and the majestic San Francisco Peaks. Beautiful

The core of the Milky Way peers between the needles of pine trees in Coconino National Forest, west of Flagstaff.

A billowing tree sits below a sky full of stars in Coconino National Forest, west of Flagstaff.

forest roads generally take you toward the northwest, with sharp turns to the north and west along the route as you make gentle climbs and fast downhill runs. Just 0.44 mile north of the Lava River Cave turnoff, exit FR 171 west to FR 812 and find a nice spot in the grass to camp. Watch as the stars come out, and be amazed by the sheer amounts of stars you can see from camp. Conclude your first day by spotting satellites and shooting stars as they carry light across the skies.

Start your second day with a unique side trip to the Lava River Cave. Created by an underground lava flow nearly 700,000 years ago, the mile-long Lava River Cave normally sits at a chilly 35°F to 45°F, even in summer! Make the rocky descent into the dark mouth of the cave, located just 0.4 mile east of FR 171. Keep your helmet on as a bump cap, and explore the cave's depths, with some chambers

> The scenic San Francisco Peaks are the remnants of a stratovolcano that have been eroded downward over time.

and passages large enough to drive a truck through. After the cave, head back to camp, pack up, and begin your second day of riding by heading first northwest then west on FR 171. Reach FR 144 a few miles after the Pumpkin Center, then head north for 1.55 miles. Turn east on FR 910 for a very challenging climb up Bull Basin Mesa for almost 8 miles. At times, you may need to dismount your bike and hike-a-bike to get over the steep rocky hills. Finish the climb strong and take a well-deserved break before ripping down FR 760 after a hairpin turn to the north through a gorgeous mountainside forest.

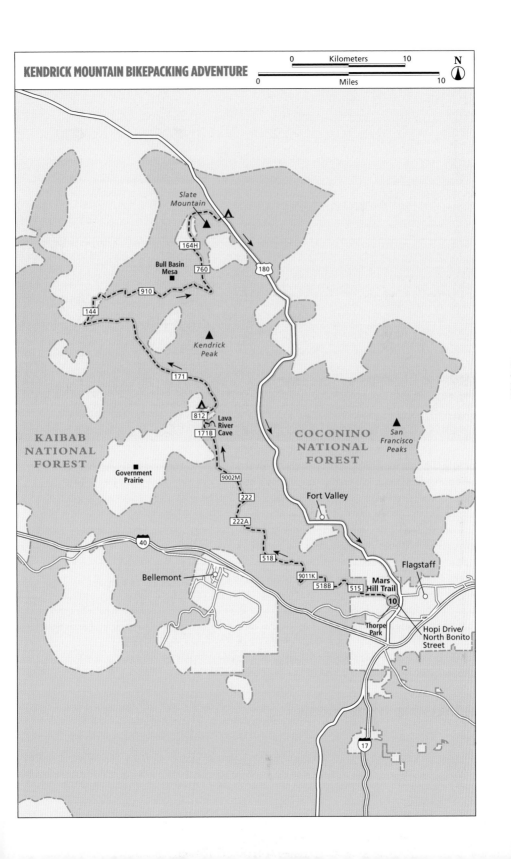

KENDRICK MOUNTAIN BIKEPACKING ADVENTURE

0 — Kilometers — 10

0 — Miles — 10

N

Slate Mountain

164H

Bull Basin Mesa

760

910

180

144

▲ *Kendrick Peak*

171

812

Lava River Cave

1718

KAIBAB NATIONAL FOREST

9002M

■ **Government Prairie**

222

▲ *San Francisco Peaks*

COCONINO NATIONAL FOREST

222A

Fort Valley

518

Flagstaff

Bellemont

9011K

518B

515

Mars Hill Trail

40

10

Thorpe Park

Hopi Drive/ North Bonito Street

17

A row of ponderosa pines stands before
the core dust lanes of the Milky Way.

Before FR 760 turns west, take a small connecting road north for 0.3 mile to FR 164H, where you will circle Slate Mountain to the north for 3.66 miles to US 180. After more than 27 miles of riding, make camp somewhere in the fields around the FR 164H/US 180 junction.

Another peaceful night of camping will leave you in awe of the night skies over Northern Arizona. The next morning, gather your camping gear, load your bike, and begin the journey back toward Flagstaff. Head southeast on US 180 and be sure to stay safely on the shoulder all the way until you reach Flagstaff. The paved road back slowly climbs to an elevation just over 8,000 feet, levels off, and then makes an exhilarating descent through the forests to Fort Valley and the Flagstaff area. After 27.45 miles, exit US 180 to Piute Road and then continue south on Hopi Drive/North Bonita Street to return to the neighborhood east of Thorpe Park. After 77 miles of adventure through the forest, you'll be very happy to get back to your car and enjoy some good food to celebrate the journey.

MILES AND DIRECTIONS

0.0 Start from the south side of the Coconino County Community Services Center and ride west then north on the Thorpe Park Gravel Track for 0.5 mile.

0.5 Turn left and head west on the Mars Hill Trail for 1.5 miles.

2.0 Continue west on FR 515 for 2.72 miles.

4.72 At the junction with FR 518B, turn right and head north then west on FR 518B for 1.39 miles.

6.11 Continue west then southwest on FR 9011K for 1.03 miles.

7.14 Make a sharp hairpin turn and head north on FR 518, which generally heads northwest for 6.33 miles.

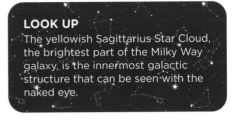

LOOK UP
The yellowish Sagittarius Star Cloud, the brightest part of the Milky Way galaxy, is the innermost galactic structure that can be seen with the naked eye.

13.47 At the junction with FR 222A, continue north on FR 222A for 1.87 miles.

15.34 Turn left and head northwest on FR 222 for 0.77 mile.

16.11 At the fork, turn right and head northwest on FR 9002M for 1.83 miles.

17.94 Reach FR 171; turn right, heading north on FR 171 for 2.6 miles.

20.54 Turn right on FR 171B to go east for 0.41 mile to the Lava River Cave.

20.95 Reach the Lava River Cave. Return to FR 171 by heading west on FR 171B for 0.41 mile.

21.36 Turn right, back on FR 171, and head north for 0.44 mile.

21.8 Head west on FR 812 to find camping in the grassy fields about 0.25 mile ahead.

22.05 Reach the camping area. Return to FR 171 by heading east on FR 812 for 0.25 mile.

22.3 Turn left back onto FR 171 and head north then west for 10.84 miles.

33.14 At FR 144, turn right and head north on FR 144 for 1.55 miles.

34.69 Just after a stock tank, turn right onto FR 910 and head east, climbing steeply up Bull Basin Mesa for 7.93 miles.

42.62 At a hairpin turn, head north on FR 760 for 3.18 miles of downhill riding.

45.8 Before FR 760 turns west, head north on a small unnamed track for 0.1 mile; connect with FR 191 briefly for 200 feet and then turn left, heading northwest on FR 164H. FR 164H will go around Slate Mountain from north to east for 3.7 miles.

49.5 Reach the junction of US 180 and FR 164H and make camp in the fields near the road junction. For the third day of riding, head southeast toward Fort Valley and Flagstaff on US 180's shoulder for 27.45 miles.

76.95 Exit US 180 in Flagstaff at Piute Road; turn right, heading west toward Hopi Drive for 0.15 mile.

77.1 Turn left on Hopi Drive and head south for 0.6 mile, continuing south as the road becomes North Bonito Street. At this point you will be back in the residential neighborhood just east of Thorpe Park.

77.7 Arrive back at the trailhead.

The crescent moon and Venus are the first to
shine through the twilight at Southern Arizona's
Ironwood Forest National Monument.

SOUTHERN ARIZONA

PICTURE FORESTED SKY ISLANDS RISING TO THE CLOUDS above an ocean of rolling grassy hills and saguaro-studded cliffs; this is Southern Arizona. Ancestral Sonoran Desert People have resided in Southern Arizona for millennia, with the first people in the area at least 7,500 years ago. Dark skies and astronomy are no stranger to Southern Arizona. Generations of stargazers have enjoyed the darkness of this region, from the eyes of Native Americans to the mirrors of large mountaintop telescopes. The unique geography, dark skies, and rich cultural history make Southern Arizona a top destination for astrotourism.

The beautiful "sky islands" of southeastern Arizona are isolated mountain ranges that rise significantly from the deserts and grasslands, harboring unparalleled biodiversity. Elevation differences can be as great as 6,000 feet between mountain highs and valley lows. In summer, temperatures can vary considerably between 115° in the deserts and 75° in the mountains. Major sources of water in the region include the Santa Cruz River, the San Pedro River, and their tributaries. Like most of Arizona, Southern Arizona experiences a fifth season: the wet monsoon summer after the notoriously hot and dry early summer. Biannual seasons of precipitation water the land with soaking winter rains and powerful monsoon storms in summer. Solid monsoon rains transform Southern Arizona, sprouting grassy fields, wildflowers, and thick leaves running up the spiky strands of an ocotillo. The Chihuahuan and Sonoran Deserts meet in Southern Arizona, adding a variety of flora and fauna to the region.

A variety of life-forms are supported by Southern Arizona's sky islands, with alpine forests found on tall mountain ranges like the Santa Catalina Mountains north of Tucson. Animals that thrive in the mountains are black bears, mountain lions, exotic coatis, many species of birds, and rare jaguars near the Mexican border. Downslope of the pines, forests of oak and piñon-juniper are met by rolling fields of grass. The wide-open grasslands of Southern Arizona transition to upper- and lower-desert species such as saguaro cacti, palo verde, javelinas, and Gila monsters. Due to high temperatures in summer, many animals in the region live a nocturnal life. Bats, moths, tarantulas, owls, and nighthawks can be observed while stargazing, adding excitement to the experience. It's dazzling to watch nighthawks and bats dance across the night sky to capture their prey.

Astronomy has played an important role in the history and economy of Southern Arizona due to an abundance of dark skies in the region. Major astronomical observatories include Kitt Peak National Observatory, Whipple Observatory, and the Mt. Lemmon SkyCenter Observatory. Kitt Peak National Observatory is the largest observatory complex in Arizona, featuring a diverse array of optical, infrared, solar, and radio telescopes to study the cosmos. The University of Arizona in Tucson plays a major role in local astronomy. The school is a leader in astronomy education and a major contributor of scientific research. Mirrors for some of the largest telescopes in the world are produced at the Richard Carris Mirror Lab, located underneath Arizona Stadium. The Carris Mirror Lab produced mirrors for the large binocular telescope at the Mount Graham International Observatory in Southeastern Arizona.

Millions of acres of public land are accessible for recreation across the dark skies of Southern Arizona. Several International Dark Sky Parks have been certified in the region by the International Dark-Sky Association, headquartered in Tucson. Dark Sky Parks include Chiricahua National Monument, Kartchner Caverns State Park, Oracle State Park, and Tumacácori National Historical Park. Each park possesses unique recreational opportunities in the dark, such as night hiking, camping, and cave tours! As Arizona's population grows, these parks and future parks become more important for preserving a natural night sky for all.

Archaeological evidence suggests that people have inhabited Southern Arizona for at least 7,500 years. As the climate warmed and dried out after the most recent ice age, agriculture was adopted and crops from Mesoamerica, such as corn, beans, and squash, helped fuel these ancient peoples. Crops were irrigated with water from canals that diverted water from rivers like the Santa Cruz near modern-day Tucson. Local game sources like deer and rabbit were hunted for protein, and wild plants such as saguaro fruit and mesquite beans were harvested for food. Ancestors of the Tohono O'odham, Hopi, and Zuni tribes are sometimes popularly referred to as "Hohokam." It's important to know that "Hohokam" is not an actual name of a tribe but a reference likely to the O'odham word Huhugam, which can be translated as "ancestors." Ancestral Sonoran Desert People traded excess crops and shell jewelry with other tribes for copper bells, iron pyrite mirrors, obsidian, shells, piñon nuts, turquoise, and even parrots from faraway places in Mesoamerica.

The earliest known Spanish activities in Arizona occurred in 1539 with Fray Marcos de Niza and famously in 1540 with Coronado's expedition. Systematic exploration of Southern Arizona by the Spanish occurred in the 1690s when they encountered villages of the O'odham, Sobaipuri, and Apache. The Spanish established religious missions, presidios, and ranches in Southern Arizona. Famous Spanish missions that can be visited today include the Mission San Xavier del Bac and Mission San José de Tumacácori. European diseases, conflict with the Spanish colonial forces, and conflict with the US government contributed to the tragic loss of countless Native Americans in Southern Arizona.

Today, the dominant Native American tribe in the region is the Tohono O'odham tribe. The Tohono O'odham nation to the southwest of Tucson encompasses 2.8 million acres, making it as large as the state of Connecticut and the second-largest in Arizona. Millions of people live in the cities and towns across Southern Arizona, including Tucson, Sierra Vista, Bisbee, Tombstone, Benson, and Nogales. Each community in Southern Arizona is unique, offering diverse culture, personalities, and food. A diverse economy of copper mining, defense manufacturing, agriculture, astronomy, and international trade with Mexico keep many Southern Arizonan's busy.

Stargazers should not miss a trip down to Southern Arizona to enjoy its abundant night skies and diverse landscapes. The stars can be enjoyed from a sky island, from a grassy hill, or under the skyward arms of a giant saguaro. In this chapter you'll be guided through ten unique places under a starry sky with a variety of recreation modalities. International Dark Sky Parks explored in this chapter include Chiricahua National Monument, Kartchner Caverns State Park, and Oracle State Park. Whether you are camping at Chiricahua, traversing Oracle's rolling hills, or spelunking the inner reaches of Kartchner Caverns, you're sure to have an awesome experience under the night skies of Southern Arizona.

11 SABINO CANYON NIGHT HIKE

Discover the nocturnal wonders of Sabino Canyon, Southern Arizona's riparian oasis just outside Tucson, by hiking or biking Upper Sabino Canyon Road.

Activity: Night hike or bike
Location: 5700 North Sabino Canyon Rd., Tucson
Start: Upper Sabino Canyon Road; GPS: N32 18.634' / W110 49.345'
Elevation gain: 687 feet
Distance: 7.6 miles out and back
Difficulty: Easy
Hiking time: 2–4-hours
Seasons/schedule: Open year-round; good in all seasons
Timing: New moon to a quarter moon
Fees and permits: Fee for access to the Sabino Canyon Recreation Area trailhead; see fs.usda.gov/recarea/coronado/recarea/?recid=75425 for current fee amounts.
Trail contacts: Coronado National Forest, 5700 North Sabino Canyon Rd., Tucson 85750; (520) 749-8700; fs.usda.gov/recarea/coronado/recarea/?recid=75425; email: sm.fs.scrd@usda.gov
Dog-friendly: No; dogs not allowed due to bighorn sheep management policies
Trail surface: Paved

Land status: National forest
Nearest town: Tucson, Arizona
Other trail users: Backpackers, cyclists, trail runners, shuttles/buses
Maps: Santa Catalina Ranger District maps available online at fs.usda.gov/main/coronado/maps-pubs
Water availability: Yes; at the visitor center and some shuttle stops; seasonally available in creeks and pools (must be treated before use)
Special considerations: Mountain lions, coyotes, bobcats, javelinas, and venomous reptiles are present in Sabino Canyon. Flash flooding can occur at any time of year, especially in monsoon season, from late June through September. Do not attempt to cross any bridges in the canyon if floodwaters are running over the spans; wait until the flood waters recede.
Other: The Sabino Canyon Crawler sometimes offers special summer-nights shuttle tours in Sabino Canyon; check their website (sabinocanyoncrawler.com) for availability.

FINDING THE TRAILHEAD
From Tucson, take North Sabino Canyon Road to its intersection with East Sunrise Drive. On the right, about 200 feet north of the intersection, is the main entrance to the Sabino Canyon Recreation Area parking lot with a fee station. The paved Upper Sabino Canyon Road begins just north of a roundabout located west of the visitor center. From the trailhead you can ride the shuttle or hike for 3.8 miles on Upper Sabino Canyon Road to stop #9. Trailhead GPS: N32 18.634' / W110 49.345'

THE ADVENTURE
Sabino Canyon is an old favorite hiking spot for many Arizonans and adventurous tourists. Sabino Creek serves as the backbone for the riparian habitat within Sabino Canyon, supporting diverse wildlife and lush vegetation in the midst of the Sonoran Desert. Make an escape from the heat of the day and explore

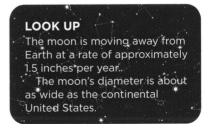

LOOK UP
The moon is moving away from Earth at a rate of approximately 1.5 inches per year.
The moon's diameter is about as wide as the continental United States.

Top: Mighty saguaro rake their giant arms across the stars over lower Sabino Canyon.
Bottom: A long-dead tree stands tall in the middle of Sabino Creek after dark.

this canyon on a pleasant 7.6-mile out-and-back night hike or bike ride, just 30 minutes from downtown Tucson. A surprisingly starry sky and peaceful atmosphere soundtracked by Sabino Creek, crickets, frogs, and chirping bats will leave you in awe. Begin your adventure at sunset or after dark from the start of Upper Sabino Canyon Road, just west of the visitor center.

Hike or ride toward the northeast on the flat paved road along a beautiful Sonoran Desert landscape featuring saguaros, moths, and bats. After 0.9 mile you reach the top of a hill and see Sabino Canyon ahead and its riparian corridor below you. Continue north on the road and descend into Sabino Canyon, listening for the sounds of Sabino Creek and its amphibian residents. Restrooms, benches, picnic tables, and water fountains are

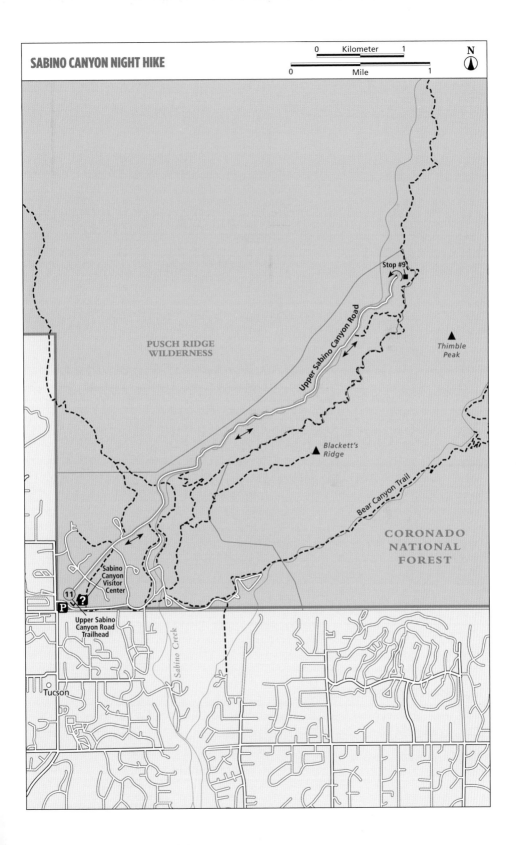

SABINO CANYON NIGHT HIKE

Kilometer

Mile

N

PUSCH RIDGE
WILDERNESS

Stop #9

Thimble
Peak

Upper Sabino Canyon Road

Blackett's
Ridge

Bear Canyon Trail

CORONADO
NATIONAL
FOREST

Sabino
Canyon
Visitor
Center

11

Upper Sabino
Canyon Road
Trailhead

Sabino Creek

Tucson

Hundreds of stars shine over Sabino Canyon and a moonlit bridge crossing Sabino Creek.

present at many of the nine shuttle stops along the road, making breaks very convenient. Several small side trails from the main road and bridges over Sabino Creek offer views of waterfalls and calm reflective pools.

> The Santa Catalina Mountains north of Tucson are 12 million years old.

Grand views of Thimble Peak and the surrounding canyons poking into the starry night sky can be found as you meander up the canyon. The steady uphill climb finally ends 3.8 miles up Sabino Canyon Road at shuttle stop #9, the last stop. From the roundabout at stop #9, take a break and see the lights of Tucson in the distance. At stop #9 you'll also see how much darker it is on this side of the canyon.

When ready, head south, back to the Sabino Canyon Visitor Center the same way you came on Upper Sabino Canyon Road. Cyclists will have a blast riding downhill, but be mindful of others, wildlife, and sharp corners near the bridges. As you head back to the trailhead, notice how some stars become harder to see due to light pollution. Arrive back at the roundabout near the visitor center to complete your trip; head south into the parking lot to return to your vehicle.

MILES AND DIRECTIONS

0.0 Head north through Sabino Canyon on Upper Sabino Canyon Road for 3.8 miles to the stop #9 roundabout.

3.8 Reach the stop #9 roundabout. When ready, head back down Upper Sabino Canyon Road toward the south for 3.8 miles to the visitor center.

7.6 Arrive back at the trailhead.

12 SAGUARO NATIONAL PARK WEST—DESERT DISCOVERY TRAIL STARGAZING AND ASTROPHOTOGRAPHY

Saguaro National Park West's Desert Discovery Trail is an easy 0.3-mile walk along a paved, wheelchair-accessible path lined with saguaros. This family-friendly trail is great for anyone looking for an easy getaway under the stars near Tucson. The Tucson Mountains to the east block some of Tucson's light pollution, allowing you to see and photograph many more stars than you ever could in town.

Activity: Walking and stargazing
Location: Saguaro National Park West, 2700 North Kinney Rd., Tucson
Start: Desert Discovery Trail parking lot; GPS: N32 15.755' / W111 12.629'
Elevation gain: 0 feet
Distance: 0.3-mile loop
Difficulty: Easy
Hiking time: 5–10 minutes to complete one loop
Seasons/schedule: Any season; open 24 hours a day
Timing: No moon to a quarter moon
Fees and permits: Entrance fees are required and can be paid online or at the visitor center; see nps.gov/sagu/planyourvisit/fees.htm for details.

Trail contacts: Saguaro National Park West, 2700 North Kinney Rd., Tucson 85743; (520) 733-5158; email: nps.gov/sagu/contacts.htm
Dog-friendly: Yes
Trail surface: Paved
Land status: National park
Nearest town: Tucson, Arizona
Other trail users: Bikes and horses not allowed on the trail
Maps: Park maps available online at nps.gov/sagu/planyourvisit/maps.htm
Water availability: None
Special considerations: Temperatures at night in the winter can be very cold; dress appropriately and bring plenty of water

FINDING THE TRAILHEAD

Saguaro National Park has two districts flanking Tucson—the Rincon Mountain District (commonly known as Saguaro National Park East) to the east and the Tucson Mountain District (commonly known as Saguaro National Park West) to the west. Use caution when searching for directions online for Saguaro National Park to avoid going to the wrong district. There are multiple ways to access Saguaro National Park West, but here we describe how to get there from central Tucson. From Tucson, drive west on Speedway Boulevard for 11.5 miles over Gates Pass to Kinney Road, where you will turn right. Head northwest on Kinney Road for 5.8 miles until you see a sign for the Desert Discovery Trail parking lot, located on your left around 100 feet after the sign. Trailhead GPS: N32 15.755' / W111 12.629'

THE ADVENTURE

At first, pulling into the Desert Discovery Trail parking lot, especially at night, can look ominous. Your headlights will light up the thorny plants, and the sky above will look pitch black, creating a less than inviting scene. Be brave, open the door, step out, and look up; just like that, you will remember why you came as thousands of stars come into

Top: A saguaro, the Milky Way, and a thrust bubble from a Trident rocket come together in the night skies over Saguaro National Park West.
Bottom: The setting winter Milky Way silhouettes a large saguaro cactus at the start of the Desert Discovery Trail.

SAGUARO NATIONAL PARK WEST—DESERT DISCOVERY TRAIL STARGAZING AND ASTROPHOTOGRAPHY

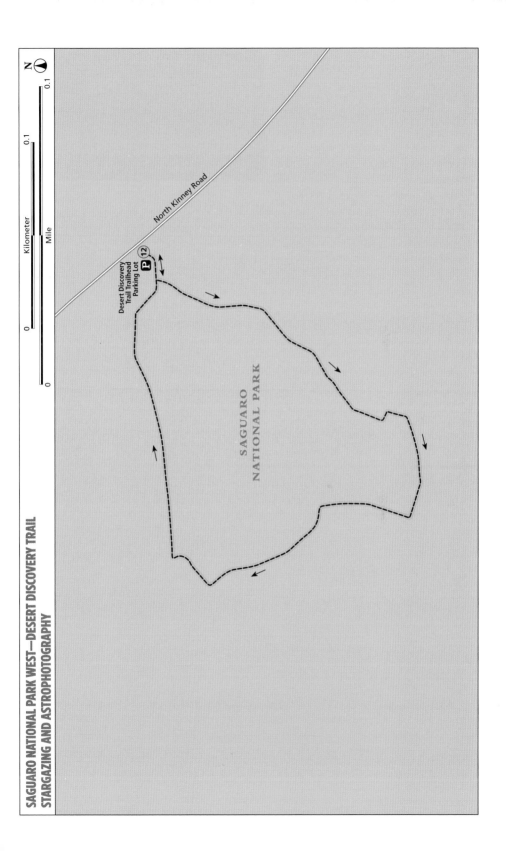

view. The paved Desert Discovery Trail starts at the parking lot and leads you to one of the oldest saguaros, standing at the fork in the loop. Clockwise and counterclockwise are the only possible directions for exploring the flat, 0.3-mile path through this beautiful section of Sonoran Desert. Saguaro National Park West protects around 25,000 acres of dry, low-elevation desert that includes plant

species like saguaro cactus and ocotillo and animal species like bats, lizards, and desert tortoises. Several education signs and a few benches are scattered along the trail, providing opportunities to learn about the desert and stare at the skies above.

The night sky experience at the Desert Discovery Trail is rewarding, especially considering its proximity to the major light-pollution source of Tucson. I recommend using a red-bulb flashlight to limit the loss of night vision and help you watch your step on the path. Although views of the stars at the eastern and northern horizons are limited by low mountains and light pollution, thousands of stars and full constellations are visible overhead, to the west, and to the south. The Milky Way core and galactic dust lanes can be enjoyed from this location, a real treat for anyone who has not seen such details before. When your eyes are fully adjusted to the night, the walking path will be fairly visible thanks to light pollution from Tucson and distant Phoenix creeping over the mountains to the north and east.

The Sonoran Desert landscape on the Desert Discovery Trail provides plentiful photo compositions for astrophotography. Saguaros are the most iconic subject to photograph against fields of stars, and the light pollution can provide lighting for the cacti, revealing details of their pleated bodies. As you photograph or admire the saguaros, remember that it takes the cactus an average of fifty to seventy-five years to grow just one arm! Enjoy as many laps as your heart desires around this great place to learn about the desert and appreciate its beauty. Once ready to go, locate the exit to the parking lot on the eastern side of the loop.

MILES AND DIRECTIONS

0.0   Start the Desert Discovery Trail from the north side of the parking lot. At the fork 30 feet west of the parking lot, choose to go either north or south on the paved loop (our map shows clockwise). Stay on the paved portion of the path at all times for safety and to ensure the health of the desert.

0.3   Complete a loop at the Desert Discovery Trail once you have reached the fork in the path that goes to the parking lot. Exit here and arrive back at the trailhead, or complete as many loops as desired.

To achieve more even lighting on your landscape subjects, like a saguaro cactus, diffuse the light using a coffee filter or a piece of white paper in front of your flash or other light source and point it toward your subject.

13 ORGAN PIPE CACTUS NATIONAL MONUMENT CAR CAMPING AND NIGHT HIKE

Camp and hike under the stars in Organ Pipe Cactus National Monument, the only place where you can see wild organ pipe cactus in the United States. The Twin Peaks Campground is a clean, quiet, and comfortable developed campground with hundreds of sites available to tent and RV campers alike. Night hike on the Desert View Trail through a collection of organ pipe cacti for beautiful starry vistas.

Activity: Car camping and night hike

Location: Organ Pipe Cactus National Monument; GPS: N31 56.579' / W112 48.672'

Campground: Twin Peaks Campground; GPS: N31 56.551' / W112 48.677'

Start: Desert View trailhead; GPS: N31 56.627' / W112 48.789'

Elevation gain: 162 feet

Distance: 1.2-mile loop

Difficulty: Moderate due to a short climb

Hiking time: About 45 minutes

Seasons/schedule: Open year-round; best in late fall, winter, and early spring

Timing: No moon to a quarter moon

Fees and permits: Park entrance fees and nightly camping fees apply; see nps.gov/orpi/planyourvisit/fees .htm for current fees.

Trail and campground contacts: Organ Pipe Cactus National Monument, 10 Organ Pipe Dr., Ajo 85321; (520) 387-6849; nps.gov/orpi/index.htm

Dog-friendly: Yes, in the campground; dogs not allowed on the Desert View Trail

Trail surface: Dirt and rock

Land status: National park

Nearest town: Lukeville, Arizona

Other trail users: Photographers, trail runners

Suitable camp setups: RVs, cars, trucks, tents, fifth wheels, vans

Maps: Organ Pipe Cactus NM map available online at nps.gov/orpi/planyourvisit/maps.htm

Facilities: Grills, shaded picnic tables; solar showers, flush toilets, sinks, drinking water; black water dump station, gray water station

Water availability: Yes; water is available at the Organ Pipe Cactus NM Visitor Center and the Twin Peaks Campground. Water and sewer hookups are not available for RVs; however, a dump station and a freshwater station are available at the southern side of the campground.

Special considerations: Camping reservations are required prior to arrival at the Twin Peaks Campground. Flush toilets, a gray water rinsing station, and solar showers are available at the campground. Leashed pets are allowed on the Palo Verde Trail and on the campground perimeter trail, but are not allowed on the Desert View Trail. This park is located on the international border with Mexico and is a safe place to visit. However, be aware that illegal crossings and drug smuggling may occur along the border at any time. Summer temperatures in the day can exceed 115°F, and winter nighttime temperatures can be below freezing.

Other: The Desert View Trail has several benches where stargazers can sit and take a break.

A mature organ pipe cactus on the Desert View Trail reaches high for thousands of stars in the night sky.

FINDING THE CAMPGROUND AND TRAILHEAD

From Why, Arizona, head south on AZ 85 for 22.1 miles. Turn right on Puerto Blanco Drive toward Organ Pipe Cactus National Monument's Kris Eggle Visitor Center. After stopping at the visitor center to pay entrance fees, continue west on Puerto Blanco Drive and then turn south on Twin Peaks Road for 1.3 miles toward the Twin Peaks Campground entrance gate. To get to the Desert View trailhead, head west on Twin Peaks Road for 0.2 mile from the entrance to the campground. The Desert View Trail is a loop that you can start from either the western or eastern side of the parking lot. Campground GPS: N31 56.551' / W112 48.677'; trailhead GPS: N31 56.627' / W112 48.789'

THE ADVENTURE

Organ Pipe Cactus National Monument is a special place in Southern Arizona. Also designated as a UNESCO International Biosphere Reserve in 1976, Organ Pipe is the only place in the United States where you can see wild organ pipe cacti. In Southern Arizona and northern Mexico, these beautiful cacti rise out

Organ pipe cacti can live to be 150 years old. They produce creamy white flowers that only open at night.

ORGAN PIPE CACTUS NATIONAL MONUMENT CAR CAMPING AND NIGHT HIKE

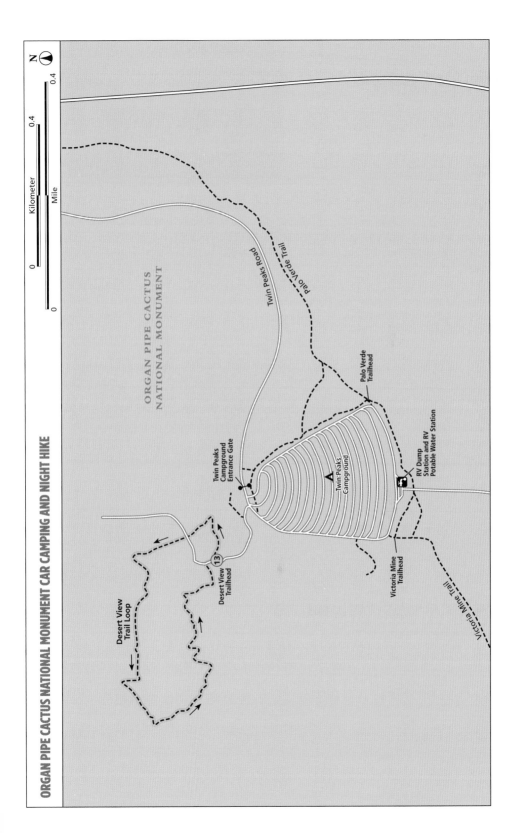

of the Sonoran Desert with dozens of octopus-like arms. Dark starry skies prevail at this monument, which is far from large cities and significant sources of light pollution. The monument's Twin Peaks Campground and nearby Desert View Trail provide you with an unparalleled opportunity to hike and camp with the organ pipe cactus under rich, starry skies.

Pitch your tent or park your RV in your reserved site at Twin Peaks Campground and enjoy the warm afternoon sun leading up to sunset. To enjoy a truly dark night sky while you hike the Desert View Trail, leave your camp sometime after the sun dips below the horizon. As dusk settles over the valley, find your way to the northern entrance to the campground and walk west on the Twin Peaks Road for 0.2 mile until you reach the Desert View trailhead. You may start the 1.2-mile loop heading east or west; however, going east first will allow more time for full darkness before you reach the high point of the hike. Notice the first stars poking through the twilight as you make your way past organ pipe cacti that are over one hundred years old.

As the sky fades from deep blue to fields of stars, scale the hill on the western side of the loop. Topping the hill, crowned with mature organ pipe and saguaro cacti, is the highlight of this hike. The views from the high point of the Desert View Trail are unbeatable, and under a starry sky, you may feel like you're just a few steps from the heavens. Relax on one of the benches at the top of the hill, spot your favorite constellations with great clarity, and learn new constellations with your favorite star chart app. Continue down the Desert View Trail from the hill toward the trailhead, watching your step for any snakes or tarantulas crossing the trail.

Return to the trailhead and walk 0.2 mile on Twin Peaks Road southeast to the campground. Try walking with no flashlight, using only starlight or moonlight to see the road ahead; you'll be amazed with how bright starlight alone can be. While at camp, enjoy a nice dinner with your family with the Milky Way floating overhead. By the time you go to bed, you should feel more connected to the night sky and the Sonoran Desert around you.

MILES AND DIRECTIONS

0.0   Start from the entrance to Twin Peaks Campground and head west; then curve north on Twin Peaks Road to the Desert View trailhead.

0.2   Arrive at the Desert View trailhead. Head either west or east to start the 1.2-mile Desert View Trail loop (our map shows counterclockwise).

1.4   Complete a loop on the Desert View Trail and head south then east for 0.2 mile on Twin Peaks Road toward Twin Peaks Campground.

1.6   Arrive back at the Twin Peaks Campground entrance and head back to your campsite.

14 IRONWOOD FOREST NATIONAL MONUMENT CAR CAMPING AND NIGHT HIKE

Embark on a car camping adventure to a desert forest of ironwood trees at Ironwood Forest National Monument. Located approximately 25 miles northwest of Tucson, this monument enjoys dark night skies suspended over iconic Ragged Top Mountain and its surrounding Sonoran Desert valleys. Watch the sunset at a high-up view of Ragged Top revealing thousands of stars overhead with the yip-yap of coyotes calling in the distance.

Activity: Car camping and night hike

Location: Ironwood Forest National Monument; GPS: N32 28.069' / W111 28.520'

Campground (dispersed camping): GPS: N32 28.279' / W111 29.391'; GPS: N32 28.443' / W111 29.899'

Start: Car camping site; GPS: N32 28.279' / W111 29.391'

Elevation gain: 245 feet

Distance: 5.25–6.25 total miles out and back

Difficulty: Moderate for an off-trail scramble to the top of a hill overlooking Ragged Top Mountain

Hiking time: About 3 hours

Seasons/schedule: Open year-round; best in late fall, winter, and spring

Timing: No moon to a quarter moon

Fees and permits: None for camping or BLM land access. Arizona State Trust Land permit required to access certain areas of the monument. See asld.secure.force.com/recreationalpermit/ to purchase a recreational permit online.

Trail and campground contacts: Ironwood Forest National Monument, Tucson Field Office, 3201 East Universal Way, Tucson 85756; (520) 258-7200; blm.gov/national-conservation-lands/arizona/ironwood

Dog-friendly: Yes, under control

Trail surface: Dirt

Land status: Bureau of Land Management and Arizona State Trust Land

Nearest town: Marana, Arizona

Other trail users: Trucks, cars, UTVs/ATVs, dirt bikes; mountain bikers, walkers, runners, photographers, birders

Suitable camp setups: Cars, trucks, vans, small RVs, fifth wheels, tents

Maps: BLM Ironwood Forest National Monument map available at blm.gov/visit/ironwood

Facilities: None

Water availability: None

Special considerations: Daytime summer temperatures can exceed 115°F, and winter nighttime temperatures can fall well below freezing. Flash floods can occur at any time and in any season. Venomous reptiles, scorpions, and venomous spiders inhabit the monument. The monument is within a travel corridor for migrants who have illegally crossed the international border with Mexico. US Customs and Border Protection units patrol this area by ground and air. Ironwood Forest National Monument has no paved roads. West Silverbell Road changes to a graded dirt road that crosses several dry washes after entering the monument. This road is normally passable for carefully driven passenger vehicles; call the Bureau of Land Management for current road conditions.

Other: All camping in the monument is dispersed and does not include any facilities.

FINDING THE CAMPGROUND AND TRAILHEAD

From I-10, exit onto Marana Road/Sandario Road; head southwest for about 400 feet, and turn west on Marana Road. Continue on West Marana Road for 5.9 miles and then turn northwest on West Silverbell Road, following its curvy path generally west and northwest for 12.3 to 12.8 miles. At around 4.5 and 5.1 miles past where the road becomes dirt, you will find dispersed camping sites, marked by small nightly stay-limit signs, on the south side of the road. The larger group site is 5.1 miles from the start of the dirt and may be suitable for some medium-sized RVs. The hike to a hill with a view of Ragged Top Mountain starts from wherever you build camp. Campground GPS: N32 28.279' / W111 29.391' or N32 28.443' / W111 29.899'; trailhead GPS (starting from your campsite on West Silverbell Road): N32 28.279' / W111 29.391' or N32 28.443' / W111 29.899'

THE ADVENTURE

Protected for its biological and cultural significance, Ironwood Forest National Monument is a quiet reserve of the Sonoran Desert and its dark skies. This monument covers 129,000 acres, preserving stands of healthy ironwood trees—a keystone species in the desert

> **LOOK UP**
> Meteors glow different colors as they streak across the night sky based on their composition. Iron minerals glow yellow, silicates glow red, and copper glows blue or green.

that can live to be 1,500 years old. Ironwood seeds are an important food source, and the microclimates created under their canopies protect sensitive species from extreme temperatures. Archaeological finds from the prehistoric Hohokam period, such as the petroglyph-adorned Cocoraque Butte, suggest that the area has been enjoyed by humans for at least 5,000 years. Experience the wild beauty of Ironwood Forest National Monument under starry skies by camping and taking a sunset-to-night hike to a scenic view.

Watch the dust billow in your rearview mirror as you enter the monument, driving west on West Silverbell Road past tall saguaros and stands of ironwood and palo verde trees. Some of the best dispersed campsites on West Silverbell Road are located on the south side of the road 4.5 and 5.1 miles from the start of the dirt section. Rugged sights of Ragged Top Mountain can be enjoyed from these campsites both day and night. After establishing your camp, settle in to the quiet of this space and admire the ghostly gray bark and little green leaflets of a nearby ironwood tree. About 90 minutes before sunset, pack up your day hiking pack and head east on Silverbell Road for a sunset-to-night hike up a hill with a view of Ragged Top Mountain.

Depending on which campsite you start from, walk 1.65 to 2.15 miles east on relatively flat West Silverbell Road until you reach Pipeline Road, minding traffic on the road as you walk. Turn northwest on Pipeline Road for 0.2 mile until you reach the state trust land gate. Open then close the gate behind you, and continue northwest 0.6 mile toward a small hill to the west. Once you are closest to the small hill to the west of Pipeline Road, climb the hill off-trail, traveling on durable surfaces such as rock and watching for venomous reptiles. Reaching the top of the small hill will reward you

> Ironwood trees bloom with beautiful light pink to light purple flowers in late April to May. The wood of ironwood trees is so dense that it will not float in water. It was used by prehistoric Hohokam cultures for tools.

Top: Three saguaros stand guard at Ironwood Forest National Monument as the core of the Milky Way looms overhead.
Bottom: A tall saguaro divides the Milky Way from the moon in the dark skies of Ironwood Forest National Monument.

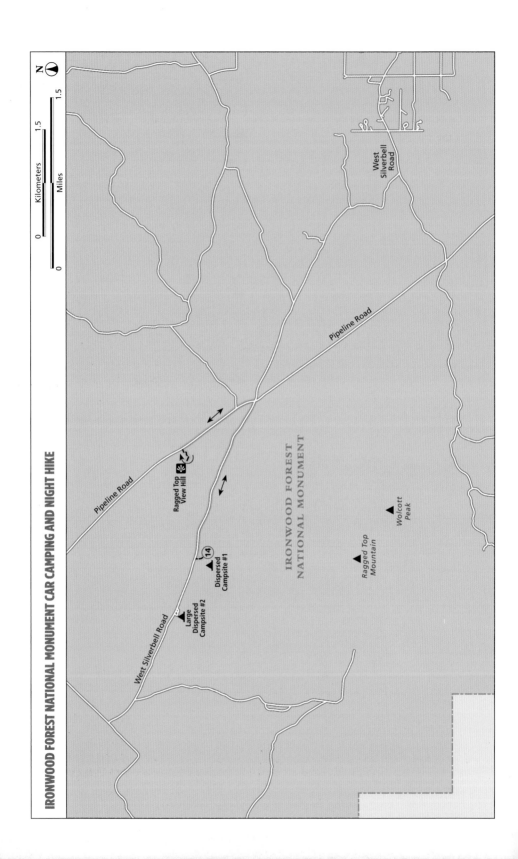

IRONWOOD FOREST NATIONAL MONUMENT CAR CAMPING AND NIGHT HIKE

with a panorama of Ragged Top Mountain over the valley and a colorful sunset. Take in the stunning view of the saguaro forest below you as you listen for distant coyotes and owls signaling the beginning of the night.

After the sun has set and released its jealous sky, watch thousands of stars make their appearance across the night. Carefully descend the hill toward Pipeline Road and walk back to camp the same way you came for 2.63 to 3.13 miles southeast then west under the twinkling stars. The dark skies of Ironwood Forest National Monument allow clear views of faint meteors and the Milky Way's spectacular presence behind Ragged Top Mountain. Night sky visibility is only limited by light pollution on the horizon in the northwest from Phoenix and the southeast from Tucson. Although night hiking in unfamiliar places may feel scary, the night sky is always a familiar sight, no matter where you are in Arizona.

Ocotillo thorns poke into the late evening skies over Ragged Top Mountain.

MILES AND DIRECTIONS

0.0 Start from your dispersed campsite on the south side of West Silverbell Road (GPS: N32 28.279' / W111 29.391') and walk east on Silverbell Road for 1.65 miles. Add 0.5 mile if coming from the larger campsite farther west (GPS: N32 28.443' / W111 29.899').

1.65 Turn sharply toward the northwest on Pipeline Road, marked with small yellow "Gas Pipeline" placards, and walk 0.2 mile to the state trust land gate.

1.85 Open and close the state trust land gate behind you and continue 0.6 mile northwest on Pipeline Road.

2.45 Reach a point on Pipeline Road closest to a small hill to the west, and hike off-trail to the top of the hill.

2.63 Top the small hill and take in the views. Return to camp the same way you came to the hill, taking Pipeline Road southeast and then West Silverbell Road to the west.

5.25 Arrive back at the trailhead/campsite.

15 ORACLE STATE PARK NIGHT HIKE

Hike through rolling grassy hills under the stars at Oracle State Park, an International Dark Sky Park. Climb the granite overlook trail to gain expansive views of the boulder-strewn landscape and a dome of stars above.

Activity: Night hike
Location: Oracle State Park, 3820 East Wildlife Dr., Oracle
Start: American Avenue trailhead parking lot; GPS: N32 37.292' / W110 44.786'
Elevation gain: 346 feet
Distance: 4.3-mile lollipop
Difficulty: Moderate due to a steep descent
Hiking time: About 2 hours
Seasons/schedule: Open year-round; good any season
Dark sky designation: International Dark Sky Park
Timing: No moon to a quarter moon
Fees and permits: Fee to park at the American Avenue parking lot; see azstateparks.com/oracle/explore/facility-information for current fees.
Trail contacts: Oracle State Park, 3820 Wildlife Dr., Oracle 85623; (520) 896-2425; azstateparks.com/oracle

Dog-friendly: Yes, leashed
Trail surface: Dirt and rock
Land status: State park
Nearest town: Oracle, Arizona
Other trail users: Mountain bikers, equestrians, trail runners, photographers
Maps: Oracle State Park maps available at azstateparks.com/oracle/explore/maps
Water availability: None
Special considerations: Winter temperatures may fall below freezing at night. The Granite Overlook Trail requires a steep descent/ascent on the western side of the loop. Fees are paid in cash at a fee tube at the American Avenue parking lot and are slightly higher for nighttime parking. Venomous reptiles and other nocturnal animals may be present at night.

FINDING THE TRAILHEAD

From AZ 77, take the American Avenue (Old Highway 77) exit south for 0.3 mile. Take the first left down an unmarked road for 0.3 mile, heading east to the American Avenue parking lot; park anywhere in the lot. From downtown Oracle, take East American Avenue east then northeast for 1.5 miles. Turn right onto the unmarked road, heading 0.3 mile east to the American Avenue parking lot. Trailhead GPS (American Avenue parking lot): N32 37.292' / W110 44.786'

THE ADVENTURE

Oracle State Park features a vast landscape of rolling hills topped with boulders and oak trees. The park also features the historic Kannally ranch house, abundant wildlife, and a section of the Arizona Trail. Designated as an International Dark Sky Park in 2014, Oracle State Park provides

LOOK UP
In the winter sky, look for the golden gate of the ecliptic asterism, the gap between Taurus and the Pleiades where planets and the moon appear to cross through.

The ancient core of the Milky Way rises above Oracle State Park's rolling hills.

plentiful opportunities to see very dark night skies year-round. Take a 4.3-mile night hike to experience the landscape and Oracle's dark skies, protected from light pollution. Start this night sky adventure at the American Avenue parking lot, which is always open for exploration.

Begin your adventure at night on the 1.3-mile Mariposa Trail after paying the entrance fee at the southwest-

LOOK UP

The Milky Way core can be seen from February to November but is best seen June through August.

The Milky Way was given its name from a Greek legend that the goddess Hera sprayed milk across the night sky, giving the Milky Way its hazy appearance.

ern part of the parking lot. Follow the signs and hike south on the dirt Mariposa Trail, zigzagging up and down the grassy hills. Cresting each hill will reward you with open views of the surrounding hills and the deep night sky above. Benches along the Mariposa Trail provide excellent opportunities to relax and take long looks at the sky to focus on constellations or star clusters and the moon. Reach the paved Wildlife Drive about 0.3 mile south from a bench near a large granite outcrop and cross the road 50 feet west to the turn for the Granite Overlook trailhead parking lot.

Walk 200 feet south into the parking lot and start the next part of your adventure by taking either the eastern or western trailhead for the 1.7-mile Granite Overlook Trail. Take the eastern trailhead near an information kiosk for a gentler climb to the top of a hill with unobstructed vantages of the park and stars. Listen for small birds and coyote calls as you climb the gentle grade southeast through oak and mesquite trees. Meet with a ramada at 0.44 miles up the loop, and continue southwest then northwest for 0.66 mile

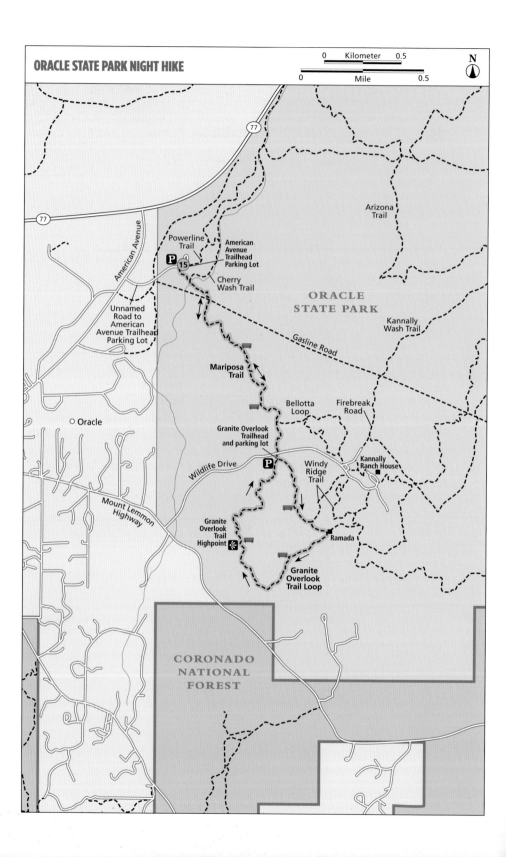

Kilometer

Mile

N

77

American Avenue

77

Powerline
Trail

P 15

American
Avenue
Trailhead
Parking Lot

Cherry
Wash Trail

Unnamed
Road to
American
Avenue Trailhead
Parking Lot

ORACLE
STATE PARK

Kannally
Wash Trail

Gasline Road

Arizona
Trail

Mariposa
Trail

Bellotta
Loop

Firebreak
Road

Granite Overlook
Trailhead
and parking lot

○ Oracle

Wildlife Drive

P

Windy
Ridge
Trail

Kannally
Ranch House

Mount Lemmon
Highway

Granite
Overlook
Trail
Highpoint

Ramada

Granite
Overlook
Trail Loop

CORONADO
NATIONAL
FOREST

Stacked boulders loom over the open, moonlit landscape of Oracle State Park.

toward the high point of the hike. The final push up to the overlook offers close encounters with tall soaptree yucca and a chance to get closer to the night sky.

Absorb the immensity of the star fields above you at the summit of the granite overlook. A bench located at the top gives you a chance to bask in the light of thousands of visible stars. Try closing your eyes for just 20 seconds and then opening them to take in the stars with even more clarity. Landmarks visible from this point are the white Kannally ranch house to the northeast of the hill and tall Mount Lemmon to the south. When ready, continue down a steep and rocky section of the Granite Overlook Trail for 0.6 mile to the north and northeast. After your descent to the western Granite Overlook Trailhead parking lot, return to the American Avenue trailhead by hiking north on the Mariposa Trail for 1.3 miles.

MILES AND DIRECTIONS

0.0 Start south on the Mariposa Trail from the American Avenue trailhead parking lot near the informational kiosk.

1.3 Arrive at Wildlife Drive; cross the road toward the south, walk 50 feet west and then 200 feet south into the Granite Overlook Trailhead parking lot. Take the eastern trailhead for the Granite Overlook Trail loop near the informational sign.

1.64 At the junction with the Windy Ridge Trail, continue south on the Granite Overlook Trail.

1.73 At the second junction with the Windy Ridge Trail, continue south on the Granite Overlook Trail toward the ramada.

2.4 Arrive at the Granite Overlook Trail summit bench. Continue north then northeast down a steep slope for 0.6 mile.

3.0 Return to the Granite Overlook parking lot at the western trailhead. Walk north then east for 250 feet to the Mariposa Trailhead. Hike north for 1.3 miles on the Mariposa Trail to the American Avenue trailhead parking lot.

4.3 Arrive back at the trailhead.

16 COCHISE STRONGHOLD CAR CAMPING AND NIGHT HIKE

Venture to the heart of the Dragoon Mountains and camp under thousands of stars at Cochise Stronghold Campground. Admire the stars above, just like legendary Apache leader Cochise did from his favorite hideout in the mountains.

Activity: RV and car camping and night hike
Location: Cochise Stronghold
Campground: Cochise Stronghold Campground; GPS: N31 55.359' / W109 58.066'
Start: Cochise Stronghold Campground; GPS: N31 55.359' / W109 58.066'
Elevation gain: 50 feet
Distance: 0.4-mile loop
Difficulty: Easy
Hiking time: About 15 minutes
Seasons/schedule: Open in fall, winter, and spring
Timing: New moon to a quarter moon
Fees and permits: Nightly campground fees; see fs.usda .gov/recarea/coronado/ ?recid=25446 for current fees.
Trail and campground contacts: Coronado National Forest, Douglas Ranger District, 1192 West Saddleview Rd., Douglas 85607; (520) 364-3468; fs .usda.gov/recarea/coronado/ recarea/?recid=25446
Dog-friendly: Yes
Trail surface: Dirt for Cochise Nature Trail. Dirt road to the campground; road paved and maintained within the campground.

Land status: National forest
Nearest town: Sunsites, Arizona
Suitable camp setups: Tents, small RVs, vans, small fifth wheels, pickup trucks, SUVs
Maps: Coronado National Forest maps available online at fs .usda.gov/recarea/coronado/ recarea/?recid=25446
Facilities: Pit toilets
Water availability: None
Special considerations: RVs and trailers longer than 16 feet should not attempt to enter the campground due to tight corners and parking spaces. No water or electric hookups are available. Black bears inhabit the area, so store food in bear boxes, by hanging, or within vehicles to avoid bear encounters. Overnight temperature in winter can be freezing. West Ironwood Road is passable to passenger cars during dry weather, but road conditions may vary depending on weather conditions.
Other: The Cochise Stronghold Campground is typically open Sept through May. All sites are first-come, first served and have a stay limit of 14 days. There are pit toilets in the campground.

FINDING THE CAMPGROUND AND TRAILHEAD

From the intersection of Dragoon Road and Cochise Stronghold Road, head south on Cochise Stronghold Road for 6 miles. Turn west on West Ironwood Road and continue for 4.5 miles. West Ironwood Road ends at the Cochise Stronghold Campground entrance, which features a paved campground road. Campground GPS: N31 55.359' / W109 58.066'; trailhead GPS: N31 55.333' / W109 58.035'

Top: Ironwood Road bends around a huge boulder on the drive into Cochise Stronghold Campground.
Bottom: Eerie shadows playing across a boulder in the moonlight resemble a skull in the foothills of Cochise Stronghold.

COCHISE STRONGHOLD CAR CAMPING AND NIGHT HIKE

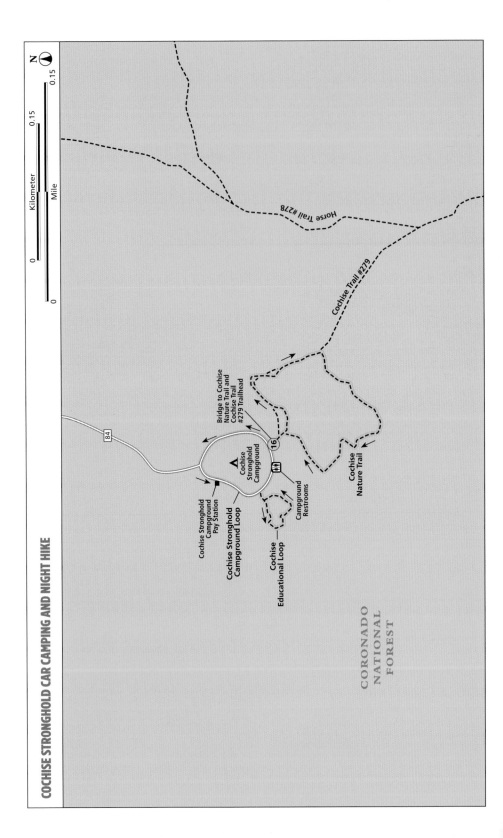

The moon and stars shine through a canopy of oak trees at Cochise Stronghold.

THE ADVENTURE

Nested deep in the Dragoon Mountains, Cochise Stronghold captures a special place in the hearts of people who visit this rugged and historic area. Cochise Stronghold is a natural fortress of tall granite cliffs, giant boulders, and shady groves of oak trees. In the 1800s, Chiricahua Apache chief Cochise and his followers took advantage of their knowledge of this rugged landscape to launch raids on their enemies. Starry skies also take refuge in the Dragoon Mountains, offering modern-day campers with a view of the night sky much like what Chief

> Chief Cochise launched fierce raids on the US Army from his stronghold to avenge his slain followers.

Cochise would have seen generations ago. Experience the night at Cochise Stronghold Campground by pitching your tent or parking your small camping rig under a canopy of oak trees and stars.

After selecting your campsite and paying the fee, take some time to enjoy the quiet of Cochise Stronghold Campground. Hear the oak trees gently rustle their leaves in the breeze and the call of Mexican jays as they explore the forest for food. Trails surrounding the campground, like the 4.5-mile Cochise Trail #279 and the 0.4-mile Cochise Nature Trail, give campers plenty to explore before and after dark. After the sun goes down on your campsite and the stars emerge, walk toward the southern part of the campground to the Cochise Nature Trail to enjoy a beautiful walk under the stars. The Cochise Nature

Trail begins by crossing a small bridge spanning a wash.

Once you have crossed the bridge, start the Cochise Nature Trail toward the left, generally heading clockwise on the loop. This easy dirt trail features stairs and will take you from the canopy of trees to a canopy of thousands of stars in a matter of minutes. Open views of the sky will showcase the tall granite peaks of Cochise Stronghold and give you the opportunity to appreciate full constellations. Enjoy this hike under a quarter moon to see rich star fields and the striking landscape in detail. Crest the high point of the Cochise Nature Trail and descend the trail toward the campground bathrooms to start the short 0.10-mile educational loop. The paved educational loop features informational signs so you can learn about the cultural and natural history of the area.

Cochise Stronghold is a special place for dark skies, animals, and people alike. As you enjoy your nights at Cochise Stronghold, consider how many people have called this area their special place for generations. Do your part to care for the campground; be sure not to abandon campfires or leave food and other smelly items accessible to bears. Some people claim to feel Chief Cochise's spirit in the charismatic rocks of the Dragoon Mountains, where he is buried for all time. Everyone should feel the spirit of the night sky's awesome beauty at Cochise Stronghold.

MILES AND DIRECTIONS

0.0 Start the Cochise Nature Trail in a clockwise direction at the southeastern side of the campground by crossing over a bridge.

0.4 Complete the nature trail loop and arrive back at the campground.

17 CHIRICAHUA NATIONAL MONUMENT CAR CAMPING AND NIGHT HIKE

Camp under the stars and explore the wonderful balanced rocks of Chiricahua National Monument, an International Dark Sky Park.

Activity: Car camping and night hiking

Location: Chiricahua National Monument, 2856 East Rhyolite Creek Rd., Willcox

Campground: Bonita Canyon Campground; GPS: N32 00.667' / W109 21.324'

Start: Echo Canyon Trailhead; GPS: N32 00.718' / W109 18.953'

Elevation gain: 525 feet

Distance: 3.4 miles out and back

Difficulty: Moderate due to steep stairs and sections of trail

Hiking time: About 1.5 hours

Seasons/schedule: Open year-round; best in spring, summer, and fall

Dark sky designation: International Dark Sky Park

Timing: No moon to a quarter moon

Fees and permits: Nightly camping fees; see nps.gov/chir/planyourvisit/bonita-canyon-campground.htm for current fees. All campsites are reservable.

Trail and campground contacts: Chiricahua National Monument, 12856 East Rhyolite Creek Rd., Willcox 85643; (520) 824-3560; nps.gov/chir/index.htm

Dog-friendly: Yes, leashed and under control in Bonita Canyon Campground. Dogs are not allowed on the Echo Canyon Trail.

Trail surface: Dirt and rock

Land status: National monument and federally designated wilderness

Nearest town: Willcox, Arizona

Other trail users: Equestrians, trail runners, photographers, birders.

Suitable camp setups: RVs up to 29 feet in length, tents, fifth wheels, vans, cars, pickup trucks

Maps: Chiricahua National Monument maps available online at nps.gov/chir/planyourvisit/maps.htm

Facilities: Picnic tables, grills, ash cans, bear boxes; flush toilets, sinks; drinking water spigots; gray water dump station, trash cans. No RV hookups are available.

Water availability: Drinking water available at the campground and the visitor center

Special considerations: Ground fires are not permitted at Bonita Canyon Campground. Bears, mountain lions, and rattlesnakes inhabit the area, so bring bear spray and make noise while hiking. Overnight temperatures can be freezing at night in the winter, fall, and spring. Flash flooding can occur at any time of the year; check the forecast and also check the weather before camping and hiking. Rockfalls are common near the rhyolite pinnacles.

FINDING THE CAMPGROUND AND TRAILHEAD

From Willcox, take Maley Street/AZ 186 southeast for 31.3 miles. Once you reach AZ 181, turn left and head east for 3 miles to the Chiricahua National Monument entrance station. Go through the entrance station and head east on Bonita Canyon Road for

The word "Chiricahua" is an Opata word for wild turkey, which can be found in the Chiricahua Mountains.

Large hoodoos stand guard under the dark skies of Chiricahua National Monument.

2.7 miles until you see a sign for Bonita Canyon Campground, where you will turn left (west) into the campground. To reach the Echo Canyon Trailhead, exit the Bonita Canyon Campground and turn left to head north, east, then south again on Bonita Canyon Drive for 4.7 miles. Follow the sign for Echo Canyon Trail and Sugar Loaf Trail and turn right (west) off Bonita Canyon Drive, continuing west for 0.1 mile. Turn left (south) into the Echo Canyon Trailhead parking lot. Campground GPS: N32 00.667' / W109 21.324'; trailhead GPS: N32 00.718' / W109 18.953'

THE ADVENTURE

Tucked deep in the southeastern corner of Arizona lies a wonderland of rhyolite hoodoos at Chiricahua National Monument. Fractured and eroded into existence, the pinnacles rise stories-high like a city of

> **LOOK UP**
> Betelgeuse, a bright red supergiant star in Orion's eastern shoulder, is 950 times the size of our sun.

rocks on the sky island of the Chiricahua Mountains. Generations of people and cultures have called the Chiricahuas home, from the Chiricahua Apache tribe to modern-day park rangers. All who have ever called these mountains home slept under the same dark skies that earned Chiricahua National Monument its International Dark Sky Park status in 2021. For this adventure, call Bonita Canyon Campground your home for a couple nights and explore the hoodoos of the Echo Canyon Trail at night.

Reserve your campsite at Bonita Canyon Campground to ensure the perfect home base for your adventures in Chiricahua National Monument. Located a short drive north on Bonita Canyon Road from the visitor center, the campground is situated within a pine-oak woodland teeming with birds and wildlife. Complete with amenities like flush toilets, drinking water, and bear boxes, Bonita Canyon Campground is fully developed for your comfort and enjoyment. Take advantage of the bear boxes, and be careful how you store smelly items at the campground—this is bear country. Once you have your camp set up, it's time to gear up for a sunset-to-night hike on the Echo Canyon Trail.

An hour or two before sunset, take a scenic drive north on Bonita Canyon Drive for 4.8 miles to the Echo Canyon Trailhead. From the trailhead at the southern side of the parking lot, begin your hike southward high above the hoodoos in the pine trees.

CHIRICAHUA NATIONAL MONUMENT CAR CAMPING AND NIGHT HIKE

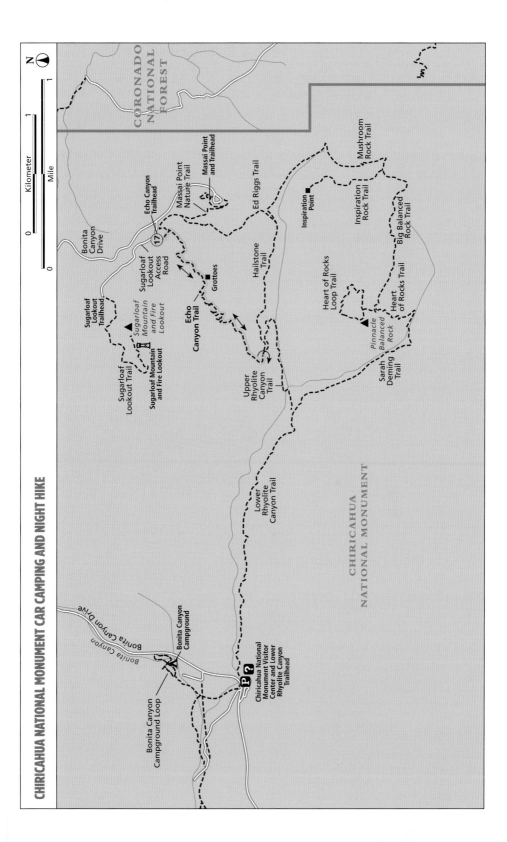

Descend the rocky trail generally southwest, gaining better and better views of the hoodoos and eventually coming up close and personal with the huge spires of rock. Around 0.55 mile from the trailhead, you'll encounter The Grottoes, a popular sheltered group of hoodoos with chunks of rock pinned between the hoodoos above your head. Continue southeast for 1.13 miles through this sunset-lit wonderland of rocks, passing between hoodoos and descending switchbacks carefully constructed by the Civilian Conservation Corps (CCC) decades ago. Emerge from the city of hoodoos and enter a small forest of trees at Echo Park, 1.25 miles down the trail. Head southeast for the remaining 0.45 mile of the trail, crossing a small creek bed and curving around a hill above a beautiful valley lined with towers of rhyolite. Finish the Echo Canyon Trail at the junction with the Hailstone and Rhyolite Trails, then turn around and begin the 1.7-mile night hike portion of this trail toward the northeast.

> Chiricahua National Monument is known for its biodiversity, including coatimundi, a small social mammal that roams the forest during the day for food.

The hoodoos at Chiricahua National Monument seem endless; however, the stars you can see in the night sky far outnumber the hoodoos. On the Echo Canyon Trail, dark, vivid skies silhouette the hoodoos. Views include complete constellations and deep-sky objects like the Andromeda galaxy. In spring and fall, look for a pillar of diffuse zodiacal light reaching for the skies alongside the hoodoos to the west after twilight. Be sure to make noise as you hike back generally northeast on the Echo Canyon Trail to alert any animals like mountain lions to your presence. Encounters with large, potentially dangerous mammals are rare; however, it's important to exercise caution while enjoying the stunning dark skies over Chiricahua National Monument.

As you hike, find places to stop and gaze at the stars. When you return to the trailhead, take a long pause to see the stars on the horizons around you. To return to Bonita Canyon Campground, simply travel back down Bonita Canyon Drive for 4.8 miles. Enjoy the night skies from your campsite before getting some rest for the night. Chiricahua National Monument offers many other trails to explore during the day or night, such as the challenging yet very rewarding Heart of Rocks Loop. Wherever you explore in Chiricahua National Monument, you are sure to make beautiful memories among the skyward hoodoos and protected night skies.

MILES AND DIRECTIONS

0.0 For the Echo Canyon Trail, start south then southeast from the Echo Canyon Trailhead.

0.55 Reach The Grottoes and continue southeast on the trail, including several areas of switchbacks, for 0.7 mile to Echo Park.

1.25 Arrive at Echo Park and continue south then southwest, curving east for 0.45 mile to the Echo Canyon–Hailstone–Rhyolite Trail junction.

1.7 Meet the end of the Echo Canyon Trail at the Echo Canyon–Hailstone–Rhyolite Trail junction. To return to the Echo Canyon Trailhead, hike generally northeast to the trailhead.

3.4 Arrive back at the trailhead.

18 LAS CIENEGAS NATIONAL CONSERVATION AREA BIKEPACKING

Bikepack through the rolling grassy hills of Las Cienegas National Conservation Area and camp under vast starry skies.

Activity: Bikepacking
Location: Las Cienegas National Conservation Area; GPS: N31 47.474' / W110 37.825'
Start: Airstrip group campsite; GPS: N31 47.474' / W110 37.825'
Elevation gain: 340 feet
Distance: 17.4-mile loop
Difficulty: Moderate due to steep climbs
Riding time: About 4 hours or 1 night
Seasons/schedule: Open year-round; best in fall, winter, and spring
Timing: No moon to a quarter moon
Fees and permits: None for BLM land. Arizona State Trust Land requires a permit to access certain areas of the monument. See asld.secure.force.com/recreationalpermit/ to buy a recreational permit online.
Trail contacts: BLM, Tucson Field Office, 3201 East Universal Way, Tucson 85746; (520) 258-7200; blm.gov/national-conservation-lands/arizona/las-cienegas
Dog-friendly: Yes
Trail surface: Maintained gravel roads to unmaintained rocky and sandy doubletrack road
Land status: National conservation area and State of Arizona conservation lands

Nearest town: Sonoita, Arizona
Other trail users: Motorcyclists, cars, trucks, RVs, UTV/ATV, equestrians, birders
Maps: Las Cienegas NCA maps available online at blm.gov/national-conservation-lands/arizona/las-cienegas
Water availability: Yes, at the Empire Ranch Headquarters
Special considerations: Las Cienegas NCA contains a working ranch; beware of cattle, and leave gates as you find them while cycling. Nighttime temperatures can fall below freezing in winter. Although an encounter is unlikely, undocumented migrants pass through this area at times; US Customs and Border Protection operates in the area. Rattlesnakes inhabit the area. Camping is allowed only in preexisting campsites.
Other: Reducing tire pressure can provide a smoother ride on rocky trails. Some sections of the route are very sandy and may require you to dismount your bike for a short distance. Some sections of this route cross Arizona State Trust Land and require a recreation permit for access.

FINDING THE TRAILHEAD

From AZ 83, take Empire Ranch Road/BLM 6900 northeast for 3 miles to a junction with BLM 6901. Turn north onto BLM 6901 and continue north for 1 mile. Take the first turn to the west onto BLM 6902; head 100 feet west and then turn right (north). Park your vehicle near the restroom for the Airstrip group site. This is where you will begin your bikepacking adventure. Trailhead GPS: N31 47.474' / W110 37.825'

Cienega Creek is one of the last valley-bottom wetlands in the southwestern United States.

THE ADVENTURE

The rolling grassy hills of Las Cienegas National Conservation Area (NCA) look more like a scene from the American Midwest than Arizona. Las Cienegas harbors perennial Cienega Creek, galleries of cottonwood trees, rare marshlands, and vast grasslands that

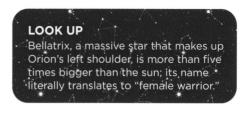

LOOK UP
Bellatrix, a massive star that makes up Orion's left shoulder, is more than five times bigger than the sun; its name literally translates to "female warrior."

stretch for miles. Dark skies find their refuge at this conservation area with stars and constellations burning brightly in the sky with little light pollution. For this bikepacking adventure, load up your bicycle with camping gear, and ride through the grasslands on a short 17-mile loop.

Start your adventure in the daytime near the Airstrip group site just a mile north of the historic Empire Ranch Headquarters. Park in a large lot near the Airstrip site restrooms, where you can safely leave your vehicle for the trip. Kick off this adventure by heading south from the Airstrip group site and then turning left (northeast) onto BLM 6901, passing cattle and rolling pastures. Continue northeast on BLM 6901, making a left at the first junction 1 mile up the route, a left 2.5 miles up the route at the second junction, and a right 3.75 miles up the route at the third junction. After crossing Cienega Creek and 1 mile of passing galleries of cottonwood trees and a marsh, you will reach the northern end of the loop, which also affords access to the Ag Fields group campsite.

As BLM 6910 ends in a group of mesquite trees, begin the challenging part of the route on BLM 6914, heading generally southeast for 4 miles. The first 4 miles of BLM 6914 to Cinco Canyon offer solitude and grand views of the grasslands on a doubletrack road that is rocky and steep in some places. After reaching Cinco Canyon, BLM 6914 turns southwest and continues for 3 miles through more open grasslands and eventually meet its end at BLM 6900. Near the junction, make a quick detour down BLM 6919 for 0.3 mile to the historic Hummel ranch house and then backtrack to BLM 6900. Head west on the graded BLM 6900 for 1.3 miles, pass a beautiful marsh area, and take the southern turnoff for the Cieneguita camping area. After 13.75 miles of riding, this undeveloped campground perched on a high grassy plain makes a great place to pitch your tent and stargaze after dark.

Enjoy a beautiful sunset backlighting the Santa Rita Mountains and casting golden light on the blades of grass. As the night skies open wide over Las Cienegas, absorb the bright starlight and enjoy views of the deep universe above. In the distance, experience the sounds of the Wild West, listening for the sounds of crickets, cattle, and coyotes. Complete the loop by departing the Cieneguita camping area and return to BLM 6900. Head northwest for 1.25 miles and then turn north on BLM 6901 for 1 mile toward the Airstrip group site. Return to your vehicle. When you are ready, leave the same way you arrived at the Airstrip group site.

MILES AND DIRECTIONS

0.0   Start from the Airstrip group site parking area and head southeast for 0.25 mile to BLM 6901.

0.25   Turn left on BLM 6901 and head northeast for 4.5-miles.

"Las Cienegas" is Spanish for "the marshlands."

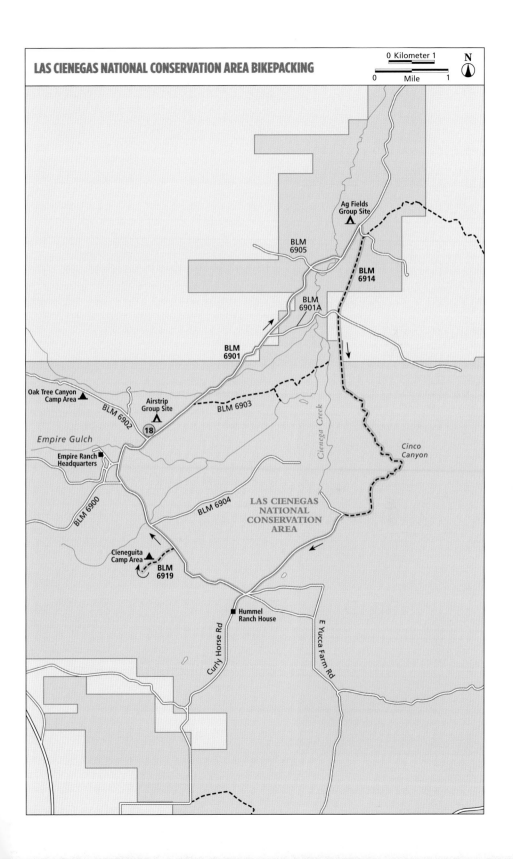

0 Kilometer 1

0 Mile 1

N

Ag Fields
Group Site

BLM
6905

BLM
6914

BLM
6901A

BLM
6901

Oak Tree Canyon
Camp Area

BLM 6902

Airstrip
Group Site

18

BLM 6903

Empire Gulch

Empire Ranch
Headquarters

Cienega Creek

*Cinco
Canyon*

BLM 6900

BLM 6904

LAS CIENEGAS
NATIONAL
CONSERVATION
AREA

Cieneguita
Camp Area

BLM
6919

Hummel
Ranch House

Curly Horse Rd

E Yucca Farm Rd

A field of stars hangs over the vast moonlit fields of grass at Las Cienegas National Conservation Area.

The Milky Way streaks the sky as blades of grass reach for the stars at Las Cienegas National Conservation Area.

4.75 Make a sharp right onto BLM 6914 and head southeast then southwest for 7.05-miles.

11.8 Arrive at the junction with BLM 6900 and 6919; go south onto BLM 6919 toward the Hummel ranch house for 0.3 mile.

12.1 See the Hummel ranch house then head back on BLM 6919 to BLM 6900 for 0.3 mile.

12.4 Turn left and head northwest on BLM 6900 for 1.35 miles.

13.75 Turn left and head southwest on BLM 6900C to the Cieneguita camp areas and select a campsite.

14.95 After camping, return to BLM 6900 and head northwest for 1.24 miles.

16.19 At the junction with BLM 6901, head north for 1 mile.

17.2 Arrive back at the junction with BLM 6902; turn left (west) toward the Airstrip group site.

17.4 Arrive back at the trailhead.

19 UNIVERSITY OF ARIZONA MT. LEMMON SKYCENTER— STARGAZING WITH THE EXPERTS

Stargaze and learn the night sky with professional astronomers at the University of Arizona's Mt. Lemmon SkyCenter at the peak of Mount Lemmon. Enjoy unparalleled views of galaxies and nebulae far away through one of the largest publicly available telescopes in the United States.

Activity: Stargazing and astronomical education

Location: University of Arizona's Mt. Lemmon SkyCenter

Start: Mt. Lemmon SkyCenter, 9800 East Ski Run Rd., Mount Lemmon

Difficulty: Easy

Adventure time: About 5 hours

Seasons/schedule: Open early fall, winter, and late spring

Timing: Any time

Fees and permits: SkyNights stargazing program tickets can be purchased online at skycenter .arizona.edu/content/tickets.

Contacts: University of Arizona Steward Observatory, 933 North Cherry Ave., Tucson 85719; (520) 626-8122; skycenter.arizona.edu

Dog-friendly: No dogs allowed. Contact the Mt. Lemmon SkyCenter with service animal inquiries.

Trail surface: Paved paths and roads

Land status: USDA Forest Service and University of Arizona property

Nearest towns: Tucson, Summerhaven

Maps: Mt. Lemmon SkyCenter map available online at skycenter.arizona .edu/content/maps-and-directions

Water availability: Yes

Special considerations: Dress warmly for cold overnight temperatures any time of the year. In winter, dress for extremely low temperatures and be prepared to walk on icy surfaces. Ice may be present on the Catalina Highway (Mount Lemmon Scenic Byway) on the drive up to the SkyCenter. Two to seven days' cancellation notice must be given by phone or email (mtlemmon .skycenter@gmail.com), depending on group size. (**Note:** SkyNights programs may be canceled due to weather conditions; ticket holders will receive a full refund.) Allow 1.5 to 2 hours to get from Tucson to the meetup location. Arrive at the meetup location at least 15 minutes before the scheduled program start time. SkyCenter staff cannot accommodate late arrivals. No gas is available on Mount Lemmon.

FINDING THE MEETUP LOCATIONS

For stargazing programs Mar–Oct, take Catalina Highway 24.5 miles to East Ski Run Road. Turn right on East Ski Run Road and travel west for 3.1 miles to a closed gate next to the Mount Lemmon trailhead parking lot. Park on the road shoulder in front of the gate until your guides let you into the SkyCenter, just 0.2 mile ahead of the gate. For stargazing programs in winter, Nov–Feb, drive 24.5 miles up Catalina Highway. Turn right on East Ski Run Road and travel west for 1.5 miles to the Iron Door Restaurant. Park on the north side of the road at the restaurant and wait for your guides to pick you up and take you to the SkyCenter in a University of Arizona shuttle. Do not park on the south side of the road by the ski lift; you risk your vehicle being locked in while you are attending the program. Meetup locations GPS (Mar–Oct): N32 26.449' / W110 47.146'; (Nov–Feb): N32 26.918' / W110 46.868'

Stars shine over the observatory dome of the Schulman telescope at the University of Arizona's Mt. Lemmon SkyCenter.

THE ADVENTURE

Sitting high above Tucson, the peak of Mount Lemmon has had many uses over the decades. Formerly the Mount Lemmon Air Force Station, the military scanned the skies with radar for enemy aircraft and missiles during the Cold War. Today, everyone can search the skies for stars, planets, and galaxies far, far away at the University of Arizona's Mt. Lemmon SkyCenter. On this adventure, explore the night sky like you've never before with the popular SkyNights stargazing program. Hosted by professional astronomers from the University of Arizona's Steward Observatory, you will learn about the wonders of the night sky using state-of-the-art telescopes.

The adventure begins with a scenic drive all the way up Mount Lemmon from Tucson. At the beginning of the 5-hour SkyNights program, you will group up and learn some of the history of the site. Next you will step into one of the large on-site telescope domes to learn about the telescope and some interesting star facts. While visiting the telescope, you may observe a distant star shining in the daytime! Then it's time for a light

LOOK UP

The Milky Way galaxy is part of the Local Group, a small galaxy cluster containing around eighty galaxies, including the Andromeda galaxy.

The Local Group is part of the larger Virgo Supercluster, a massive galaxy cluster of at least one hundred galaxy groups and clusters.

> The Catalina Sky Survey, based on Mount Lemmon, searches nightly for potentially hazardous near-Earth objects (NEOs) such as asteroids and comets.

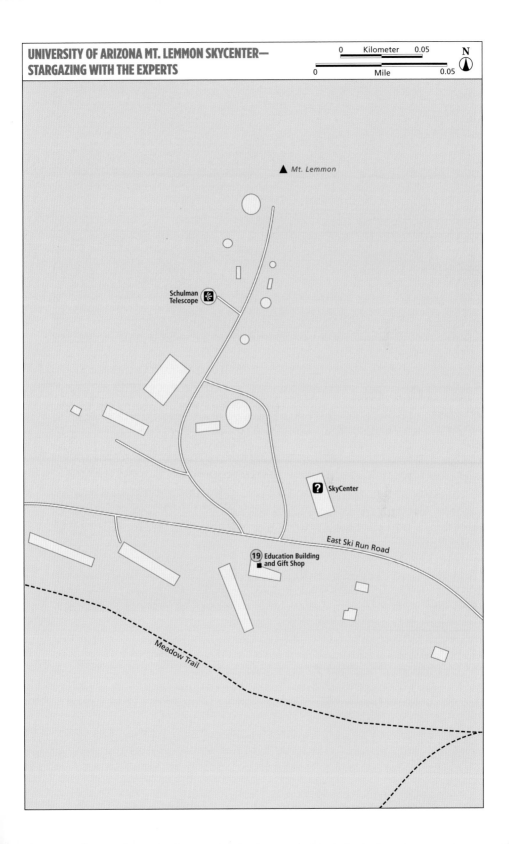

0   Kilometer   0.05

0   Mile   0.05

N

▲ Mt. Lemmon

Schulman
Telescope

SkyCenter

East Ski Run Road

19 Education Building
and Gift Shop

Meadow Trail

A pair of telescope domes peer into the night sky at the Mt. Lemmon SkyCenter.

dinner and an in-depth astronomy presentation about our own solar system at an indoor educational center. People of all ages will enjoy learning about the planets and get the opportunity to ask questions in an inviting atmosphere.

Around sunset, you'll move over to a mountaintop view of the wide valleys west of the Santa Catalina Mountains. Here you'll get a chance to calibrate your pair of binoculars and start getting excited for the stars to come out. Throughout twilight, you'll return to the education center and get a chance to buy memorabilia at the gift shop or relax. After dark, you'll bundle up and reemerge from the education center to travel to one of the telescopes for deep-sky viewing. Astronomers will point the 32-inch Schulman and/or 24-inch Phillips telescopes for extraordinary views of the heavens.

Visitors can view wonderful objects millions of light-years away, like the Sombrero galaxy and dazzling star clusters. It's a humbling experience to see an entire galaxy in an eyepiece,

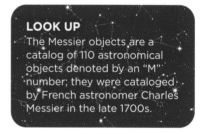

LOOK UP
The Messier objects are a catalog of 110 astronomical objects denoted by an "M" number; they were cataloged by French astronomer Charles Messier in the late 1700s.

and it certainly makes you wonder if anyone out there is looking back at you. The final part of the stargazing experience includes a full laser-guided tour of the constellations like Ursa Major and asterisms like the Big Dipper. You'll also be treated to seasonal constellations like Scorpius and Orion. To conclude the experience, you'll be shuttled back to your vehicles by your hosts; from there you'll take the windy road back down to Tucson or your nearby cabin. By the end of the night, you should have learned a lot from the knowledgeable staff and gotten to know our amazing stellar neighborhood.

20 KARTCHNER CAVERNS CAVE TOUR AND NIGHT HIKE

Explore the hidden world of dripping stalactites, giant caverns, and cave bacon at Kartchner Caverns State Park. Trade dark caves for dark skies on a 3-mile sunset-to-night hike to see for yourself why this is an International Dark Sky Park.

Activity: Cave tour and night hiking
Location: Kartchner Caverns State Park, 2980 South Hwy. 90, Benson
Start: Foothills Loop Trailhead; GPS: N31 50.158′ / W110 20.975′
Elevation gain: 563 feet
Distance: 3.05-mile loop
Difficulty: Moderate due to steep ascents and descents on rocky terrain
Hiking time: About 2 hours
Seasons/schedule: Open year-round; best in late fall, winter, and spring
Dark sky designation: International Dark Sky Park
Timing: No moon to a quarter moon
Fees and permits: Park entrance and cave tour reservation fees required; entrance fees waived when a cave tour or campsite/cabin has been reserved. Check azstateparks.com/kartchner/explore/facility-information for current fee information.
Trail contacts: Kartchner Caverns State Park, 2980 South Hwy. 90, Benson 85602; (520) 586-4100; azstateparks.com/kartchner
Dog-friendly: No dogs allowed in the cave; leashed dogs allowed on the trail
Trail surface: Dirt and rock
Land status: State park
Nearest town: Benson, Arizona
Other trail users: Hikers, photographers, trail runners
Maps: Interactive and downloadable maps available online at azstateparks.com/kartchner/explore/maps

Water availability: Yes; water is available at the visitor center.
Special considerations: In warm months, spiders, scorpions, and rattlesnakes may be present on the trail; keep a close eye on the trail at all times, and use a strong headlamp. Javelinas, snakes, deer, bobcats, and mountain lions are present in the park. Winter temperatures may be freezing overnight. Monsoon storms can produce intense rain, lightning, and destructive winds; check the forecast before hiking. For cave tours, the Rotunda/Throne Room are open year-round; the Big Room is only open Oct 15 to Apr 15 due to the presence of roosting bats. Although not required, reservations are strongly recommended; tours fill up quickly, especially on weekends. Arrive 15 minutes before your cave tour; park rangers cannot accommodate late arrivals. If you have been in any other caves or mines prior to your visit, do not wear the same clothes or shoes to prevent the spread of white-nose syndrome, a fatal fungal disease for bats. Video or photography is not allowed inside a cave unless authorized by permit or when on a special photography tour of the cave. Electronic devices, food, drinks, and other items are not allowed in the cave. Age restrictions are in place for cave tours; check the park website for details.

FINDING THE TRAILHEAD
From I-10 in Benson, take AZ 90 south for 8.9 miles; following the signs for Kartchner Caverns, turn right into the park. Drive west into the park and follow signs for the visitor center. The Foothills Loop Trailhead is located just southwest of the visitor center and is signed. Trailhead GPS: N31 50.158′ / W110 20.975′

The Milky Way stretches over a century plant and the Whetstone Mountains just west of Kartchner Caverns State Park.

THE ADVENTURE

When Gary Tenen and Randy Tufts discovered pristine caves on the eastern slopes of the Whetstone Mountains in 1974, they decided to keep their discovery secret to preserve the area's natural and scientific value. A slow but intentional preservation process followed, creating one of the most popular and beloved places in Arizona: Kartchner Caverns State Park. Water, gravity, and calcium combined in total darkness to create cave formations like chandeliers of stalactites, decorated columns, and delicate soda straws. In an effort to preserve the darkness that falls over the park every night, Kartchner Caverns State Park was certified as an International Dark Sky Park in 2017. On this adventure, you will combine all of Kartchner Caverns' assets by taking a tour of the caves and then embarking on a fun sunset-to-night hike on the Foothills Loop Trail.

The standard cave tour begins with a brief presentation on the natural history of the caves and how they were discovered in 1974 by Randy Tufts and Gary Tenen. After a summary of the etiquette rules for the cave and touching a "get it out of your system rock," you'll step onto a tram and make your way to the cave entrance. Next you'll pass

LOOK UP

Every star you can see with your naked eye is bigger and brighter than our own sun.

The color of a star indicates its temperature, with blue stars like Sirius being much hotter than red stars like Betelgeuse.

Humans with great vision and ideal viewing conditions free of light pollution can only see 2,000 to 2,500 stars in the sky.

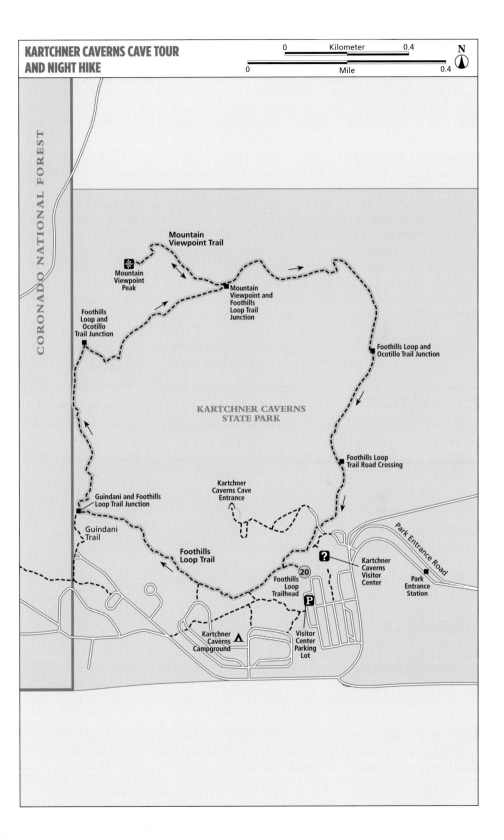

KARTCHNER CAVERNS CAVE TOUR
AND NIGHT HIKE

0   Kilometer   0.4
0   Mile   0.4

N

CORONADO NATIONAL FOREST

Mountain
Viewpoint Trail

Mountain
Viewpoint
Peak

Foothills
Loop and
Ocotillo
Trail Junction

Mountain
Viewpoint and
Foothills
Loop Trail
Junction

Foothills Loop and
Ocotillo Trail Junction

KARTCHNER CAVERNS
STATE PARK

Foothills Loop
Trail Road Crossing

Kartchner
Caverns Cave
Entrance

Guindani and Foothills
Loop Trail Junction

Guindani
Trail

Foothills
Loop Trail

Park Entrance Road

Kartchner
Caverns Visitor
Center

Park
Entrance
Station

Foothills
Loop
Trailhead

20

P

Visitor
Center
Parking
Lot

Kartchner
Caverns
Campground

through a tunnel and enter the warm humidity of the real cave for an exciting tour of its beautiful features. Sparking totems will dazzle your eyes, and in moments of deafening silence, all you'll be able to hear is water dripping from ceiling to floor. Once you complete this amazing tour, step out aboveground and take some time to enjoy daytime activities like browsing the gift shop or grabbing dinner nearby.

Return to Kartchner Caverns 30 minutes before sunset for a 3-mile hike on the Foothills Loop. Starting near the visitor center, take the loop in a clockwise direction and head to the left (west) to begin the loop. A steady climb for 1.36 miles west then north around the hills containing Kartchner Caverns will bring you to the Mountain Viewpoint trail junction. Take this quick, 10-minute side trip west to the top of a small mountain and watch the rest of the twilight fade over the Whetstone Mountains. Take some time up here or down at the Foothills Loop junction to take in the dark skies over Kartchner Caverns.

From the Mountain Viewpoint, you can see light pollution from the highways, Sierra Vista, Willcox, and Tucson, but over the park it's dark, and the stars have a chance to shine. Dust lanes and star clusters of the Milky Way are clearly visible to the naked eye from this high vantage. Keep an eye out for satellites and shooting stars while gazing at your favorite constellations. When you're ready to complete the loop, head east on the Foothills Loop down a hill, then go south and cross a few washes for 1.17 miles back to the visitor center. When you finish up your hike on the Foothills Loop, you may even get to see some of the same bats that call Kartchner Caverns home buzzing around the parking lot.

MILES AND DIRECTIONS

0.0 Start from the Foothills Loop Trailhead and take the loop in a clockwise direction. Turn left and head west on the Foothills Loop for 0.6 mile to the Guindani Trail junction.

0.6 At the junction, continue north on the Foothills Loop Trail for 0.37 mile up a hill to the Ocotillo Trail junction.

0.97 From the Ocotillo Trail junction continue east on the Foothills Loop for 0.39 mile to the Mountain Viewpoint Trail junction.

1.36 Head west up the Mountain Viewpoint Trail for 0.26 mile.

1.62 Summit a small mountain, then return to the Foothills Loop Trail by hiking back east on the trail for 0.26 mile.

1.88 Head east down a hill then south crossing some washes on the Foothills Loop Trail back to the visitor center for 1.17 miles.

3.05 Arrive back at the trailhead.

The light of the Milky Way core breaks through the
night skies over Kartchner Caverns State Park

Orion and a train of winter constellations tower in the
skies over Cathedral Rock near Sedona in Central Arizona.

CENTRAL ARIZONA

CENTRAL ARIZONA IS A LAND OF DIVERSITY, with one foot in the hardy Sonoran Desert and the other in verdant pine forests. Desert mountains guarded by saguaro dominate part of the landscape, however, follow the Verde River upstream to rolling grasslands, red-rock canyons, and forests climbing up to the Mogollon Rim. Despite heavy light pollution from Phoenix, Central Arizona has the most International Dark Sky Communities in the state, with municipalities like Sedona stepping up to protect the night sky. The region has been a cultural center for thousands of years, from ancient Hohokam civilizations to the modern-day state capital in Phoenix, the largest city in the state. The diverse geography, dark skies, and rich history of Central Arizona make it a great place to have a stargazing adventure.

Connected to Arizona's other four regions, Central Arizona contains a unique piece from each region. The hot Sonoran Desert dominates the region's west and south and is characterized best by mountains like the Superstitions, covered in iconic saguaro cactus. Moving north from the desert heat, you'll find magical places like the red-rock country around Sedona and oak forests riding above rolling grasslands. Seven thousand feet up to the east, the Mogollon Rim hosts one of Arizona's most beautiful forests and supports outstanding rivers like Oak Creek and the Salt River. Both day and night, the beauty of Central Arizona can be accessed through abundant public lands such as the Tonto and Coconino National Forests.

In spite of extreme light pollution from the Phoenix metroplex, Central Arizona is also the beginning of a dark sky corridor leading up to the Grand Canyon. Starry skies are found throughout the national forests and wilderness areas of the region, including Tonto National Monument, an International Dark Sky Park. Institutions like Arizona State University contribute significantly to astronomical research, and local astronomy organizations give the public the opportunity to attend star parties. Dark skies are further supported by Central Arizona's certified International Dark Sky Communities found along the Verde River Valley, including Fountain Hills, Sedona, Big Park/Village of Oak Creek, and Cottonwood. In contrast to the dark sky communities, extreme light pollution from Phoenix and its suburban sprawl blots out all but a handful of bright stars for its residents. People have always lived here in a big way, so let's turn back the clock to reveal Central Arizona's rich cultural history.

Central Arizona's human history dates back thousands of years, weaving a story of resiliency and survival leading up to the modern-day boom of desert cities like Phoenix and Mesa. Native Americans in the Hohokam culture were masters of the Sonoran Desert, digging sophisticated canal systems along the Salt and Gila Rivers for crop irrigation. Villages of thousands of people stretched from the Phoenix Valley to the Tucson Valley, but the Hohokam cultures mysteriously disappeared, dispersing themselves into such modern-day tribes as the Tohono O'odham. For more than 11,000 years, the Sinagua

Three giant saguaro cacti rise out of Sonoran Desert National Monument against a backdrop of bright stars.

and their Yavapai and Apache descendants inhabited the Verde River Valley and the red-rock canyons near Sedona. With the arrival of European Americans to Central Arizona in the 1800s, the five "Cs" that fueled Arizona's rapid economic growth came to fruition: cattle, cotton, citrus, copper, and climate. The economic core of Arizona resides in the sprawling cities of Phoenix, Mesa, Scottsdale, and Chandler, which attract people from across the country to move in and start new lives in the Sonoran Desert.

Abundant public lands and Dark Sky Communities protect Central Arizona's starry skies, making it a great place to have an adventure under the night sky. In this chapter, explore the mysterious Superstition Mountains or relax under the stars by Oak Creek at Red Rock Crossing. Thanks to the International Dark Sky Community movement, you can see hundreds of stars in the skies right over the sidewalks of Sedona. An interesting cultural history creates space to think about all those who gazed upon a star over the region thousands of years ago. Over the course of this chapter, you'll embark on ten adventures under the night sky to see for yourself why Central Arizona is a great place to stargaze.

21 SUPERSTITION MOUNTAINS BACKPACKING

Backpack through the Superstition Wilderness, known for its legends of the Lost Dutchman's buried treasure, lonely ghosts, and stark desert beauty. Here you will discover the treasures of golden sunsets and dark skies in the rugged Superstition Mountains east of Phoenix.

Activity: Backpacking

Location: Superstition Wilderness of the Tonto National Forest

Start: Boulder Canyon Trail #103 trailhead; GPS: N33 32.040' / W111 25.370'

Elevation gain: Approximately 1,114 feet

Distance: 20.1-mile lollipop

Difficulty: Strenuous due to steep rocky climbs

Hiking time: 2–3 days

Seasons/schedule: Open year-round but very hot in summer; best in late fall, winter, and early spring

Timing: No moon to a quarter moon

Fees and permits: None

Trail contacts: Tonto National Forest, Mesa Ranger District, 5140 East Ingram St., Mesa 85205; (480) 610-3300; fs.usda.gov/recarea/tonto/recarea/?recid=35393

Dog-friendly: Yes

Trail surface: Dirt and rock

Land status: National forest and federally designated wilderness

Nearest town: Apache Junction, Arizona

Other trail users: Day hikers, trail runners, photographers, horses and stock animals

Maps: Official maps of the Superstition Wilderness are available online at fs.usda.gov/detail/tonto/specialplaces/?cid=fsbdev3_018739. Other reliable maps include Beartooth Publishing's Superstition Wilderness and National Geographic Trails Illustrated #851: Superstition and Four Peaks Wilderness Areas.

Water availability: Water is not available at the trailhead but is seasonally available in the backcountry. Boulder Creek, La Barge Creek, and the Second Water Spring are major sources of water along this route. Backpackers should carry at least 1 extra gallon of water and check with the Mesa Ranger District on water availability in the wilderness.

Special considerations: For safety, backpackers should notify at least the Canyon Lake Marina staff of their vehicle information and trip details, such as an estimated exit date from the wilderness. Mountain lions, cholla cactus, and venomous reptiles and insects inhabit the wilderness. Extreme heat and limited water make hiking in the summer very dangerous in this wilderness area.

Other: Trailhead parking is available across the street at the Canyon Lake Marina and Campground dirt parking lot at 16802 AZ 88, Apache Junction.

FINDING THE TRAILHEAD

From Apache Junction, take AZ 88 East, also known as the Apache Trail, toward the northeast for approximately 14 miles to the Canyon Lake Marina and Campground. The Canyon Lake Marina and Campground offers free parking to hikers and backpackers in a dirt parking lot to the north of AZ 88 East, about 100 feet past the second one-way bridge. The trailhead for Boulder Canyon Trail #103 is located across AZ 88 from the Canyon Lake Marina parking lot; look for brown trailhead signs across the highway. Trailhead GPS: N33 32.040' / W111 25.370'

THE ADVENTURE

The very name of the Superstition Wilderness evokes mystery and imagination to all who explore its rugged desert landscape. Driving the Apache Trail/AZ 88 East to the trailhead is an adventure itself, offering beautiful views of the Superstition Mountains and Canyon Lake's deep blue waters. Dark skies can be enjoyed throughout the wilderness as a welcome relief from the heavy light pollution from Phoenix to the west. Saguaro, palo verde, and other classic Sonoran Desert species dominate the landscape of colorful canyon walls and legendary pinnacles like Weaver's Needle. Start the 20.1-mile backpacking journey into the Superstition Wilderness with Boulder Canyon Trail (#103), across from the Canyon Lake Marina.

The first 2.5 miles of the Trail #103 will take you over steep saguaro-studded hills to the edge of a ragged cliff for incredible views of LaBarge Canyon, Battleship Mountain, and Weaver's Needle. After taking in the view, descend switchbacks to the floor of the canyon and cross LaBarge Creek to take a pleasant stroll past some campsites along the Boulder Canyon Trail. About 4.25 miles from the trailhead, you will come to the junction with Second Water Trail (#236), where you may find seasonal water flow from Second Water Canyon to the west. Crisscross Boulder Creek south on Trail #103 for 1.5 miles through a rocky canyon until you reach the Calvary Trail (#239) junction. Take a steep climb to the southeast at the start of the Calvary Trail and then level out for a 3.2-mile journey deep into the Superstitions through riparian areas to the junction with the Dutchman Trail (#104) at Marsh Valley. After hiking more than 9 miles to this point, you may want to set up camp in the Marsh Valley area or further up Trail #104 near the junction with the Bull Pass Trail (#129).

Battleship Mountain rises dramatically from LaBarge Canyon into a sea of stars in the Superstition Mountains.

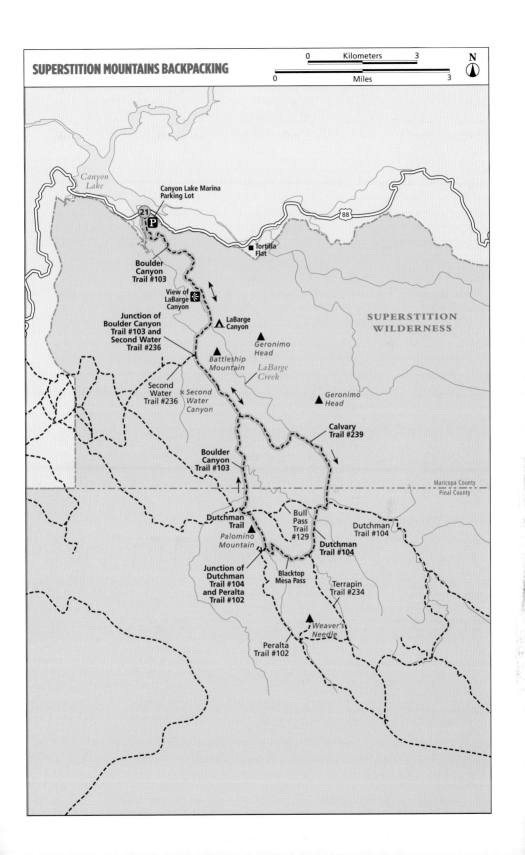

SUPERSTITION MOUNTAINS BACKPACKING

0 Kilometers 3

0 Miles 3

N

Canyon Lake

Canyon Lake Marina
Parking Lot

21

P

88

■ Tortilla
Flat

**Boulder
Canyon
Trail #103**

View of
LaBarge
Canyon

**Junction of
Boulder Canyon
Trail #103 and
Second Water
Trail #236**

LaBarge
Canyon

*Geronimo
Head*

**SUPERSTITION
WILDERNESS**

*Battleship
Mountain*

*LaBarge
Creek*

Second
Water
Trail #236

× *Second
Water
Canyon*

▲ *Geronimo
Head*

**Calvary
Trail #239**

**Boulder
Canyon
Trail #103**

Maricopa County
Pinal County

**Dutchman
Trail**

Bull
Pass
Trail
#129

**Dutchman
Trail #104**

▲ *Palomino
Mountain*

**Dutchman
Trail #104**

**Junction of
Dutchman
Trail #104
and Peralta
Trail #102**

Blacktop
Mesa Pass

Terrapin
Trail #234

▲ *Weaver's
Needle*

Peralta
Trail #102

Weaver's Needle stands at 4,555 feet above sea level and was created as a result of weathering and erosion of the volcanic tuff rock.

Legends of the Lost Dutchman Gold Mine say that the shadow of Weaver's Needle points to a rich vein of gold. Although gold has never been officially found by thousands of treasure hunters over the decades, the legend still lives to this day.

As night sweeps over the Superstitions, enjoy wide views of the starry skies hanging over you, with tall mountains and light pollution from Phoenix in the west being the only limits to visibility. Waking up at different times of the night and night hiking along some of the nearby trails can provide different perspectives of the night sky and Weaver's Needle silhouetted in the distance. Constellations such as the Pleiades and the faint smudge of the Orion Nebula can be easily identified with the naked eye for this backcountry stargazing experience. Once camp is packed up, take the Dutchman Trail (#104) for about 3 miles to hook up and over Blacktop Mesa Pass, featuring more impressive views of the towering Weaver's Needle. Just about 0.5 mile past Palomino Mountain on Trail #104, you will meet Boulder Canyon Trail (#103). Take Trail #103 north 7.6 miles to the Boulder Canyon Trailhead at Canyon Lake. Be aware that the first 1.8 miles northbound on Trail #103 are overgrown and faint in some areas, requiring route-finding skills and a map or GPS to relocate the trail.

Most of the return hike along Trail #103 will be downhill and a retrace of the hike in; however, the most challenging part will be a 500-foot ascent up switchbacks to the view of LaBarge Canyon. Conquer the switchbacks, take a breather, and continue the remaining 2.5 miles to the Boulder Canyon Trailhead at Canyon Lake. More adventures can easily be made throughout the Superstition Mountains by using one of its many accessible trailheads. Exiting the Superstitions will leave you with an unforgettable stargazing experience and a peace that only the wilderness can provide.

MILES AND DIRECTIONS

0.0   Start on Boulder Canyon Trail (#103), generally heading south from the trailhead across AZ 88 from Canyon Lake Marina and Campground's dirt parking lot.

0.75   Reach the Superstition Wilderness sign on Trail #103.

1.2   Reach a 360-degree view of the Superstition Mountains and Canyon Lake on Trail #103.

2.5   Arrive at a ragged cliff on Trail #103 overlooking LaBarge Canyon, Battleship Mountain, and Weaver's Needle to the south. Start down steep switchbacks toward LaBarge Creek and Battleship Mountain. Campsites are available near Trail #103 and LaBarge Creek.

3.7   Ascend an unnamed pass on Trail #103 to the north of Battleship Mountain, heading southwest.

4.25   Intersect Second Water Trail (#236), where you may see water in Second Water Canyon to the west. Continue southeast on Trail #103, crossing Boulder Creek multiple times, for 1.5 miles until you reach the intersection of Calvary Trail (#239).

5.75   Meet with the junction of Boulder Canyon Trail (#103) and Calvary Trail (#239). Head left (east) on Trail #239 on a steep uphill climb.

Orion and the outer bands of the Milky Way shine over Weaver's Needle and the Superstition Mountains.

6.8 Briefly curve northwest on Trail #239 toward Malpais Mountain until you reach LaBarge Creek.

7.25 At LaBarge Creek, the Calvary Trail curves upstream toward the southeast and then the south, crossing LaBarge Creek several times on a gentle uphill grade for 1.75 miles.

9.0 Reach the southern end of the Calvary Trail (#239) at the junction with the Dutchman Trail (#104) near Marsh Valley. Head south then west on the Dutchman Trail (#104) toward the Bull Pass Trail (#129). Campsites are available in the Marsh Valley area near Trail #104.

9.4 Arrive at the junction of Dutchman Trail (#104) and the Bull Pass Trail (#129); continue south on Trail #104 toward Weaver's Needle. Campsites are available near the junction of Trails #104 and #129.

10.3 Continue west on Trail #104 at the junction with the Terrapin Trail (#234) for 1.2 miles. For this section of the Dutchman Trail, you will climb and then descend Blacktop Mesa Pass toward blocky Palomino Mountain.

11.5 Intersect the Peralta Trail (#102) and continue northwest and downhill toward Palomino Mountain on the Dutchman Trail (#104). Some campsites are available along Trail #104 heading northwest toward Palomino Mountain.

12.25 Hike west on Trail #104 at the junction with Bull Pass Trail (#129).

12.35 Meet the junction of Trail #104 and the Boulder Canyon Trail (#103) and turn north on Trail #103 to begin a 7.6-mile trek generally north to the Boulder Canyon Trailhead at Canyon Lake. The Boulder Canyon Trail crosses Boulder Creek many times heading north; the trail itself is faint and overgrown in areas. As you hike, look out for cairns; follow them to stay on the trail.

14.35 Reach the junction of Boulder Canyon Trail (#103) and Calvary Trail (#239); continue northwest on Trail #103 for 1.5 miles, crossing Boulder Creek many times until you reach Second Water Trail (#236).

15.85 Continue to LaBarge Canyon on Trail #103 after arriving at the junction with Second Water Trail. Hike 4.25 miles generally to the north on Trail #103 to Canyon Lake the same way you entered the Superstition Wilderness. The hike is mostly downhill; however, there is a steep 500-foot uphill climb through switchbacks to a ragged cliff overlooking LaBarge Canyon.

20.1 Arrive back at the trailhead.

LOOK UP
Look for the Pleaides open star cluster in the winter sky by drawing an imaginary line from the belt of Orion to the right until you spot a small, dipper-like pattern of bright blue stars.

22 SONORAN DESERT NATIONAL MONUMENT NIGHT MOUNTAIN BIKING

Feel the cool wind on your face as you ride your mountain bike under stars through Sonoran Desert National Monument to Margies Cove. After getting to Margies Cove, wander into the North Maricopa Mountain Wilderness and experience the splendors of a dark sky.

Activity: Mountain biking
Location: Sonoran Desert National Monument
Start: South Woods Road exit from AZ 85; GPS: N33 07.882' / W112 38.851'
Elevation gain: 308 feet
Distance: 11.3 miles out and back
Difficulty: Moderate due to deep sand in areas
Riding time: About 1.25 hours
Seasons/schedule: Open year-round; best in fall, winter, and spring
Timing: No moon to a quarter moon
Fees and permits: None
Trail contacts: Bureau of Land Management, 21605 North 7th Ave., Phoenix 85027; (623) 580-5500; blm.gov/visit/sonoran-desert-national-monument
Dog-friendly: Yes
Trail surface: Dirt and sand
Land status: Bureau of Land Management and federally designated wilderness
Nearest town: Gila Bend, Arizona

Other trail users: UTV/ATVs, SUVs, backpackers, hikers, equestrians, other MTB riders
Maps: Bureau of Land Management map available online at blm.gov/visit/margies-cove-west-trailhead
Water availability: None
Special considerations: Extreme heat in summer can persist into the night at this location, and temperatures can be freezing at night in winter. Venomous reptiles and insects exist in Sonoran Desert National Monument. Release some air from your tires for a more cushioned ride along the road to Margies Cove. Flash flooding can occur at any time of year, especially during the summer monsoon.
Other: The Margies Cove West Campground is free; it has three campsites with fire rings and a pit toilet. Bicycles are not allowed past the gate at the Margies Cove West Trailhead into the North Maricopa Mountains Wilderness.

FINDING THE TRAILHEAD
From Gila Bend, take AZ 85 north for 15.5 miles to South Woods Road. Exit east onto South Woods Road, and park near the cattle guard shortly after the start of the dirt road. Unload your bike and begin your ride west and then north on BLM 8001. Trailhead GPS: N33 07.882' / W112 38.851'

THE ADVENTURE
Sonoran Desert National Monument protects thousands of acres of untouched lower-elevation desert, including species like saguaros, ironwood trees, and families of bighorn sheep. Located near Phoenix and Gila Bend, the skies here are dark enough to see the Milky Way's dust lanes, despite the presence of light pollution. Instead of driving, take your mountain bike for a night ride to the monument's heartlands at Margies Cove.

Wild saguaro grows in unique
shapes at Margies Cove.

SONORAN DESERT NATIONAL MONUMENT NIGHT MOUNTAIN BIKING

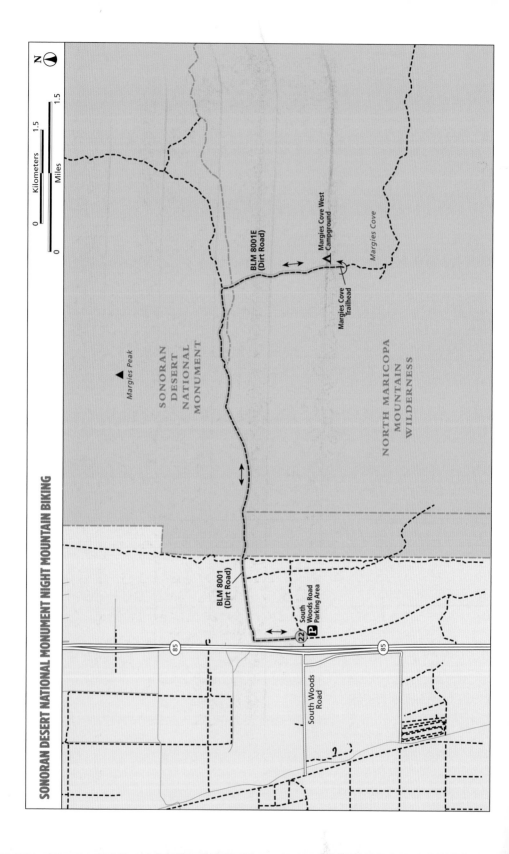

Riding a bike to Margies Cove under a dark sky is an incredibly freeing experience—you can feel the wind in your face and watch the stars move from behind the mountains.

Start your ride by exiting AZ 85 onto South Woods Road; park your vehicle in the dirt just 600 feet from the exit. Get your bike lights on, strap on your helmet, and follow a small sign to start on unmaintained dirt BLM 8001, heading west for a very short distance. BLM 8001 then runs north for 0.5 mile and then turns sharply east, continuing straight for 3.78 miles up a slight incline through the desert, crossing sandy washes and passing large ironwood trees. Enjoy the stars hanging above you as you set a strong pace through the sandy washes until you reach a sign for Margies Cove West Campground on the right. Turn south onto BLM 8001E and cruise on a slight downhill decline to Margies Cove for 1.3 miles.

Arrive at the peaceful Margies Cove West Campground and Trailhead from your 5.65 mile ride and dismount your bike for a look up at the stars. In this dark valley protected by low mountains on all sides, the stars and light pollution to the northeast from Phoenix are the only significant sources of light. Near the Margies Cove West Trailhead, there is a pit toilet, primitive campground, and an informational sign about the North Maricopa Mountain Wilderness. The Margies Cove Trail goes into the North Maricopa Mountains Wilderness, where you must explore on foot. In the area near the trailhead, you will find saguaros and remnants of old cattle operations and shot-up water tanks.

Once you're satisfied with your exploration of the Margies Cove area, return to the trailhead, mount your bike, and head north on BLM 8001E. Set a solid pace for your slight climb for 1.3 miles up BLM 8001E until you reach BLM 8001 and turn west. Have a fun and fast ride on BLM 8001, floating through the desert on a downhill grade while stealing glances at the sky above. The sounds of the highway and smell of farms in the distance will begin to return as you accelerate toward AZ 85 for 3.8 miles. Carefully corner south to the section of BLM 8001 that parallels AZ 85 and return to your vehicle.

MILES AND DIRECTIONS

0.0   Start from a small dirt parking area on South Woods Road just 600 feet east of AZ 85. Find a small black road sign for BLM 8001 that's labeled "Margies Cove West," with an arrow pointing west. Take BLM 8001 for 0.05 mile west.

0.05   Turn north on BLM 8001 and continue for 0.5 mile, paralleling AZ 85.

0.55   Turn east on BLM 8001, following signs for Margies Cove West for 3.8 miles on a slight uphill grade through sandy washes and past low mountains.

4.35   Turn south on BLM 8001E, following signs for Margies Cove West. Continue south on BLM 8001E for 1.3 miles on a slight downhill slope.

5.65   Arrive at the Margies Cove West Campground and Trailhead at the end of BLM 8001E. (**Option:** If desired and prepared with a map, explore further [on foot only] south on the Margies Cove Trail into the North Maricopa Mountain Wilderness, generally heading south then southeast.) Return to your vehicle on South Woods Road by following the reverse directions: 1.3 miles north on BLM 8001E, 3.8 miles west on BLM 8001, 0.5 mile south on BLM 8001 parallel to AZ 85, and 0.05 mile east to the parking area near South Woods Road and BLM 8001.

11.3   Arrive back at the trailhead.

23 WATSON LAKE NIGHT HIKE

Watch the sunset and stars dance on Watson Lake through a sunset-to-night hike around the lake. Listen for owls and coyotes as you travel the wonderland of granite knolls and oak trees.

Activity: Night hike
Location: Watson Lake Park, 3101 Watson Lake Park Rd., Prescott
Start: Hilltop Ramada Parking Lot; GPS: N34 35.414' / W112 25.234'
Elevation gain: 175 feet
Distance: 4.8-mile loop
Difficulty: Moderate due to steep rock scrambles
Hiking time: About 2.5 hours
Seasons/schedule: Open year-round but with limited winter hours; best in spring and summer
Timing: Any time of the month
Fees and permits: Parking fees required; see prescott-az.gov/recreation-area/watson-lake-park/ for current fees.
Trail contacts: City of Prescott Recreation Services, 824 East Gurley St., Prescott 86301; (928) 777-1552; prescott-az.gov/recreation-area/watson-lake-park/
Dog-friendly: Yes, leashed
Trail surface: Dirt and rock
Land status: City park

Nearest town: Prescott, Arizona
Other trail users: Runners, mountain bikers, equestrians, rock climbers, photographers
Maps: Watson Lake Loop Trail map available online at prescott-az.gov/recreation-area/watson-lake-loop-trail/
Water availability: Yes; water fountains near the Watson Lake south boat ramp
Special considerations: Watson Lake Park typically closes at 6 p.m. in winter, which makes it more difficult to explore at night. The Watson Lake Loop Trail is exposed, with vertical drops and steep slopes in some areas. Look for white dots painted on the rocks to guide you along the trail. Start the hike around an hour before sunset to enjoy both a sunset and a night hike.
Other: Overnight camping is available in the summer months at Watson Lake Park.

FINDING THE TRAILHEAD

From downtown Prescott, go east on Gurley Street for 1.2 miles to AZ 89; turn north onto AZ 89. Continue north on AZ 89 for 3.6 miles to a roundabout, where you will turn east at the first exit onto Watson Lake Park Road. Pay the parking fee and drive southeast on Watson Lake Park Road to a large ramada and parking lot at the top of a hill. Trailhead GPS: N34 35.414' / W112 25.234'

THE ADVENTURE

Only 5 miles from downtown Prescott lie the deep blue waters and beautiful granite dells of Watson Lake Park. A dark sky can be enjoyed at this reservoir despite the impact of light pollution from Prescott and Prescott Valley on the southern and eastern horizons. Abundant hiking opportunities are available to explore Watson Lake's many coves and granite bluffs under the starry night sky. Take the Watson Lake Loop Trail on a fun 4.8-mile sunset-to-night hike to

LOOK UP
Due to the vast distances light has to travel across space, our view of the stars and planets in the night sky allows us to look back in time.

A starry sky reflects in the calm waters of Watson Lake.

see the lake and stars from every angle. Start your hike from a remarkable view of Watson Lake at the Hilltop Ramada near the western shore of the lake.

Start your hike an hour before sunset, heading north on the Watson Lake Loop with an astonishing view of Watson Lake's rounded granite hills. Following spray-painted white dots on the rocks, the trail zigzags north between boulders and high up over coves, gaining striking views of the lake's northern shore. Along the northern side of the loop, you will turn east, dip down into a small valley, pass two junctions for the Flume Trail, and cross Granite Creek over a small footbridge just below the Watson Lake Dam. At around 1.3 miles, the trail begins to head south and southwest on steep climbs through the granite dells and across small creeks. At this point of the hike, the sun will be close to setting, painting the sky in gradients of yellow and orange.

Take a short 0.15-mile detour on the Treehouse Loop Trail, 1.9 miles from the trailhead, offering lovely views from the top of a granite outcrop of the setting sun and Watson Lake to the west. Rejoin the Watson Lake Loop Trail and continue south for 0.35 mile before breaking off onto the Peavine Trail, a flat dirt path that goes straight southwest for 1.1 miles. Enjoy the flat easy walk down the road and spot the first planets and stars that begin to poke through the twilight. By the time you reach the Watson Woods, the stars should be shining through the large cottonwood trees as you walk over the Granite Creek Bridge. At about 3.6 miles, the loop turns generally northeast, following AZ 89 along beautiful trees and passing the Watson Lake south boat ramp.

See hundreds of stars and long views of the lake and Prescott as you hike the remaining 0.5 mile from the southern boat ramp to the Hilltop Ramada parking lot where you started. Hear the call of coyotes across the lake and watch the stars shimmer in its calm reflective waters. Stop at the rocky view of Watson Lake just east of the parking lot and look all around for constellations and stars reflected in the lake's many coves. Enjoy your rest under the stars at a bench or take some time to photograph the scenes around you after completing the 4.8-mile loop. When ready to leave, simply walk west to the Hilltop Ramada parking lot to your vehicle.

WATSON LAKE NIGHT HIKE

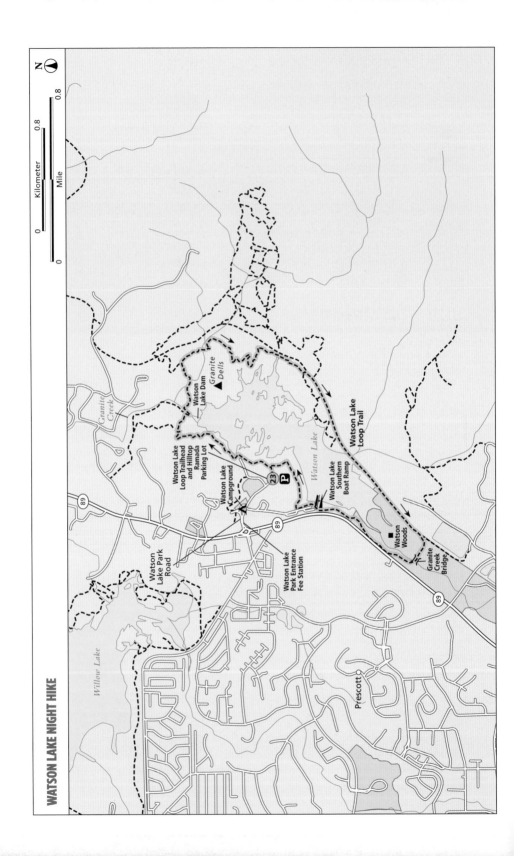

Moonlight washes over the Granite Dells around Watson Lake.

MILES AND DIRECTIONS

0.0 Start from the Hilltop Ramada parking lot at Watson Lake Park, heading east then generally north on the Watson Lake Loop Trail. Follow the white dots spray-painted on the rocks.

0.7 The Watson Lake Loop trail descends a steep hill heading north and then turns east, passing two Flume Trail junctions.

0.9 Cross Granite Creek below the Watson Lake Dam on a small footbridge. Climb northeast and continue east on the Watson Lake Loop Trail, climbing up and down the granite dells.

1.3 Reach the junction with an unnamed trail and continue southeast then southwest for 0.6 mile on the Watson Lake Loop Trail, passing another unnamed trail that connects to the Peavine Trail.

1.9 Arrive at the junction with the Treehouse Loop and Watson Lake Loop Trails and head west on the Treehouse Loop for 0.15 mile, climbing over large boulders.

2.05 Finish the Treehouse Loop Trail and rejoin the Watson Lake Loop Trail, continuing southwest for 0.35 mile, passing a second unnamed trail that connects to the Peavine Trail.

2.4 Reach an unnamed trail junction on the Watson Lake Loop Trail; head east to the Peavine Trail for 100 feet. Walk southwest on the flat dirt path of the Peavine Trail for 1.1 miles.

3.5 Turn west off the Peavine Trail toward Watson Woods and the Discovery Trail. Cross Granite Creek on a large footbridge about 0.15 mile from the Peavine junction.

3.65 The Discovery Trail turns north and continues generally north for 0.65 mile to the southern Watson Lake boat ramp.

4.3 Arrive at the southern Watson Lake boat ramp from the Discovery Trail and hike north along the Watson Lake Loop Trail toward the northeast. The trail will curve around to the north for 0.5 mile until you reach the Hilltop Ramada parking lot.

4.8 Arrive back at the trailhead.

LOOK UP
In dark skies, you can see two to seven meteors per hour streak across the stars.

24 LOWER SALT RIVER STARGAZING DRIVE

Take a scenic night drive following the Salt River on the Bush Highway to Saguaro Lake. Stop at seven recreation areas along the Salt to experience the night skies of this important riparian corridor.

Activity: Scenic drive and stargazing
Location: Lower Salt River, downstream of Saguaro Lake
Start: Granite Reef Recreation Area; GPS: N33 30.871' / W111 40.888'
Elevation gain: 409 feet
Distance: 20.0-mile point-to-point drive
Difficulty: Easy
Driving time: About 1.5 hours
Seasons/schedule: Open year-round; great in any season
Timing: No moon to a quarter moon
Fees and permits: Recreation fees required; see fs.usda .gov/detail/tonto/passes-permits/?cid=fsbdev3_018733 for current fees.

Trail contacts: Tonto National Forest, 5140 East Ingram St., Mesa 85205; (480) 610-3300; fs.usda.gov/tonto
Dog-friendly: Yes, leashed and under control
Road surface: Paved
Land status: National forest
Nearest town: Mesa, Arizona
Other road users: UTV/ATVs, motorcycles, bicycles
Maps: Tonto National Forest maps available online at fs .usda.gov/recarea/tonto/null/ recarea?recid=35395&actid=43
Water availability: None
Special considerations: Wild horses are present along the Lower Salt River and along the Bush Highway; drive with caution. Stay at least 50 feet away from wild horses.

FINDING THE STARTING POINT

From Mesa, take Power Road north until it becomes the Bush Highway. Continue northbound on the Bush Highway and start the scenic drive by pulling into the Granite Reef Recreation Area, about 0.8 mile from the start of the Bush Highway. For the rest of the drive, continue east then eventually north to Saguaro Lake, taking the pullouts for six other locations. Starting point GPS (Granite Reef Recreation Area): N33 30.871' / W111 40.888'

THE ADVENTURE

The Salt River is a refuge for animals and people escaping the summer heat of Central Arizona and Phoenix's light pollution. The Bush Highway runs along a section of the Lower Salt River, making for a scenic drive from Mesa to Saguaro Lake. Although this adventure is in Phoenix's backyard, you can still enjoy relatively dark skies the further east you go on the Bush Highway. For this adventure, drive to seven stops along the highway to experience increasingly dark skies and the beauty of the Lower Salt River.

Start your drive at night and make your first stop at Granite Reef Recreation Area, which features reflections of Red Mountain across a small lake. Take some time here to look at the stars and note the strong light pollution from the Phoenix area. Once ready, continue east on the Bush Highway for 2.65 miles; turn north on Phon D. Sutton Road toward the recreation area parking lot. Walk down to the Salt River to the north of the parking lot, and take in the sounds and smells of the river gently passing in front of you.

The Bulldog Cliffs hang high over the Lower Salt River under a starry night sky.

Now it's time to make your way just upriver to the Coon Bluff Recreation Area to see a forest of mesquite trees and a tranquil view of the Salt River. Backtrack south on Phon D. Sutton Road to the Bush Highway and head east for 1.05 miles; turn left onto North Coon Bluff Road. The Coon Bluff Recreation Area sits between a

> The 200-mile-long Salt River gets its name for a section of large salt deposits that it flows over further upstream.

small hill and the Salt River in a beautiful grove of mesquite trees. Views of the stars at Coon Bluff are slightly limited by the forest and Coon Bluff, so take a short 0.25-mile hike south to the top of the bluff to gain great starry views of the Salt River and the distant Four Peaks. Drive back to the Bush Highway and head 1.25 miles farther east toward the Goldfield Recreation Area. Head north then west on Goldfield Road to reach the Goldfield Recreation Area, where you can meditate on the banks of the river under the stars.

For your next stop, drive back to the Bush Highway and head 2.45 miles east on a windy road to the Pebble Beach Recreation Area. Pebble Beach offers plenty of parking and areas to enjoy the stars in darker skies by lying down on a picnic blanket. Head back to the Bush Highway and head east for 1.75 miles to the Water Users Recreation Area for dramatic views of the giant Bulldog Cliffs hanging over the Salt River. Walk down to the Salt River from the parking lot to witness the stars and the towering cliffs reflected in this lazy section of the river. For the finale of the scenic drive, get back on the highway and drive east then north for 1.6 miles toward the Saguaro del Norte Recreation Area.

Make your way 0.95 mile east on FR 206 along the shores of Saguaro Lake to the far eastern side of Saguaro del Norte Recreation Area. Park and walk down to the lake or step foot on a pier and experience the magic of the darkest sky available on this scenic drive. From the lake you can see the stark difference between light pollution to the southwest from Phoenix and the dark starry skies over the Superstition Mountains to the southeast. Take the opportunity to appreciate these dark skies and identify your favorite constellations shining above the waters of Saguaro Lake. When ready, head back to the Phoenix area by driving west to the Bush Highway and then south and west on the highway to Mesa.

LOWER SALT RIVER STARGAZING DRIVE

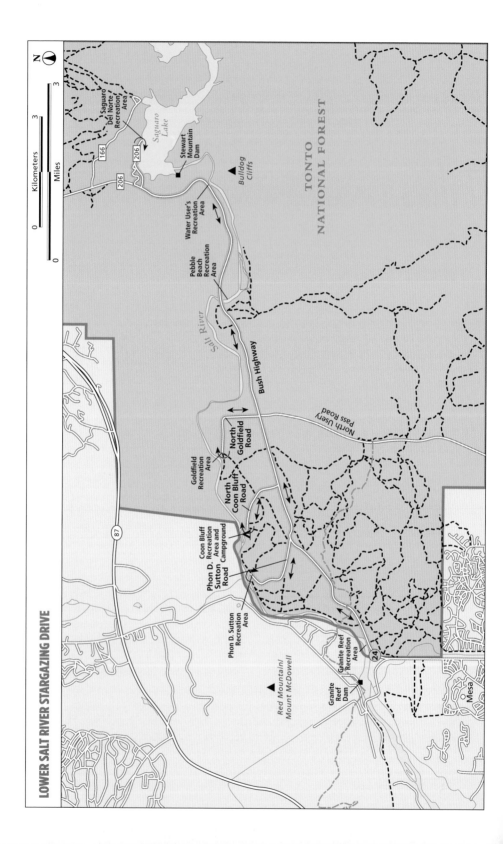

MILES AND DIRECTIONS

0.0 Start the drive from the Granite Reef Recreation Area.

> Wild horses inhabit the Lower Salt River and can be seen any time of the year.

2.65 Turn left on Phon D. Sutton Road and continue northwest then northeast for 1.3 miles.

3.95 Reach the Phon D. Sutton Recreation Area parking lot and walk north to see the Salt River. Backtrack southwest then southeast on Phon D. Sutton Road for 1.3 miles to return to the Bush Highway.

5.25 Turn left on the Bush Highway and drive east for 1.05 miles to North Coon Bluff Road.

6.3 Turn left onto North Coon Bluff Road and drive northwest for 1.1 miles to the Coon Bluff Recreation Area.

7.4 Arrive at the Coon Bluff Recreation Area parking lot next to a mesquite forest. (**Option:** Hike 0.25 mile toward the south to the top of Coon Bluff.) Backtrack southeast 1.1 miles to return to the Bush Highway.

8.5 Turn left and head east on the Bush Highway for 1.25 miles to North Goldfield Road.

9.75 Turn left onto North Goldfield Road and head north then west for 1.4 miles to the Goldfield Recreation Area.

11.15 Arrive at the Goldfield Recreation Area and walk north for about 500 feet to view the Salt River. Backtrack east then south on North Goldfield Road for 1.4 miles to the Bush Highway.

12.55 Turn left onto the Bush Highway and continue east for 2.45 miles to the Pebble Beach Recreation Area.

15.0 Turn right toward the Pebble Beach Recreation Area and park in any of the parking lots about 0.25 mile to the south of the turnoff. Return to the Bush Highway by driving north the same way you entered Pebble Beach.

15.5 Turn right onto the Bush Highway and continue east for 1.75 miles toward the Water User's Recreation Area.

17.25 Turn right into the Water User's Recreation Area and park in any of the parking lots 0.1 mile to the south. Walk downhill to the south for about 500 feet to reach the Salt River and view the Bulldog Cliffs. Return to the Bush Highway by driving north the same way you entered the Water User's Recreation Area.

17.45 Turn right onto the Bush Highway and continue northeast then north for 1.6 miles toward the Saguaro del Norte Recreation Area.

19.05 Turn right and drive east into the Saguaro del Norte Recreation Area for 0.95 mile; park in one of the parking spaces on the eastern end of the recreation area.

20.0 Arrive at Saguaro Lake; access the lake by walking down to one of the piers or taking any of the user trails down to the lake from the parking areas. (**Option:** Return to the Bush Highway by driving west up a windy road for 0.9 mile. Return to Mesa by driving south then west on the Bush Highway for 12.0 miles.)

OTHER ADVENTURES IN THE AREA

The Salt River can be floated with a kayak, stand-up paddleboard, or an inner tube at night.

25 RED ROCK CROSSING NIGHT HIKE

Hear the rush of Oak Creek and watch the stars rise behind Cathedral Rock at Red Rock Crossing near Sedona. Take an easy 10-minute night hike down to Red Rock Crossing and experience the magic of a dark sky over an iconic landscape.

Activity: Night hiking and stargazing

Location: Red Rock Crossing of Oak Creek; GPS: N34 49.472' / W111 48.177'

Start: Baldwin Trailhead; GPS: N34 49.331' / W111 48.444'

Elevation gain: 66 feet

Distance: 1.0 mile out and back

Difficulty: Easy

Hiking time: About 20 minutes

Seasons/schedule: Open year-round; all seasons

Timing: No moon to a quarter moon

Fees and permits: Day-use fees required; see fs .usda.gov/detail/coconino/ home/?cid=stelprdb5416207 for current fees.

Trail contacts: Coconino National Forest, Red Rock Ranger District, PO Box 20429, Sedona 86341-0429; (928) 203-2900; fs .usda.gov/recarea/coconino/ recarea/?recid=54892

Dog-friendly: Yes

Trail surface: Dirt and rock

Land status: National forest

Nearest town: Village of Oak Creek, Arizona

Other trail users: Mountain bikers, equestrians, trail runners, photographers

Maps: Coconino National Forest Red Rock Ranger District maps available online at fs.usda.gov/detail/coconino/ recreation/?cid=stelprd3851843

Water availability: Water is available in Oak Creek all year; however, it should be filtered and treated before using.

Special considerations: Large animals such as deer, bobcats, and javelinas rely on Oak Creek for water and may be found near the creek at night. Rattlesnakes and venomous insects also inhabit the area, so use caution when night hiking. Storms can cause flash floods at any time of the year, so only attempt this trail during dry weather and with a dry forecast. During the winter months, ice can form on the rocks of Red Rock Crossing.

Other: Verde Valley School Road becomes a somewhat rough dirt road for the last 1.1 miles to the Baldwin Trailhead. Day-use fees may be paid at an electronic payment kiosk on the west side of the Baldwin Trailhead parking lot.

FINDING THE TRAILHEAD

From the Village of Oak Creek, take Verde Valley School Road west from AZ 179 for 4.9 miles. Verde Valley School Road will go west then head north and eventually become a graded dirt road about 1.1 miles from the Baldwin Trailhead. The trailhead parking lot is located on the left near a Forest Service restroom and electronic payment kiosk for Coconino National Forest Red Rock Passes. The Baldwin Trailhead is located to the northeast, across Verde Valley School Road from the parking lot. Trailhead GPS: N34 49.331' / W111 48.444'

Sedona was named for Sedona Miller Schnebly, a homesteader who moved to the area in 1899.

Orion's Belt and the Orion Nebula rise over Cathedral Rock near Sedona.

THE ADVENTURE

The name Sedona alone conjures up beautiful sights of Central Arizona's beloved red rock country. Even if you haven't visited, the iconic formations of Cathedral Rock and the clear waters of Oak Creek take residence in your mind. For this adventure you will create star-studded memories of majestic Cathedral Rock at the Red Rock

LOOK UP
Find Messier #4 with binoculars or a telescope by locating bright orange Antares in the constellation Scorpius and looking next to the star for a globular cluster of more than 100,000 stars.

Crossing of Oak Creek. Just a 0.5-mile hike will transport you through a woodland to the edge of the gentle waters of Oak Creek under a mosaic of thousands of stars. Begin your adventure by starting a 1.0-mile round-trip night hike from the Baldwin Trailhead.

Arrive after dark at the Baldwin Trailhead and start the Baldwin Trail (#191) into a woodland by crossing Verde Valley School Road to the east. Head east for 0.3 mile down a gentle dirt trail, taking some time to get comfortable with your surroundings. You may hear small animals rustling in the vegetation nearby and crickets singing gently into the night. Looking upward, you will be treated to dark skies protected by the nearby IDA-certified Dark Sky Communities of Sedona and Village of Oak Creek. After coming down a small set of rock steps on the Baldwin Trail, you arrive at a small three-way trail junction, where you will turn left (west) on the Red Rock Crossing Trail (#191B).

Head west on the Red Rock Crossing Trail for about 250 feet; at a small brown trail arrow sign, turn right (north) on a user trail into the sycamore trees. This small 0.09-mile user trail may not be on a map or show up on your GPS; however, it is well worn into the landscape and will lead you to the slickrock of Red Rock Crossing. Follow the trail toward the sounds of rushing water; eventually you will pop out on the southern

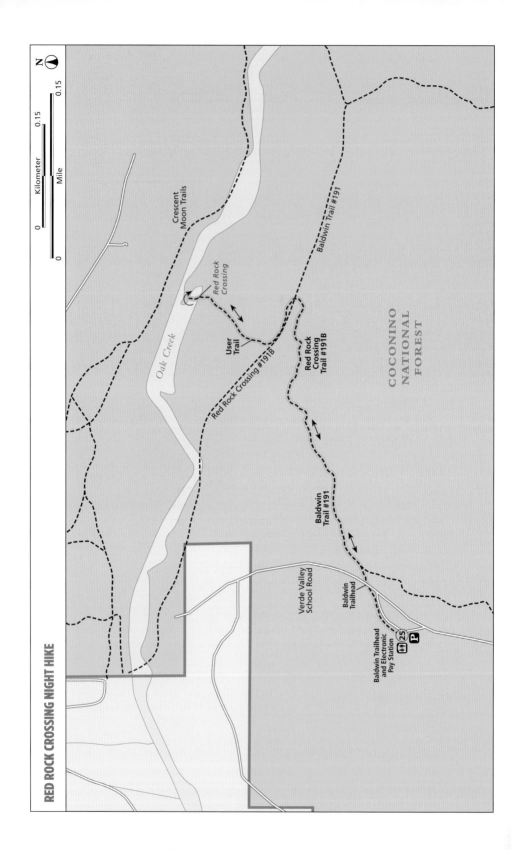

RED ROCK CROSSING NIGHT HIKE

Crescent
Moon Trails

Oak Creek

Red Rock
Crossing

User
Trail

Red Rock Crossing #191B

Red Rock
Crossing
Trail #191B

Baldwin Trail #191

COCONINO
NATIONAL
FOREST

Baldwin
Trail #191

Verde Valley
School Road

Baldwin
Trailhead

Baldwin Trailhead
and Electronic
Pay Station

N

0   Kilometer   0.15   0.15

0   Mile

P 25

The Milky Way arches over Oak Creek and Cathedral Rock at Red Rock Crossing.

Venus shines bright above Cathedral Rock, reflecting in a still pool at Red Rock Crossing near Sedona.

banks of Oak Creek. Depending on the water level, this is where you can break out of the forest and walk onto a slab of smooth red rock.

Walk out onto the slickrock and look upstream to view the sandstone towers of Cathedral Rock. Watch as star after star slowly break from behind the buttes, reveal-

LOOK UP

The Rho Ophiuchi cloud complex, located 460 light-years away in the constellation Scorpius, contains one of the closest star-forming regions to Earth.

ing their colors of blue, orange, and yellow. Hear the wonderful white noise of the creek flowing around you and note the stars reflecting in the many pools of water scattered on the slickrock. Few people come here at night, providing you with a peace that isn't always easy to get at this popular spot. Once you have had enough time at Red Rock Crossing, leave nature to its devices and retrace your steps to the Baldwin Trailhead for 10 to 15 minutes.

MILES AND DIRECTIONS

0.0   Start from the Baldwin Trailhead and walk east for 0.3 mile.

0.3   Arrive at the junction of the Baldwin Trail (#191) and Red Rock Crossing Trail (#191B). Turn left and head west on the Red Rock Crossing Trail for 250 feet.

0.35   Arrive at a small brown trail sign; turn right, taking an unmarked user trail north for 0.15 mile.

0.5   Arrive at Red Rock Crossing on Oak Creek, where there is a large slab of red sandstone. Retrace your steps to return to the trailhead.

1.0   Arrive back at the trailhead.

26 RED ROCK–SECRET MOUNTAIN WILDERNESS BACKPACKING

Take an epic three-day backpacking trip beneath the towering sandstone cliffs of the Red Rock–Secret Mountain Wilderness, just outside Sedona. Experience the magic of wilderness night skies and get in touch with your spiritual side in the friendly energies of the Sedona area.

Activity: Backpacking
Location: Red Rock–Secret Mountain Wilderness
Start: Brins Mesa Trailhead; GPS: N34 53.293' / W111 46.094'
Elevation gain: 630 feet
Distance: 17.3-mile double-lollipop loop
Difficulty: Moderate due to steep climbs and long distances
Hiking time: 2–3 days
Seasons/schedule: Open year-round; best in fall, winter, and spring
Timing: No moon to a quarter moon
Fees and permits: Coconino National Forest Red Rock Pass or Interagency Annual Pass required; see fs.usda.gov/detail/coconino/recreation/?cid=stelprdb5416207 for current fees.
Trail contacts: Coconino National Forest, Red Rock Ranger District, PO Box 20429, Sedona 86341-0429; (928) 203-2900; fs.usda.gov/recarea/coconino/recarea/?recid=54892
Dog-friendly: Yes, leashed and under control
Trail surface: Dirt and rock

Land status: National forest and federally designated wilderness
Nearest town: Sedona, Arizona
Other trail users: Equestrians, mountain bikers, photographers, day hikers, trail runners
Maps: Red Rock Ranger District interactive and downloadable maps available at fs.usda.gov/detail/coconino/recreation/?cid=stelprd3851843
Water availability: No reliable water sources within the wilderness; pack 1 gallon per person, per day.
Special considerations: Some sections of the trail around Mescal Mountain are on an exposed rocky slope. Venomous reptiles, javelinas, and mountain lions inhabit the area. Rockfalls can occur at any time near canyon walls. Cultural sites and artifacts are found throughout the wilderness; be considerate and respectful of these important resources. Camping is limited to the wilderness area; the best camping is available on Brins Mesa. Drive carefully on the dirt section of Park Ridge Road leading to the Brins Mesa Trailhead.

FINDING THE TRAILHEAD

From AZ 89A in Sedona, head north on Jordan Road for 0.8 mile. Turn west onto West Park Ridge Drive and continue west then northwest for 0.7 mile to the Brins Mesa Trailhead, at the end of the road. Trailhead GPS: N34 53.293' / W111 46.094'

THE ADVENTURE

One of the best ways to explore Sedona's famous red rocks, lush forests, and mystical energy vortices is by backpacking into the Red Rock–Secret Mountain Wilderness. This expansive wilderness protects 43,950 acres of colorful canyons, stunning sandstone pinnacles, and dark night skies. Opportunities for nightly solitude abound in this wilderness

Moonlight washes over the Red Rock–Secret Mountain Wilderness as the core of the Milky Way shines through the night sky.

with relatively few backpackers. This adventure will take you on a 17.3-mile double lollipop loop through the heart of this beautiful area. Start your adventure 2 hours before sunset at the Brins Mesa Trailhead, located at the northern edge of Sedona.

About 3 million years ago, the Colorado Plateau uplifted; erosion by wind, rain, and snow created the rock formations found around Sedona.

Incredible views of Sedona's famous red rocks are available right from the Brins Mesa Trailhead. Make your way to the western side of the parking lot and start up the Brins Mesa Trail, generally northwest, for 1.4 miles. This steep section of trail will get your heart beating and reward you with great views of the sandstone cliffs. Take the final rocky steps to the top of Brins Mesa, revealing a large grassy meadow perfect for pitching a tent. Find a place free of prickly pear to pitch your tent and enjoy the expansive views of the wilderness. Thanks to the International Dark Sky Communities of Sedona and Village of Oak Creek, you can enjoy a wonderful night sky in the wilderness while also seeing the dim city lights below you.

In the morning, leave your camp set up as a base camp and take a delightful day hike to Mescal Mountain, located 4.0 miles west of Brins Mesa. Start west down the Brins Mesa Trail for 2.25 miles until you reach Dry Creek Road. The trail starts out with open views of the windswept sandstone peaks but eventually transitions to a shady trail in dense forest. At the West Brins Mesa Trailhead, cross Dry Creek Road to the west and hike southwest for 1.75 miles on the Chuckwagon Trail. Emerge from the forest and cross Long Canyon Road to the west and transition to the Mescal Connector Trail on the south side of the Long Canyon Trailhead.

The loop around Mescal Mountain rewards you with amazing views of wild red rock country. Hike southwest on the Mescal Connector Trail for 0.3 mile then continue on the Mescal Trail for 2.15 miles. Take a right turn at all trail junctions as you meander west then north on Mescal Trail to the Deadman's Pass Trail. Hiking alongside Mescal Mountain's wall of sacred red sandstone and views of distant mountains like Capitol Butte will have you savoring every moment. After meeting the Deadman's Pass Trail, turn right and head northeast for 0.9 mile on a gentle incline to the Long Canyon Trail. Meander southeast on Long Canyon Trail for 1.0 mile to arrive back at the Long Canyon Trailhead. Finish the day hike by retracing your steps to camp northeast on the Chuckwagon Trail for 1.75 miles and then east on the Brins Mesa Trail for 2.25 miles.

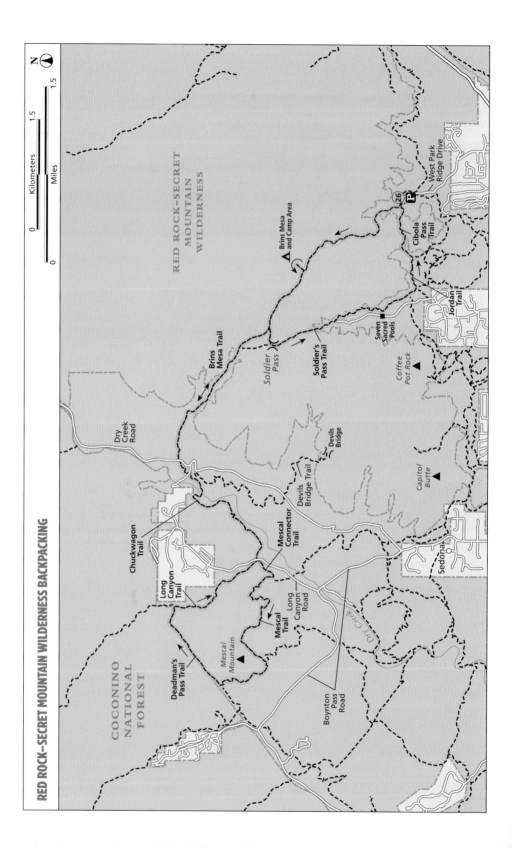

RED ROCK–SECRET MOUNTAIN WILDERNESS BACKPACKING

COCONINO
NATIONAL
FOREST

RED ROCK–SECRET
MOUNTAIN
WILDERNESS

Deadman's Pass Trail

Mescal Mountain

Mescal Trail

Long Canyon Trail

Chuckwagon Trail

Mescal Connector Trail

Long Canyon Road

Boynton Pass Road

Dry Creek Road

Brins Mesa Trail

Soldier Pass

Soldier's Pass Trail

Devils Bridge Trail

Devils Bridge

Brins Mesa and Camp Area

Seven Sacred Pools

Coffee Pot Rock

Capitol Butte

Sedona

Cibola Pass Trail

Jordan Trail

West Park Ridge Drive

26

Dry Creek

N

Kilometers
0   1.5

Miles
0   1.5

Enjoy another beautiful starry night from camp on Brins Mesa and get some rest.

The next day, pack up camp and begin the finale of the backpacking trip, heading west once more on the Brins Mesa Trail for 0.6 mile. Take the Soldier's Pass Trail west then south for 1.5 miles through a scenic red rock canyon until you

> Iron oxidation created the red sandstone found around Sedona and the Red Rock–Secret Mountain Wilderness.

reach the Seven Sacred Pools, a beautiful series of tinajas carved out of the sandstone. From the pools, continue hiking south on the Soldier's Pass Trail for 0.4 mile until you reach the Jordan Trail, just past a surprising sinkhole. Head east on the Jordan Trail for 0.35 mile and then take the Cibola Pass Trail further east for 0.7 mile. The Cibola Pass Trail provides wonderful views of the Cibola Mitten and ultimately ends back at the Brins Mesa Trailhead, where your journey began. Whether or not you believe in Sedona's energy vortices, the serenity of the Red Rock–Secret Mountain Wilderness will surely cast a spell on you.

MILES AND DIRECTIONS

0.0 Start from the Brins Mesa Trailhead and head northwest on the Brins Mesa Trail for 1.4 miles.

1.4 Reach the top of Brins Mesa and establish camp somewhere on the mesa. To continue the loop, continue northwest on Brins Mesa Trail for 2.25 miles.

3.65 Arrive at Dry Creek Road, cross the road to the west, and head southwest on the Chuckwagon Trail for 1.75 miles.

5.4 Meet Long Canyon Road, cross the road west to the Long Canyon Trailhead, and hike southwest on the Mescal Connector Trail for 0.3 mile.

5.7 Connect to the Mescal Trail and meander north then west on the trail around Mescal Mountain for 2.15 miles.

7.85 Reach the Deadman's Pass Trail; turn right and hike northeast for 0.9 mile.

8.75 Turn right on the Long Canyon Trail and hike southeast for 1.0 mile.

9.75 Arrive at the Long Canyon Trailhead and hike east across Long Canyon Road to the Chuckwagon Trail. Return to camp by retracing your steps northeast on the Chuckwagon Trail for 1.75 miles and then east on Brins Mesa Trail for 2.25 miles.

13.75 Arrive back at camp. To finish the second loop, head northwest on Brins Mesa Trail for 0.6 mile to the Soldier's Pass Trail.

14.35 Arrive at the Soldier's Pass Trail junction and head west then south on the Soldier's Pass Trail for 1.5 miles to the Seven Sacred Pools.

15.85 From the Seven Sacred Pools, continue south on the Soldier's Pass Trail for 0.4 mile.

16.25 Reach the Jordan Trail junction and head east on the Jordan Trail for 0.35 mile.

16.6 At the Cibola Pass Trail junction continue east on the Cibola Pass Trail for 0.7 mile to the Brins Mesa Trailhead.

17.3 Arrive back at the trailhead.

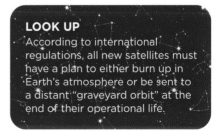

LOOK UP
According to international regulations, all new satellites must have a plan to either burn up in Earth's atmosphere or be sent to a distant "graveyard orbit" at the end of their operational life.

27 COURTHOUSE BUTTE NIGHT HIKE

Night-hike the Courthouse Butte Loop around the majestic red rock country south of Sedona. Watch stars rise and set behind the iconic sandstone monuments of Bell Rock and Courthouse Butte on this fun 3.75-mile hike under the stars.

Activity: Night hike

Location: Coconino National Forest, Courthouse Butte Loop Trail; GPS: N34 48.349' / W111 46.008'

Start: Courthouse Butte/Bell Rock Trailhead; GPS: N34 48.342' / W111 45.980'

Elevation gain: 351 feet

Distance: 3.75-mile loop

Difficulty: Moderate due to rocky ascents and descents; route-finding/map-reading abilities required at night

Hiking time: About 2 hours

Seasons/schedule: Open year-round; best in fall, spring, and early summer

Timing: Any time, any phase of the moon

Fees and permits: Red Rock Pass or America the Beautiful Pass required for trailhead parking; see fs.usda.gov/detail/coconino/recreation/?cid=stelprdb5416207 for current fees.

Trail contacts: Coconino National Forest, Red Rock Ranger District, PO Box 20429, Sedona 86341-0429; (928) 203-2900; fs.usda.gov/recarea/coconino/recarea/?recid=54892

Dog-friendly: Yes, leashed and under control

Trail surface: Dirt and rock

Land status: National forest and federally designated wilderness

Nearest towns: Village of Oak Creek, Arizona; Sedona, Arizona

Other trail users: Trail runners, hikers, mountain bikers, photographers

Maps: USDA Forest Service maps available online at fs.usda.gov/recarea/coconino/recarea/?recid=72016

Water availability: None

Special considerations: Snakes, coyotes, bobcats, mountain lions, javelinas, scorpions, and tarantulas inhabit the area. Overnight temperatures can be freezing in winter. Winter storms can produce snow and dangerously cold conditions. Summer monsoon storms can produce lightning, damaging winds, hail, and torrential rain. Flash flooding may occur whenever storms are present in the area. On the eastern side of the loop, the trail can be easily lost in the slickrock landscape, so keep an eye out for wire-cage cairns. Bring a strong headlamp to identify cairns and trails at a distance. Pack in enough water and snacks in the event you get lost. Bring a map or GPS unit in case you get lost off-trail. Mountain bikes are not allowed on the portions of trail within the Munds Mountain Wilderness.

FINDING THE TRAILHEAD

From Sedona, take AZ 179 south for 5.4 miles; turn left and head east into the Courthouse Vista parking lot. The Courthouse Butte Loop Trailhead is on the south side of the parking lot. Trailhead GPS: N34 48.342' / W111 45.980'

THE ADVENTURE

Courthouse Butte and Bell Rock act as gatekeepers to Central Arizona's red rock country south of Sedona. As seen from the southern approach into Sedona from AZ 179, these hulking buttes of red-orange sandstone stand tall in the Munds Mountain Wilderness. At nightfall, a wonderfully dark sky emerges over the mystical landscape. A night hike on the Courthouse Butte Loop Trail is an adventure worth taking for its open views of the stars over Courthouse Butte and Bell Rock. Start this moderately challenging 3.75-mile hike from the Courthouse Vista parking lot and trailhead.

Courthouse Butte anchors the dark skies in the red rock country south of Sedona.

The trailhead parking lot offers a wonderful view of Courthouse Butte and Bell Rock under a serene night sky. Begin your hike by heading to the southern side of the parking lot to the Courthouse Butte Loop/Bell Rock Pathway Trailhead. Walk south for 0.15 mile; at the junction, turn left and hike east on the Courthouse Butte Loop Trail for 1.0 mile. Traverse sections of bare sandstone with wide-open views of the sky above the piñon-juniper forest. After 1.0 mile of heading east, the trail makes a short steady climb followed by a descent southward across the Munds Mountain Wilderness for 0.9 mile.

On the eastern side of the loop, there are large areas of slickrock mixed with washes that make route finding slightly challenging. Use your flashlight and a sharp eye to spot wire-cage rock cairns that help lead the way through this confusing part of the Courthouse Butte Loop. The stars are brightest through the eastern part of the loop because the area is better shielded from light pollution. Next, the loop heads west through a lush section of the trail, which then climbs gradually through open meadows on the south side of Courthouse Butte for 0.9 mile. The southern side of the loop is peaceful and beautiful, with calm vistas of Bell Rock silhouetted against the star fields to the west.

Reach the junction with the Bell Rock Pathway and head north on the pathway sandwiched between the highway and Bell Rock for 0.55 mile. On Bell Rock's western side, note how the iconic peak changes form to a series of pinnacles under the night sky. When you reach the junction with the Phone Trail, take the Phone Trail north for 0.25 mile back to the Courthouse Butte Trailhead to complete your hike. Before driving away, take a final look at the stars from the Courthouse Vista parking lot with your lights off. Look to Courthouse Butte and Bell Rock and remember how far you came around these sacred mountains under the beauty of the night sky.

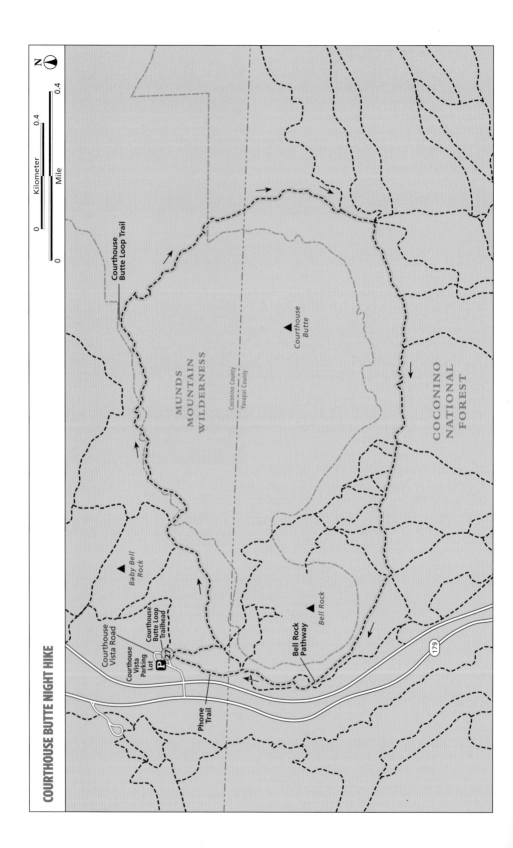

COURTHOUSE BUTTE NIGHT HIKE

Courthouse Butte Loop Trail

MUNDS MOUNTAIN WILDERNESS

Coconino County
Yavapai County

Courthouse Butte

COCONINO NATIONAL FOREST

Baby Bell Rock

Bell Rock

Bell Rock Pathway

Courthouse Vista Road

Courthouse Vista Parking Lot

Courthouse Butte Loop Trailhead

Phone Trail

179

N

Kilometer
0   0.4

Mile
0   0.4

Bell Rock and the curvy mesas west of Courthouse Butte cradle the Milky Way.

MILES AND DIRECTIONS

0.0   Start from the Courthouse Butte/Bell Rock Trailhead and head south for 0.15 mile to a trail junction.

0.15 At the junction, turn left and hike east on the Courthouse Butte Loop for 1.0 mile.

> Ponderosa pines can be found from southern Canada to Mexico and from Oklahoma to the West Coast of the United States.

1.15 Begin turning southward on the Courthouse Butte Loop Trail and look for cairns to lead you south on the trail for the next 0.9 mile.

2.05 At the junction with the Big Park Loop, continue west on the Courthouse Butte Loop Trail for 0.9 mile.

2.95 Arrive at the Bell Rock Pathway junction; head north on the Bell Rock Pathway for 0.55 mile between Bell Rock and AZ 179.

3.5   Reach the Phone Trail Junction; head northeast on the Phone Trail for 0.25 mile to the Courthouse Butte Trailhead.

3.75 Arrive back at the trailhead.

28 OAK FLAT CAMPGROUND CAR CAMPING

Visit the homelands of the Apache tribe at Oak Flat Campground, where dark skies and people have found their home for generations. Long held a sacred homeland to the Apache, enjoy the scenery and the night skies that make this a special place in Central Arizona.

Activity: Car camping
Location: Oak Flat Campground; GPS: N33 18.457' / W111 03.041'
Difficulty: Easy
Seasons/schedule: Open year-round; best in fall, winter, and spring
Timing: No moon to a quarter moon
Fees and permits: None
Campground contacts: Tonto National Forest, 7680 South Six Shooter Canyon Rd., Globe 85501; (928) 402-6200; fs.usda.gov/recarea/tonto/recarea/?recid=35345
Dog-friendly: Yes, under control
Land status: National forest
Nearest town: Superior, Arizona
Suitable camp setups: Tents, RVs, fifth wheels, vans, trailers

Maps: USDA Forest Service map available online at fs.usda.gov/recarea/tonto/recarea/?recid=35345
Facilities: Pit toilets, fire rings, picnic tables; 16 first-come, first-served campsites
Water availability: None
Special considerations: No trash services are available at the campground. Some land near the campground is privately owned. Respect any cultural artifacts you come across and leave them where you find them. Be cautious of mountain lions, venomous reptiles, and venomous insects that are present in the area. Make sure all campfires are dead out and ashes are cool to the touch.

FINDING THE CAMPGROUND

From Superior, drive east on US 60 for 3 miles; turn right (south) onto FR 469. Continue south then west on FR 469 for 1 mile; turn left (south) into Oak Flat Campground. Campground GPS: N33 18.457' / W111 03.041'

THE ADVENTURE

Just behind the imposing cliffs of Apache Leap east of Superior is Oak Flat Campground. This small campground is filled with mature oak trees that have seen generations of Apache and recreationists alike take shelter under their shady branches. Oak Flat, also known to the Apache as *Chi'chil Biłdagoteel*, has long been regarded as the homeland of the Apache people. The area still serves as the site where girls and boys experience their traditional coming-of-age ceremonies. Take your own journey to Oak Flat to enjoy a dark starry sky while camping in this culturally significant area.

The 4-mile drive from Superior to Oak Flat is especially scenic as US 60 winds its way through the reddish rocky spires of Queen Creek Canyon. The dirt roads of Oak Flat Campground, suitable for passenger cars, make it feel like a dispersed

LOOK UP
The closer a satellite is to Earth, the faster it must go around the planet to stay in orbit. Satellites in low earth orbit must travel 17,000 miles per hour to stay in orbit.

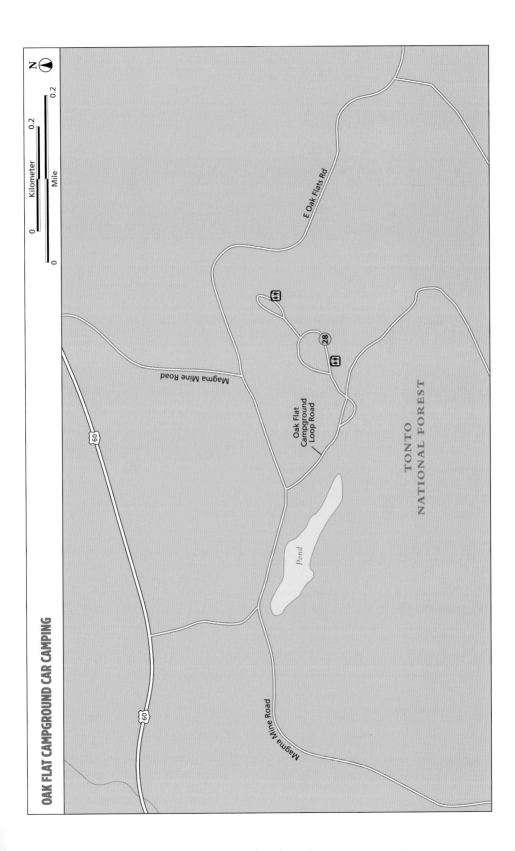

OAK FLAT CAMPGROUND CAR CAMPING

N

0   Kilometer   0.2   0.2

0   Mile

60

60

Magma Mine Road

Magma Mine Road

E Oak Flats Rd

28

Oak Flat
Campground
Loop Road

Pond

TONTO
NATIONAL FOREST

The branches of an oak tree reach for the stars at Oak Flat Campground.

campground, providing a more adventurous feeling for campers. Once you have selected one of
the sixteen free campsites, notice all the natural
assets of this area. Hear the oak leaves rattling in
the wind and the call of all kinds of birds in the
trees around you. Take a walk around the campground to see more of the large oak trees, and
take a short walk 0.15 mile to the west to see a
beautiful seasonal pond.

LOOK UP
Mintaka, the westernmost
star in Orion's Belt is not
just one star but actually a
complex system of five stars.

As night falls over Oak Flat, take another walk around the campground to see stars
gleaming in the sky. Light pollution from Phoenix and a mining operation to the west
will impede some of your views of the stars. Night sky views to the south, east, and north
are unobstructed by light pollution and will provide a rich star-viewing experience for
you. Take the short walk to the pond just west of the campground to experience the
beauty of stars reflecting in the water. Hear the sounds of frogs and crickets calling into
the night at the water's edge to connect with a place that has been sacred for a long time.
Once you are ready, return to your campsite and get a great night's rest as the Earth makes
its way to the next day. As the next day comes, you may want to explore further in the
area. Some great areas to explore include reflective Hackberry Pond, about 1.35 miles
from the campground south on Magma Mine Road and Lower Devil's/Ga'an Canyon,
about 5.0 miles south.

White clay found around Oak Flat is used in traditional coming-of-age
ceremonies to paint Apache girls white, symbolizing their molding into
women.

29 WOODS CANYON LAKE—SPILLWAY CAMPGROUND CAR CAMPING

Camp at Woods Canyon Lake, a forested reservoir high up on Arizona's Mogollon Rim, and discover a pristine night sky. Fish to your heart's content, and be amazed at the slow dance of stars reflected in the calm waters of the lake at nightfall.

Activity: Car camping
Location: Woods Canyon Lake Recreation Area, Spillway Campground; GPS: N34 19.969' / W110 56.281'
Difficulty: Easy; paved roads to the campground
Seasons/schedule: Open Apr 29–Oct 31; best May through Sept
Timing: No moon to a quarter moon
Fees and permits: Nightly camping fees required; reservations can be made online.
Campground contacts: Apache-Sitgreaves National Forest, Black Mesa Ranger District, 2748 East AZ 260, PO Box 968, Overgaard 85933; (928) 535-7300; fs.usda.gov/detail/asnf/home/?cid=stelprdb5211204
Dog-friendly: Yes, leashed and under control
Land status: National forest
Nearest town: Payson, Arizona
Suitable camp setups: Tents, cars, trucks, vans, trailers, small RVs up to 16 feet in length
Maps: USDA Forest Service map available online at fs.usda.gov/recarea/asnf/recarea/?recid=80835

Facilities: Picnic tables, campfire grills; pit toilets, drinking water, trash services; boat ramp
Water availability: Yes
Special considerations: Some campgrounds, like the Spillway Campground in the Woods Canyon Lake Recreation Area, have size limitations for RVs. Woods Canyon Lake Area campgrounds are very popular, so consider reserving a campsite, arriving early, or arriving on weekdays when more sites are available. Elk, bears, and skunks inhabit the area. Only electric boat motors are allowed on the lake. Fishing licenses are required for those over the age of 10.
Other: Several other campgrounds are available in the Woods Canyon Lake Recreation Area, including Rim, Aspen, Crook, Mogollon, and Woods Canyon Group Campground. This trip description will focus on the Spillway Campground, which is located on the eastern side of the lake. Campground hosts are available at the Spillway Campground.

FINDING THE CAMPGROUND

From Payson, drive northeast on AZ 260 for 29.2 miles. Turn left onto Rim Road/FR 300 and head north then west for 3.3 miles. From Rim Road, turn right and head north on Woods Canyon Road for 1.1 miles. Follow signs for the Spillway Campground and turn right off Woods Canyon Road, proceeding to the campground 0.3 mile ahead. Campground GPS: N34 19.969' / W110 56.281'

WOODS CANYON LAKE—SPILLWAY CAMPGROUND CAR CAMPING

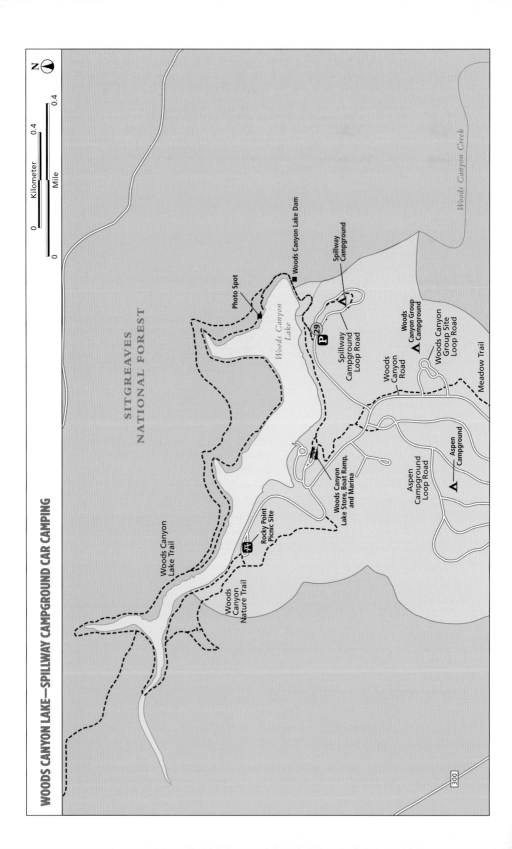

The setting crescent moon and a sky full of stars cast a cool blue glow over the still waters of Woods Canyon Lake.

THE ADVENTURE

Nestled 7,500 feet high on the Mogollon Rim, Woods Canyon Lake's peaceful waters reflect the sky and its pine-forested shoreline. Created by the damming of Woods Canyon Creek, the small lake hosts a recreational paradise for anglers, photographers, hikers, and campers alike. Pleasant summer days and cool, starry nights make Woods Canyon Lake an ideal place for a summer camping trip. The Spillway Campground is one of several campgrounds located in the Woods Canyon Lake Recreation Area; however, it's the closest to the lake. Begin your adventure to Woods Canyon Lake by making a reservation at the Spillway Campground ahead of your visit.

Driving through the open ponderosa pine forests of the Mogollon Rim en route to Woods Canyon Lake will ignite your spirit of adventure. Upon arrival at the Spillway Campground, you will find shady campsites featuring picnic tables, flat tent pads, and campfire grills for your enjoyment. Once your campsite is set up, make your way north of the campground to the rocky shores of the lake for some daytime fun. Take a short 0.5-mile walk north across the earthen dam to the northeastern side of the lake, string up a hammock, and catch some fish or the best light with your camera. If you're wanting an easy hike, take the 3.7-mile trail around the whole lake and see its many different coves and small creeks.

As you watch birds of prey dive toward the lake, watch the sun slowly plunge past the horizon and prepare for a brilliant night of stargazing from the lakeshore. Whether you stay at the lake through sundown or go after dinner, you will be amazed at the sheer variety of stars. Thousands of orange,

LOOK UP

Dark Lunar Maria, visible on the near side of the moon, is solidified lava created by volcanic activity incited by asteroid bombardment on the far side of the moon.

A pile of logs meets a cascade of stars reflecting above the forested shores of Woods Canyon Lake in Central Arizona.

yellow, blue, and white stars jewel the night skies above the still waters of the lake. If you time your trip for a crescent moon, take a look at how large it appears above the trees and its clear reflection in the water. Best of all, witness the grandeur of the Milky Way's marbled dust lakes stretching across the entire sky and slipping into the trees.

Other activities you may want to try by the lake are night fishing, long-exposure photography, or deep sky viewing with binoculars or a telescope. When you're ready to turn in for the night or make some s'mores by the fire, take the short walk back to the Spillway Campground. Remember to leave your campsite in better condition than you found it at the end of your trip. By the end of your camping trip, you'll probably have a new favorite spot in Arizona's Rim Country. One thing you will definitely take home from this trip are unforgettable memories of the Mogollon Rim's stunning night skies.

> Bald eagles and ospreys can be found nesting in the tall trees surrounding Woods Canyon Lake.

30 MOGOLLON RIM—RIM LAKES VISTA NIGHT HIKE

Watch the Milky Way drift across the sky from the Rim Lakes Vista Trail, a paved pathway on the edge of the Mogollon Rim. This scenic path through the trees is wheelchair accessible and has several inspiring viewpoints of the Rim Country's dark skies.

Activity: Night hiking
Location: Mogollon Rim; GPS: N34 18.644' / W110 56.442'
Start: Rim Lakes Vista Trailhead at the Woods Canyon Vista parking lot; GPS: N34 18.899' / W110 56.674'
Elevation gain: 68 feet
Distance: 1.75 miles out and back
Difficulty: Easy due to a paved trail with gentle grading
Hiking time: About 30 minutes
Seasons/schedule: Open Apr through Oct, weather permitting; best in late spring, early summer, and early fall
Timing: No moon to a crescent moon
Fees and permits: None
Trail contacts: Apache-Sitgreaves National Forest, Black Mesa Ranger District, 2748 East AZ 260, PO Box 968, Overgaard, AZ 85933; (928) 535-7300; fs.usda.gov/detail/asnf/home/?cid=stelprdb5211204

Dog-friendly: Yes, leashed and under control
Trail surface: Paved
Land status: National forest
Nearest town: Payson, Arizona
Other trail users: Trail runners, hikers, photographers
Maps: USDA Forest Service maps available online at fs.usda.gov/recarea/asnf/recarea/?recid=44765
Water availability: None
Special considerations: No water or restrooms are present at the trailheads. Use extreme caution around the sheer drop-offs on the canyon rim. The trail is inaccessible in winter due to snow. Bears, elk, deer, skunks, and snakes are present in the area. Monsoon storms in the summer can produce lightning, torrential rain, and strong winds. The Mogollon Rim is frequently struck by lightning during storms; get off the rim if lightning is seen within 10 miles.

FINDING THE TRAILHEAD

From Payson, take AZ 260 East for 29.2 miles; turn left to head north then west on FR 300/Rim Road. Head west on FR 300 for 3.2 miles and turn left into the Woods Canyon Vista parking lot, just before the turnoff for Woods Canyon Lake. The trailhead for the Rim Lakes Vista Trail (#622) is located on the southeastern side of the parking lot. Trailhead GPS: N34 18.899' / W110 56.674'

THE ADVENTURE

The Mogollon Rim of Central Arizona is a top destination for anyone escaping Arizona's notorious summer heat. One of the best qualities of Rim Country is the dark skies that prevail over its lush pine forests. On this adventure, mix high altitude with starry skies and take a relaxing night hike

> Tiny glowworms can be found crawling on the Rim Lakes Vista Trail, emitting a little cyan-colored light.

along the edge of the Mogollon Rim on the Rim Lakes Vista Trail. Located a little over 30 minutes from Payson, this paved trail weaves in and out of the woods, affording

MOGOLLON RIM—RIM LAKES VISTA NIGHT HIKE

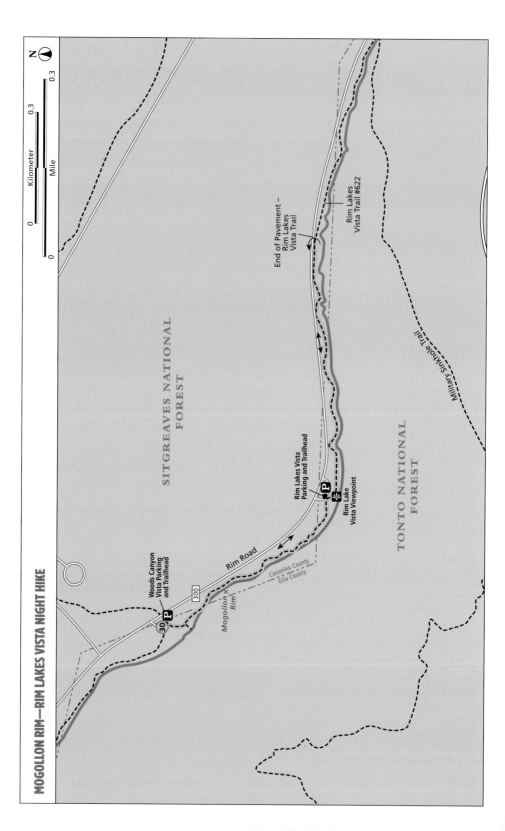

N

Kilometer
0   0.3

Mile
0   0.3

SITGREAVES NATIONAL
FOREST

TONTO NATIONAL
FOREST

Woods Canyon
Vista Parking
and Trailhead

P

30
300

Rim Road

Mogollon Rim

Coconino County
Gila County

Rim Lakes Vista
Parking and Trailhead

P

Rim Lake
Vista Viewpoint

End of Pavement –
Rim Lakes
Vista Trail

Rim Lakes
Vista Trail #622

Military Sinkhole Trail

stunning views of the night sky over a sprawling forest. Begin this easy adventure from the Rim Lakes Vista Trailhead at the Woods Canyon Vista parking lot, just south of Woods Canyon Lake.

Get to the Rim Lakes Vista Trailhead at night or 30 minutes after sunset to enjoy twilight on the first half of your walk. Hear the crickets and feel the cool mountain breeze as you start down the Rim Lakes Vista Trail, heading southeast for 0.4 mile. The walking is easy on this paved path through the woods with some stretches free of trees, offering an exciting view over the rim to horizons far away. At the Rim Lakes Vista Viewpoint and parking lot, walk about 10 feet south of the path to get out of the trees and take a good look at the plentiful stars in the southern skies. When ready, leave this amazing view and walk another 0.47 mile east on the Rim Lakes Vista Trail to see some more great views of the Milky Way through the trees.

The core of the galaxy begins to set over the forest and the cars heading west to Payson on AZ 260, as seen from the Rim Lakes Vista Trail.

The halfway point of this hike is marked by the sudden end of the paved part of the trail in the forest. Turn around and head west the same way you came for 0.88 mile toward the Woods Canyon Vista parking lot. A second stop at the Rim Lakes Vista Viewpoint is always warranted, so take your time here to sit near the edge of the Mogollon Rim and stargaze. Follow the path of the Milky Way through the sky and marvel at its clarity in these dark, high-altitude night skies. After you've stargazed to your heart's content, finish your walk along the rim by hiking 0.4 mile northwest to the trailhead.

MILES AND DIRECTIONS

0.0 Start from the Rim Lakes Vista Trailhead at the Woods Canyon Vista parking lot. Head east on the Rim Lakes Vista Trail for 0.4 mile.

0.4 Reach the Rim Lakes Vista Viewpoint. Continue east on the Rim Lakes Vista Trail for 0.47 mile.

0.87 Reach the end of the paved section of the Rim Lakes Vista Trail. Turn around and head west back to the Woods Canyon Vista parking lot for 0.88 mile.

1.75 Arrive back at the trailhead.

LOOK UP

Cassiopeia can be used to find the North Star (Polaris) by using the middle part of the constellation's "W" shape to point you toward Polaris.

The North Star (Polaris) is actually a triple star system located 447.6 light-years from Earth.

The moon shines over the
beautiful forests of the
Mount Baldy Wilderness in
Eastern Arizona.

EASTERN ARIZONA

THE FORESTS AND DESERTS OF EASTERN ARIZONA POSSESS THE SPIRIT of nature in its purest form. Eastern Arizona's landscape can be characterized in three ways: painted desert up north in Navajo Nation, cool alpine forests in the White Mountains, and the great sky islands of the southeast. Darkness rules over this region, which has no large cities for hundreds of miles and plentiful public lands for people to enjoy and the stars to shine. Between the Navajo, Hopi, and Apache tribes, a significant part of the population is Native American. Eastern Arizona is the perfect place to escape back to nature, reconnect with a dark sky, and learn about the ancient cultures that came before.

The three major subregions of Eastern Arizona are wildly beautiful and contain some of the best dark skies in the state. In the central subregion are the legendary White Mountains, an alpine paradise filled with Douglas fir and the piercing bugle of an elk in the rut. To the northeast, the Navajo Nation and the painted desert feature fascinating galleries of petrified wood at places like Petrified Forest National Park. Soaring above the southeast's Chihuahuan Desert are the sky islands with unparalleled biodiversity from mountain forests to riparian canyons like Cave Creek Canyon. Recreational opportunities abound in Eastern Arizona, with millions of acres of public and tribal land available to recreate under pristine night skies.

Those pristine night skies make Arizona's east a wonderful place for astrotourism. Atop the Pinaleño Mountains is the Mount Graham International Observatory, a cutting-edge research complex featuring the large binocular telescope, one of the largest telescopes in the world. Dark skies are a given in Eastern Arizona due to its sparse population and vast wilderness areas. Although places like the White Mountains are a popular summer escape for Arizona's city slickers, it's easy to get away from the crowds and enjoy a night of solitude under a vast starry sky. Generations of Navajo astronomers have used the dark skies of Eastern Arizona to tell star stories to one another.

This is a land of small towns, mining, and the largest Native American reservation in the United States. Copper mining, agriculture, and outdoor tourism form the backbone of the economy throughout the region. The Navajo Nation near the Four Corners is the largest Native American reservation in the United States, comparable in size to West Virginia. Important cultural heritage sites in places like Canyon de Chelly National Monument show that the area has been inhabited by the Navajo and Puebloan peoples for more than 5,000 years. The Apache have called the region home for hundreds of years and formed close bonds with the Yavapai after years of suffering forced relocations together, such as the brutal winter march to Eastern Arizona's San Carlos Reservation in 1875.

Eastern Arizona is one of the most scenic places in Arizona for stargazing and outdoor recreation, and it appears this should remain the case for many years to come. Whether you are backpacking deep in the Mount Baldy Wilderness or enjoying Navajo skies from

Dark skies free of light pollution dominate over Crescent Lake in the White Mountains of Eastern Arizona.

the edge of Canyon de Chelly, there is an adventure for everyone in Eastern Arizona. Truly dark skies dominate much of the region, allowing you to elevate your stargazing to a whole new level. Experience the beauty of Native cultures in the region and empathize with their past, both for the beauty and for the pain. Come out to Eastern Arizona for a session of starry sky therapy on one of this chapter's ten trips through the region.

31 WHITE MOUNTAINS— HANNAGAN MEADOW MOONLIT SNOWSHOEING

Strap on your snowshoes and take a leisurely walk through the snow under bright moonlight. Hear the crunch of snow and ice beneath your feet and note the clarity of the stars above your head in clean mountain air.

Activity: Night time snowshoeing
Location: Hannagan Meadow; GPS: N33 38.356' / W109 19.611'
Start: Hannagan Meadow snowshoeing trailhead; GPS: N33 38.356' / W109 19.611'
Elevation gain: 47 feet
Distance: 0.64-mile loop
Difficulty: Easy; flat trail
Hiking time: About 15 minutes
Seasons/schedule: Winter
Timing: Any time of the month
Fees and permits: None
Trail contacts: Apache-Sitgreaves National Forest, 42634 US 191, Alpine 85920; (928) 339-5000; fs.usda.gov/recarea/asnf/recarea/?recid=44619
Dog-friendly: Yes, under control
Trail surface: Snow
Land status: National forest
Nearest town: Alpine, Arizona
Other trail users: Skiers
Maps: USDA Forest Service map available online at fs.usda.gov/recarea/asnf/recreation/wintersports/recarea/?recid=75391&actid=91
Water availability: None
Special considerations: Overnight temperatures are freezing, so dress in layers and bring hot drinks. Watch for falling hazards in the forest such as dead trees and large branches hung up in the trees above. Ensure that weather forecasts are clear to avoid being trapped in a disorienting snowstorm. There is no cell-phone signal at Hannagan Meadow.
Other: The Hannagan Meadow Lodge, located across from Hannagan Meadow, offers hospitable lodging, meals, and snowshoe and ski rentals; visit hannaganmeadow.com or arizonawhitemountainadventures.com/cross-country-skiing-snowshoeing.htm.

FINDING THE TRAILHEAD
From Safford, take US 191 North for 114 miles. Park at Hannagan Meadow Lodge, on the west side of the road, and cross US 191 to the wide-open Hannagan Meadow to start snowshoeing. Trailhead GPS: N33 38.356' / W109 19.611'

US 191 used to be named US 666 and was nicknamed the Devil's Highway.

THE ADVENTURE
In the vast White Mountains of Arizona, Hannagan Meadow sits in a remote section of the Apache-Sitgreaves National Forest. Very far from any significant light pollution and situated at high elevation, the meadow is the perfect place to stargaze in any season. The White Mountains live up to their name at Hannagan Meadow, with deep snow possible for weeks after snowstorms. Located off paved US 191, this location is accessible to vehicles even in the middle of winter. Experience the wonder of snowshoeing under moonlight through a forest of ponderosa pine, Douglas fir, and white aspen.

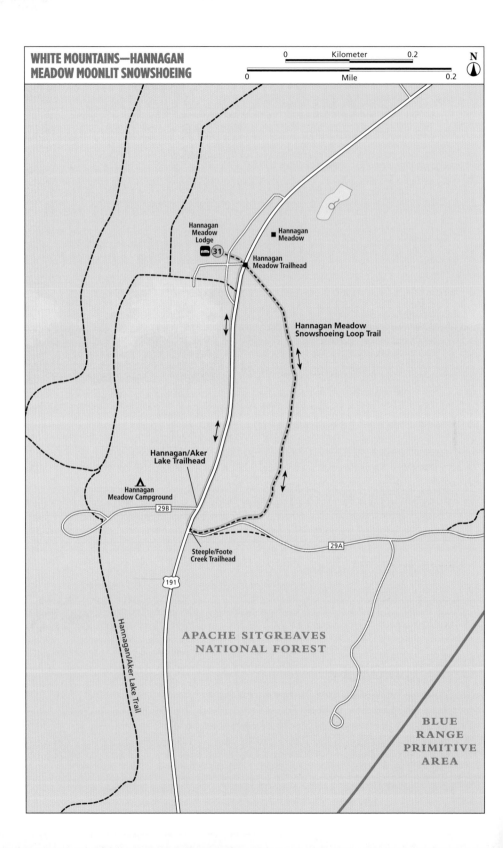

0   Kilometer   0.2

0   Mile   0.2

N

Hannagan
Meadow
Lodge

31

Hannagan
Meadow

Hannagan
Meadow Trailhead

Hannagan Meadow
Snowshoeing Loop Trail

Hannagan/Aker
Lake Trailhead

Hannagan
Meadow Campground

29B

Steeple/Foote
Creek Trailhead

29A

191

Hannagan/Aker Lake Trail

APACHE SITGREAVES
NATIONAL FOREST

BLUE
RANGE
PRIMITIVE
AREA

The footsteps of snowshoers and skiers lead onto a moonlit blanket of snow at Hannagan Meadow.

An ideal place to start your adventure is the Hannagan Meadow Lodge, located on US 191 directly across from Hannagan Meadow. Established in 1926, the Hannagan Meadow Lodge offers cabin and room accommodations in their historic lodge. Rent snowshoes from the lodge or bring your own and cross US 191 to the wide-open Hannagan Meadow as the moon hangs in the night sky. Depending on how full the moon is, it may even look like daytime outside with the moon reflecting off the snowy landscape. After strapping on your snowshoes, walk to a gap in the fence around the meadow and start out into the glowing white powder.

A headlight will hardly be necessary once your eyes adjust to the moonlit snow. Marvel at the wide views of the stars above as you head east then south through the meadow, where it begins to transition to forest. Stop breaking through the snow and enjoy the silence and the clean air filtered by the forest around you. Near the southern end of the meadow, turn to the west toward US 191. Once you reach the road, walk north along the road to the Hannagan Meadow Lodge and complete your small loop. The lodge also features a restaurant where you can warm up with a hot meal after your snowshoeing adventure.

Other groomed and marked trails branch out from the Hannagan Meadow area, including trails into the wild Blue Range Primitive Area. If desired, make your snowshoeing trip longer and access different parts of the forest by taking one of these many paths. No matter how short or long your snowshoeing trip is, you will be delighted by the magic of a moonlit winter wonderland.

MILES AND DIRECTIONS

0.0 Start from Hannagan Meadow Lodge, crossing US 191 toward a gap in the wooden fence surrounding Hannagan Meadow. Head east then south through the open meadow.

0.25 Curve west toward US 191 through a gap in the trees.

0.33 Turn north, following US 191 toward Hannagan Meadow Lodge.

0.64 Arrive back at the trailhead/Hannagan Meadow Lodge.

LOOK UP
The moon exerts very small movements on the crust of the Earth, resulting in a phenomenon called land tides.

32 WHITE MOUNTAINS— BIG LAKE CAR CAMPING

Get way out there in the White Mountains of Eastern Arizona and camp in the breezy alpine forests surrounding Big Lake. At night, see one of the best night skies in the state reflect in the calm 9,000-foot-high waters of Big Lake.

Activity: Car camping
Location: Big Lake Recreation Area, Rainbow Campground; GPS: N33 52.510' / W109 24.136'
Difficulty: Easy
Seasons/schedule: Open late spring through early fall; best in spring, early summer, and early fall
Timing: No moon to a quarter moon. Visit before and after monsoon season for reliable night-sky viewing conditions.
Fees and permits: Nightly camping fees required; see fs.usda.gov/recarea/asnf/recreation/recarea/?recid=44701&actid=29 for current fees. Some campsites are reservable; others are offered on a first-come, first-served basis.
Campground contacts: Apache-Sitgreaves National Forest, Springerville Ranger District, 165 South Mountain Ave., PO Box 760, Springerville 85938; (928) 333-6200; fs.usda.gov/detail/asnf/home/?cid=stelprdb5211223
Dog-friendly: Yes, leashed and under control
Land status: National forest
Nearest town: Springerville, Arizona
Suitable camp setups: The Rainbow and Grayling Campgrounds are suitable for tents, vans, SUVs, smaller RVs, trucks, and trailers. The Apache Trout Campground can accommodate large groups and RVs up to 82 feet long. The Brookchar and Cutthroat Campgrounds are tent-only.

Maps: Big Lake Recreation Area map available online at fs.usda.gov/recarea/asnf/recarea/?recid=80836
Facilities: Flush-toilet restrooms, hand sinks, drinking water, showers; RV dump station, fire rings, picnic tables, group campsites, and trash services at some campgrounds. No electric hookups are available in any of the campgrounds. The Big Lake Store offers supplies, boat rentals, and fishing licenses.
Water availability: Yes; drinking water available in the campgrounds
Special considerations: Bears, mountain lions, skunks, elk, and squirrels inhabit the area. For safety, food storage orders are in effect, requiring visitors to store food and toiletries in a hard-sided container at night or unless an adult is supervising the items within 100 feet. Wildfires and associated smoke are a real danger throughout fire season. Fire restrictions may be in place; check current restrictions before you have a fire. Make sure all campfires are dead out and cool to the touch. Summer monsoon storms create cloudy conditions for days at a time, which may interfere with stargazing activities. Snow may fall at any time of the year in the Big Lake Recreation Area due to its high elevation. Very limited cell-phone coverage is available in the area.

FINDING THE CAMPGROUND

From Pinetop-Lakeside, take AZ 260 east for 26 miles. Turn right and head south on AZ 273 toward the Sunrise Ski Resort for 19 miles. Turn right onto Big Lake Road and proceed into the Big Lake Recreation Area. To get to Rainbow Campground, the largest campground in the area, follow the paved Big Lake Road west for 0.7 mile; turn left into the campground. Continue down Big Lake Road to access the other campgrounds around Big Lake, including Grayling, Cutthroat, Apache Trout, and Brookchar. Campground GPS (Rainbow Campground): N33 52.510' / W109 24.136'

Side Trip: To see more beautiful alpine vistas, consider visiting Crescent Lake and the Mount Baldy Wilderness, both within 20-minute drives north of Big Lake on AZ 273.

THE ADVENTURE

The ultimate summer camping getaway can be found in the White Mountains at aptly named Big Lake. Five campgrounds offer camping opportunities along the shores of the 575-acre lake for basically anyone willing to make the journey to this Eastern Arizona gem. Fishing, hiking, and boating are some of the activities that everyone can enjoy during the day, but you should really come for what you can do after dark—stargazing! Far from light pollution at the border between open grassland and dense alpine forest, Big Lake, located a little over 4 hours east of Phoenix, is perfect for enjoying a pristine night sky. Pack your camping gear and prepare for an unforgettable trip to Arizona's high country.

One of the most beautiful sights near Big Lake is the vast subalpine grasslands dotted with deep blue lakes. Deer and elk frequent these peaceful meadows, which can turn into carpets of wildflowers during summer monsoon. Taking Big Lake Road from AZ 273, you'll approach the large blue lake from the east and start seeing signs for the campgrounds. Rainbow Campground and four other campgrounds provide hundreds of sites for campers to choose from, with amenities like fire rings, picnic tables, restrooms, and drinking water. After checking into your campsite, enjoy some daytime activities such as

A lone pine tree sits under a starry sky on the shores of Big Lake in the White Mountains of Eastern Arizona.

WHITE MOUNTAINS—BIG LAKE CAR CAMPING

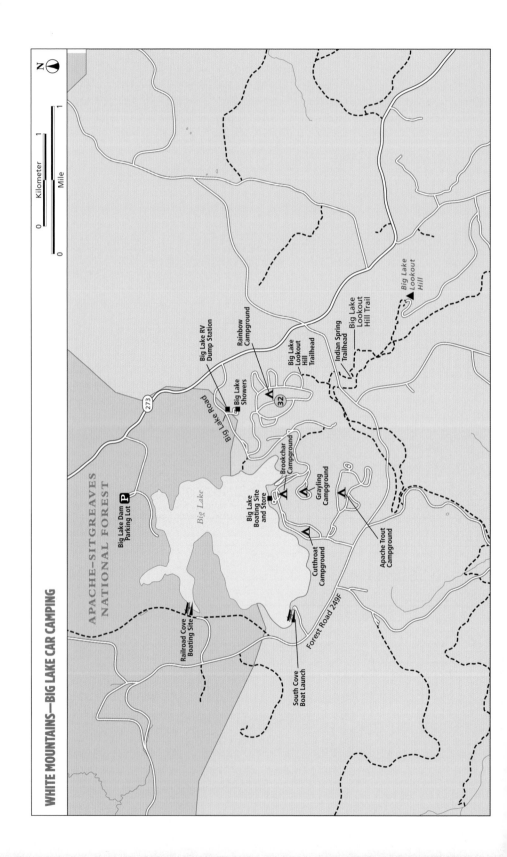

APACHE–SITGREAVES
NATIONAL FOREST

Big Lake Dam Parking Lot

Railroad Cove Boating Site

South Cove Boat Launch

Forest Road 249F

Big Lake

Big Lake Boating Site and Store

Cutthroat Campground

Brookchar Campground

Grayling Campground

Apache Trout Campground

273

Big Lake Road

Big Lake RV Dump Station

Big Lake Showers

Rainbow Campground

32

Big Lake Lookout Hill Trailhead

Indian Spring Trailhead

Big Lake Lookout Hill Trail

Big Lake Lookout Hill

N

0   Kilometer   1

0   Mile   1

fishing or a 3-mile round-trip hike up to the Big Lake Lookout Hill that starts from Rainbow Campground Loop D.

When twilight begins to fade, take a short walk down to the lake to enjoy stargazing that's free from tall trees and other obstructions. As you approach the lake, feel how the late-evening winds begin to die down and hear the quiet lapping of water on the shore. Watch an immense night sky slowly unfold above you as nautical and astronomical twilight vanish. Look in every direction as your vision adjusts to the pristine darkness; you won't find domes of light pollution this far away from civilization. In fact, all you can see at Big Lake is a dome of tens of thousands of stars, especially on a moonless night.

The dark, high-altitude skies at Big Lake make the core of the Milky Way look intimidating. The large ghostly presence of the Great Rift and dense star clouds feel close enough to touch despite being thousands of light-years away. Astrophotographers will marvel at enchanting phenomena like airglow and the enhanced clarity of galactic dust lanes when light pollution is totally absent. Dark skies like this make it hard to go back to bed, but when you're ready, simply walk back to your campsite and dream about those views of the universe. You will certainly enjoy your time camping at Big Lake no matter how many nights you stay.

LOOK UP

Our solar system sits on the edge of the Orion spur, a small arm of the Milky Way galaxy.

The core of the Milky Way is about 26,000 light-years from Earth and contains a super-massive black hole called Sagittarius A*.

The core of the Milky Way bathes in green airglow over Big Lake's rocky shoreline.

33 WHITE MOUNTAINS—CRESCENT LAKE STARGAZING AND ASTROPHOTOGRAPHY

Enjoy a magical night of stargazing and astrophotography at Crescent Lake, under the unbelievable night skies of the White Mountains. Surrounded by rolling meadows and forested hills, here you can see wide-open views of the galaxy and capture the beauty of Crescent Lake's mirrorlike reflections of a truly dark sky.

Activity: Stargazing and astrophotography
Location: Crescent Lake; GPS: N33 54.720' / W109 25.454'
Start: Crescent Lake Dam boating site parking lot; GPS: N33 54.720' / W109 25.454'
Elevation gain: 13 feet
Distance: 100 feet out and back
Difficulty: Easy
Hiking time: About 5 minutes
Seasons/schedule: Open late spring through early fall; best in late spring, early summer, and early fall
Timing: Arrive when there is no moon to a crescent moon, between 2 hours after sunset and 2 hours before sunrise.
Fees and permits: None
Trail contacts: Apache-Sitgreaves National Forest, Springerville Ranger District, 165 South Mountain Ave., PO Box 760, Springerville 85938; (928) 333-6200; fs.usda.gov/detail/asnf/home/?cid=stelprdb5211223
Dog-friendly: Yes, leashed and under control
Land status: National forest
Nearest town: Springerville, Arizona
Other trail users: Anglers
Maps: USDA Forest Service maps available online at fs.usda.gov/recarea/asnf/recarea/?recid=45159
Water availability: None
Special considerations: Bears, mountain lions, skunks, elk, and deer inhabit the area. Wildfires and associated smoke are a real danger throughout fire season. Summer monsoon storms can create cloudy conditions for days at a time, which may interfere with stargazing activities. Roads in the area will be closed in winter. FR 114 and FR 114A are dirt. The area has very limited cell-phone coverage.

FINDING THE TRAILHEAD
From Pinetop-Lakeside, take AZ 260 East for 26 miles. Turn right onto AZ 273, head southeast toward Sunrise Ski Resort for 15.6 miles, then turn right onto FR 114. Make an immediate left 60 feet from AZ 273 and park at the Crescent Lake Dam boating site parking lot. Trailhead GPS: N33 54.720' / W109 25.454'

LOOK UP
There are only 60 miles of atmosphere between the Earth's surface and space.

THE ADVENTURE
Like most places named Crescent Lake, the one in Arizona is wonderfully picturesque. What makes Arizona's Crescent Lake special is that it's located in one of the most underrated stargazing areas in the state, the White Mountains. Free of light pollution and crowds, you can easily have Crescent Lake all to yourself for stargazing and astrophotography, even in the middle of summer. This crescent-shaped reservoir is located just off AZ 273, 15 minutes north of Big Lake, making it an easy trip to add to your itinerary

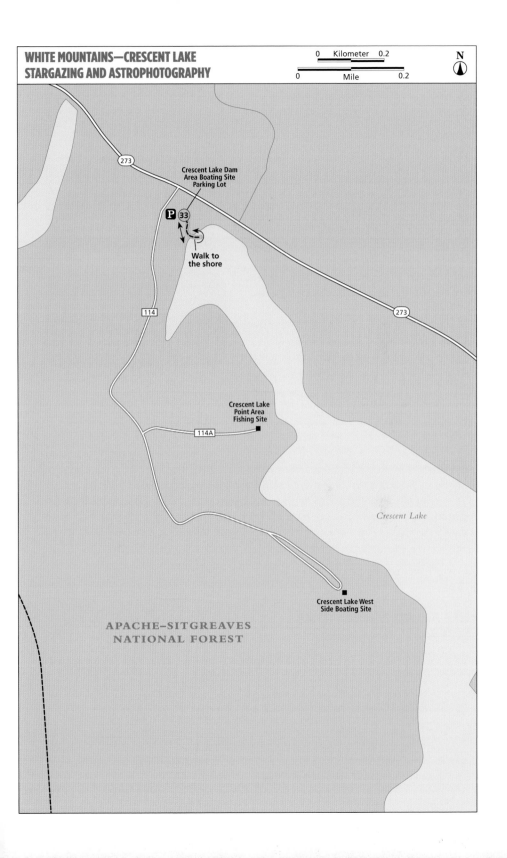

WHITE MOUNTAINS—CRESCENT LAKE
STARGAZING AND ASTROPHOTOGRAPHY

0   Kilometer   0.2

0   Mile   0.2

N

273

Crescent Lake Dam
Area Boating Site
Parking Lot

P 33

Walk to
the shore

114

273

Crescent Lake
Point Area
Fishing Site

114A

Crescent Lake

Crescent Lake West
Side Boating Site

APACHE–SITGREAVES
NATIONAL FOREST

Verdant green airglow fills the starry skies over Crescent Lake in Eastern Arizona.

while on your White Mountain summer vacation. For the best stargazing conditions, arrive at the Crescent Lake boating site parking lot when it is completely dark outside—at least 2 hours after sunset or 2 hours before sunrise.

Walk in the dark from the parking lot south to the shores of Crescent Lake. Once you arrive at the shore, turn off your lights and allow your eyes to naturally adjust to the dark. Looking south across the lake, you'll notice a few small forested hills accenting the horizon and a sky full of stars reflecting in the still waters of the lake. Nested a little over 9,000 feet elevation, the stars here will appear especially dazzling and clear. The distant calls of owls and elk may break the silence between your breaths, but do not fear; simply appreciate their presence.

If you've brought your camera for astrophotography, unpack your tripod and camera gear to capture one of the darkest night skies Arizona has to offer. Long-exposure photographs may even reveal an otherworldly green haze called airglow that can't easily be seen with the naked eye. Try incorporating airglow into your images to complement the brilliant starry skies and the Milky Way. Between images, admire the sky and truly absorb the moment—one day, you will miss these beautiful moments. As your night at Crescent Lake comes to an end, find Polaris and walk 50 feet north toward the parking lot.

LOOK UP
Airglow is the discharge of excess energy from atoms and molecules charged by the sun in the upper atmosphere.

MILES AND DIRECTIONS

0.0   Start from the Crescent Lake Dam boating site parking area and head 50 feet south toward the shore of Crescent Lake.

50 feet   Arrive at Crescent Lake. When ready, turn around and head 50 feet north, back to the parking lot.

100 feet   Arrive back at the parking area.

Lakeshores often make excellent leading lines for landscape astrophotography; use these to your advantage at Crescent Lake.

34 WHITE MOUNTAINS— MOUNT BALDY WILDERNESS BACKPACKING

Trek through lush subalpine meadows, push yourself into dense timber, and see wild night skies on a backpacking adventure in the Mount Baldy Wilderness. Guarded by sacred Mount Baldy, the tallest peak in the White Mountains, this wilderness provides an excellent opportunity for solitude in the green, high-altitude side of Arizona.

Activity: Backpacking
Location: Mount Baldy Wilderness; GPS: N33 56.097' / W109 31.594'
Start: East Baldy Trailhead; GPS: N33 55.892' / W109 29.400'
Elevation gain: 2,697 feet
Distance: 16.23-mile loop
Difficulty: Hard due to steep climbs; the trail is not cleared of hazards, with heavy timber obstacles across the trail.
Hiking time: 2–3 days
Seasons/schedule: Open late spring, summer, and early fall; best in summer and fall
Timing: No moon to a quarter moon
Fees and permits: None for the USDA Forest Service trails. Non-tribal members are not allowed to summit Mount Baldy near the western side of the backpacking loop.
Trail contacts: Apache-Sitgreaves National Forest, Springerville Ranger District, 165 South Mountain Ave., PO Box 760, Springerville 85938; (928) 333-6200; fs.usda.gov/detail/asnf/home/?cid=stelprdb5211223
Dog-friendly: Yes, leashed and under control
Trail surface: Dirt and rock
Land status: National forest and federally designated wilderness
Nearest town: Springerville, Arizona
Other trail users: Equestrians, day hikers, photographers, trail runners
Maps: USDA Forest Service maps available online at fs.usda.gov/recarea/asnf/recarea/?recid=44767

Water availability: Yes, in the East and West Forks of the Little Colorado River and small springs along the trail
Special considerations: Toward the western side of the loop, the trail has not been cleared of hazards. Trail hazards include trees fallen across the trail and large stands of dead trees, which are subject to falling at any time, especially in windy conditions. Proceed with caution on the western side of the loop; you must climb up and over fallen trees in the trail, which can be both dangerous and strenuous. Elevations on the trail range from 9,300 to 11,200 feet. Condition yourself to high elevations to prevent altitude sickness. Altitude sickness symptoms include shortness of breath, headache, dizziness, loss of appetite, and tiredness. Prepare for bears, elk, skunks, squirrels, and heavy mosquitoes (at some times of the season), which inhabit the creek-side areas. Store food 200 feet or more from camp, hanging it in a tree 10 feet off the ground and 4 feet from the trunk, or use a hard-sided bear can. Do not enter the White Mountain Apache Reservation without permission from the tribe. The best places to camp along the trail are in the large meadows on the West Baldy and the Crossover Trails.

The ghostly presence of the Milky Way lingers over the Mount Baldy Wilderness.

FINDING THE TRAILHEAD

From Pinetop-Lakeside, take AZ 260 East for 26 miles. Turn right onto AZ 273 and head southeast toward Sunrise Ski Resort for 11.7 miles. Turn right into the East Baldy Trailhead parking lot. If the lot is full at the East Baldy Trailhead, you may park 0.8 mile south at the Gabaldon Horse Camp Trailhead and take the trail west to connect to the East Baldy Trailhead. You may also park 3.5 miles north on AZ 273 at the West Baldy Trailhead and hike the loop. Trailhead GPS: N33 55.892' / W109 29.400'

THE ADVENTURE

The Mount Baldy Wilderness is the antithesis of every stereotype of Arizona's landscapes. Reminiscent of the alpine landscapes in Wyoming, this wilderness features wide-open grassy meadows and aromatic spruce-fir forests. On this adventure, backpack through 16.2 miles of this wilderness, challenging yourself to steep climbs and rewarding yourself with dramatic views of Eastern Arizona's forests. At night, fall asleep to the ramble of mountain streams as a mosaic of stars pierce dark skies free of light pollution. To begin, head to the East Baldy Trailhead in the morning and start on the East Baldy Trail to hike the loop in a clockwise fashion.

The East Baldy Trail heads westward for a relaxed 1.3 miles through a mixture of subalpine meadows and stands of aspen and fir trees. Grassy meadows accented with bouquets of wildflowers frame brief glimpses of the East Fork of the Little Colorado River. The trail exits the meadow and begins a steady ascent up a smooth trail through the woods for another 1.3 miles. Great statues of weathered sandstone will usher you up a switchback to a gorgeous view of the forests, lakes, and valleys below. Continue

LOOK UP

The fuzzy red-pink Lagoon Nebula, also known as Messier 8, is located in the Milky Way's Great Rift between the Large and Small Sagittarius Star Clouds.

WHITE MOUNTAINS—MOUNT BALDY WILDERNESS BACKPACKING

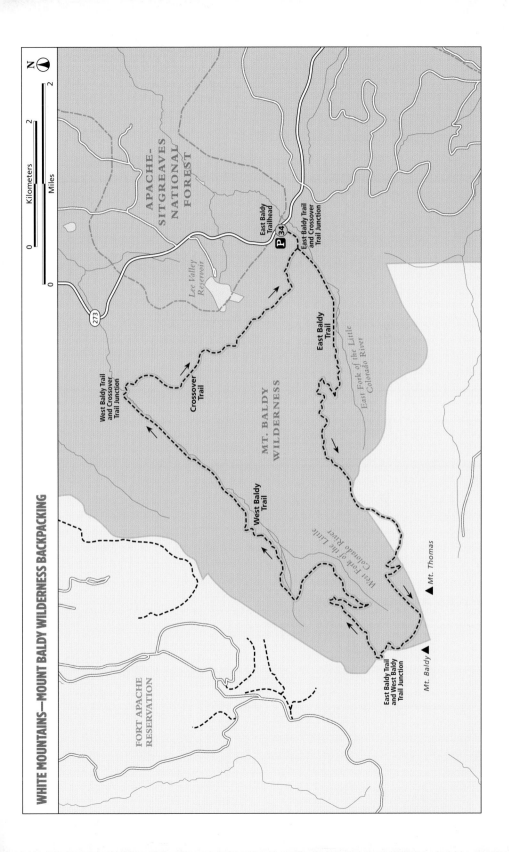

your climb west on the East Baldy Trail through the forest for nearly 3.5 miles until you reach a large stand of dead trees. Depending on how much the trail has been cleared of hazards, this may be the hardest part of your backpacking trip.

Bark beetles likely killed the majority of the trees on the saddle between Mount Baldy and Mount Thomas, creating sunny views of hundreds of trees clawing at the sky. However, if the trail has not been cleared of fallen trees, the beetles have also created a significant obstacle course for you over the next 2.5 miles. Proceed with caution over the trees in the trail as you navigate through the saddle area. Eventually you will reach the junction with the West Baldy Trail and start heading generally northeast. After getting through the downed trees, you'll enjoy a pleasant descent through healthy forest for 1.5 miles, eventually reaching the West Fork of the Little Colorado River and the return of wide-open meadows. The wide grassy valleys of the Little Colorado River's western fork provide excellent camping opportunities with chances to see a beautiful sky full of stars.

Pick a meadow on your way east on the West Baldy Trail and set up your camp for the night. As hues of twilight fade, the skies will reveal a stunningly beautiful starry sky framed by the black silhouettes of mature spruce and fir trees. These wilderness night skies feel raw and clean, with stars collectively so bright that you can see your surroundings without any artificial lighting. Enjoy the sounds of the stream rippling through the landscape, complemented by the chirps of bats all around you. Shooting stars are a common sight in night skies like this, so enjoy it all for as long as you can before going to bed.

In the morning, enjoy a nice breakfast; then, when ready to pack up camp and complete the loop, continue west down the East Baldy Trail. When you reach the Crossover Trail, turn right and head south on the trail for 3.25 miles. Over the 3.25 miles on the Crossover Trail, you will make small climbs and descents as you alternate between forest and verdant mountain meadows. A gentle descent through the woods at the end of the Crossover Trail will lead you back to the East Baldy Trail, where you will head east for 0.14 mile back to the trailhead. As you take the final steps out of the Mount Baldy Wilderness, you'll surely feel a sense of accomplishment and peace.

MILES AND DIRECTIONS

0.0 Start from the East Baldy Trailhead and head generally west for 6.8 miles to the junction with the West Baldy Trail.

6.8 Reach the West Baldy Trail and head generally northeast on the trail for 6.04 miles to the junction with the Crossover Trail.

12.84 At the Crossover Trail junction, head south and southeast on the Crossover Trail for 3.25 miles.

16.09 Arrive back at the East Baldy Trail; head east for 0.14 mile toward the East Baldy Trailhead.

16.23 Arrive back at the trailhead.

Bats can eat between 1,000 and 4,000 insects per hour while cruising the night skies for food.

35 CANYON DE CHELLY STARGAZING DRIVE

Take a scenic drive deep into the Navajo Nation and stargaze under a dark night sky at Canyon de Chelly National Monument. Dark skies and wide-open horizons make this an ideal place to stargaze after watching a sunset from the canyon rim.

Activity: Scenic drive and stargazing
Location: Canyon de Chelly National Monument; GPS: N36 08.330' / W109 30.732'
Start: Indian Route 7 from Canyon de Chelly Welcome Center; GPS: N36 09.202' / W109 32.380'
Distance: 36.0-mile out-and-back drive
Difficulty: Easy due to paved roads and short walks to viewpoints
Driving time: About 1 hour
Seasons/schedule: Open year-round; great in all seasons
Timing: Any time, any phase of the moon
Fees and permits: None
Trail contacts: Canyon de Chelly National Monument, PO Box 588, Chinle 86503; (928) 674-5500; nps .gov/cach/index.htm
Dog-friendly: No; only service animals allowed on the trails
Trail surface: Paved, dirt, and rock

Land status: National monument and Navajo Nation lands
Nearest town: Chinle, Arizona
Other trail users: Hikers, photographers
Maps: Maps available online at nps .gov/cach/planyourvisit/maps.htm
Water availability: None
Special considerations: Overnight temperatures in the winter may be below freezing. Exposed canyon rims with sheer drop-offs are present at every lookout point. Lock your possessions in your vehicle, preferably in the trunk, when left unattended to prevent theft. Keep an eye out for loose dogs and horses around the monument. Visitors cannot hike into Canyon de Chelly without a park ranger or Native guide except on the White House Trail, which may be closed due to security concerns at the trailhead.

FINDING THE STARTING POINT

From Chinle, take Indian Route 7 east to the Canyon de Chelly Welcome Center. From the welcome center, begin the scenic drive east on Indian Route 7 to all the open overlooks up to the Spider Rock Overlook. Starting point GPS: N36 09.202' / W109 32.380'

THE ADVENTURE

Sustained by lifegiving Chinle Creek and protected by massive canyon walls, the Navajo and their predecessors have lived in Canyon de Chelly for 5,000 years. Located in northeastern Arizona on the Colorado Plateau, Canyon de Chelly National Monument's red sandstone cliffs and cliff dwellings are an integral part of Navajo heritage. Today, a community of people call the canyon floor their home, where they raise sheep and harvest crops like their ancestors. Starry skies rule over Canyon de Chelly every night and certainly played a role in the development of Navajo astronomy. For this adventure, take a scenic sunset drive for 36 miles round-trip along the south rim of Canyon de Chelly and watch the stars come out over the canyon walls.

A tinaja reflects the stars as the Milky Way shines above Canyon de Chelly National Monument.

Feel the lively and kindhearted culture of the Navajo Nation as you pass through Chinle on the way to Canyon de Chelly. Begin the scenic drive an hour or two before sunset and head eastward on Indian Route 7 near the Canyon de Chelly Welcome Center. The first stop, 1.6 miles up the road, is at Tunnel Canyon Overlook, which gives you a first glimpse into the red walls of the canyon. Continue another 0.4 mile down the road to the Tseyi Overlook, a stunning view of life on the canyon floor with farm fields, Chinle Creek, and galleries of cottonwood trees. After Tseyi, continue 1.4 miles east on the road to the Junction Overlook for a wide panoramic view into the canyon and distant views of ancient ruins.

> The Hopi once lived in Canyon de Chelly and introduced peach farming in the canyon until they moved west to mesas on the present-day Hopi reservation.

A 6.9-mile drive from the Junction Overlook will take you further into the national monument to the Sliding House Rock Overlook. This overlook requires a short 0.18-mile hike down a rocky trail to a deep view into Canyon de Chelly from hundreds of feet up on the rim. At this point on your drive, the sun should be in a setting phase, so head 1.5 miles south to Indian Route 7, then 2.42 miles east on Indian Route 7, and finally turn onto Spider Rock Overlook Road and head north for 3.52 miles to the Face Rock Overlook. Arrive at the Face Rock Overlook and take a short walk to a view 1,000 feet down into the canyon. Head back to the road and go east for 1 mile to the Spider Rock Overlook parking area for twilight and stargazing.

The short 0.2-mile walk reveals an incredible view of Spider Rock, a 700-foot sandstone spire on the east side of the canyon. As Spider Rock sinks into the blackness of the canyon, let your eyes adjust to the darkness for an awesome night of stargazing. A flat horizon over the canyon rim affords perfect views of the stars. Time your visit to have the moon in the sky and see Spider Rock pointing up to the zenith. Wrap up your night at Spider Rock to make the 16.5-mile drive back to Chinle, and consider seeing the stars at the other viewpoints on the way out.

LOOK UP
The Andromeda galaxy, located near Cassiopeia, will collide with the Milky Way in 4.5 billion years.

CANYON DE CHELLY STARGAZING DRIVE

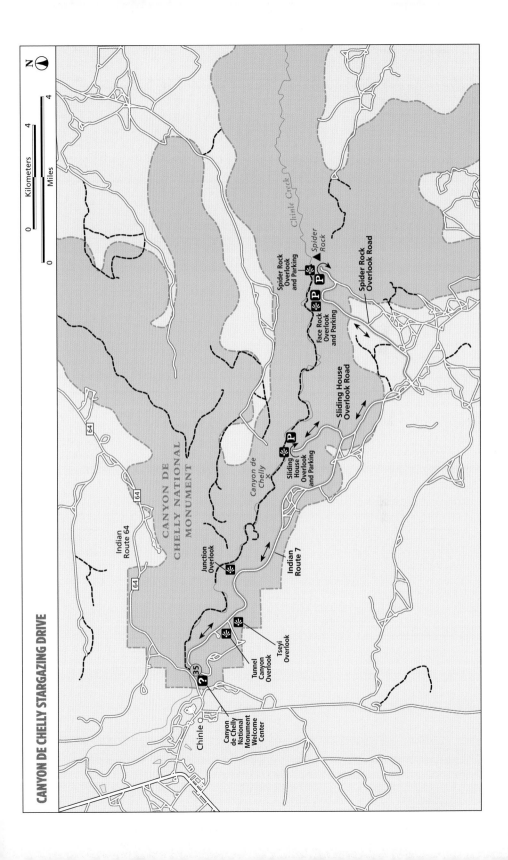

Chinle

Canyon de Chelly National Monument Welcome Center

Tunnel Canyon Overlook

Tseyi Overlook

Indian Route 64

64

64

CANYON DE CHELLY NATIONAL MONUMENT

Junction Overlook

Canyon de Chelly

Indian Route 7

Sliding House Overlook and Parking

Sliding House Overlook Road

Face Rock Overlook and Parking

Spider Rock Overlook and Parking

Spider Rock

Spider Rock Overlook Road

Chinle Creek

N

Kilometers

Miles

0   4   4

The sun sets over the south rim of Canyon de Chelly at the Sliding House Rock Overlook.

MILES AND DIRECTIONS

0.0   Start from the Canyon de Chelly National Monument Welcome Center and head east on Indian Route 7 for 1.6 miles.

1.6   Reach the Tunnel Canyon Overlook; continue east to the Tseyi Overlook 0.4 mile down the road.

2.0   Arrive at the Tseyi Overlook; continue east for 1.4 miles to the Junction Overlook.

3.4   Enjoy the views from the Junction Overlook; continue east on Indian Route 7 for 5.4 miles to the turn for Sliding House Rock Overlook Road. Turn left and head north for 1.5 miles to the Sliding House Rock Overlook parking lot.

10.3   Reach the Sliding House Rock Overlook parking lot, and make a short 0.18-mile hike north to the overlook.

10.48   Arrive at the Sliding House Rock Overlook. Turn around and head south for 0.18 mile back to the parking lot.

10.66   Return to the Sliding House Rock Overlook parking lot. Head south on the Sliding House Rock Overlook Road for 1.5 miles then east on Indian Route 7 for 2.42 miles to the turn for the Spider Rock Overlook.

14.58   Turn left and head north on Spider Rock Overlook Road for 3.52 miles to the Face Rock Overlook.

18.1   Arrive at the Face Rock Overlook; continue southeast then northeast for 1.0 mile on Spider Rock Overlook Road to the Spider Rock Overlook parking lot.

19.1   Park at the Spider Rock Overlook parking lot and head north for 0.2 mile on the paved trail to the overlook.

19.3   Arrive at the Spider Rock Overlook. Return to the Spider Rock Overlook parking lot by walking south on the paved trail for 0.2 mile.

19.5   Arrive at the Spider Rock Overlook parking lot. Return to Chinle by driving 16.5 miles back the way you came to Chinle.

36.0   Arrive back at the starting point.

According to Navajo lore, Spider Woman lives at the top of Spider Rock. Spider Woman is a master weaver who wove the universe together and taught the Navajo how to weave.

36 PETRIFIED FOREST NATIONAL WILDERNESS AREA BACKPACKING

Backpack into the Petrified Forest National Wilderness Area and discover an ancient forest of petrified wood, pristinely preserved for millions of years. Adventure into a moonscape of painted desert, and camp under one of the best dark skies in Arizona.

Activity: Backpacking
Location: Petrified Forest National Wilderness Area
Start: Painted Desert Inn Visitor Center, 1 Park Rd., Petrified Forest National Park
Elevation gain: 374 feet
Distance: 5.1-mile lollipop
Difficulty: Moderate due to steep climbs and the need for route-finding skills
Hiking time: About 4 hours
Seasons/schedule: Open year-round; best in fall, winter, and spring
Dark sky designation: International Dark Sky Park
Timing: No moon to a quarter moon
Fees and permits: Park entrance fee required. Free backcountry permit required and must be obtained from the visitor center or park headquarters by 4:30 p.m. on the day of camping. Vehicles must have permits displayed at the Painted Desert Visitor Center trailhead parking lot.
Trail contacts: Petrified Forest National Park, PO Box 2217, Attention: Petrified Forest, 86028-2217; (928) 524-6228; nps.gov/pefo/index.htm
Dog-friendly: Yes; pets must be signed up with the B.A.R.K. Ranger Program at the park.

Trail surface: Dirt, rock, and soft sand
Land status: National park and federally designated wilderness
Nearest town: Holbrook, Arizona
Other trail users: Equestrians, day hikers, backpackers, photographers
Maps: Petrified Forest National Park map available online at nps.gov/pefo/planyourvisit/maps.htm
Water availability: No water is available in the wilderness. Water is available at the visitor centers and the cafeteria next to park headquarters.
Special considerations: There are no designated or maintained trails within the wilderness; therefore, route-finding skills are necessary for navigation. You must set up camp at least 1 mile from the Painted Desert Visitor Center. Delicate soils and microbiotic crusts are present within the park, so travel only on durable surfaces or in washes/gullies. Do not collect any rocks or petrified wood from the park. Pack in and pack out all trash. Temperatures can be very hot in summer and cold in winter; prepare for the weather. Quicksand can form in washes after rainstorms.

FINDING THE TRAILHEAD

From the Petrified Forest National Park headquarters, head north on Petrified Forest Road for 2 miles. Turn right into the Painted Desert Inn Visitor Center parking lot and park. The trailhead is on the northern side of the parking lot, west of the visitor center. Trailhead GPS: N35 05.019' / W109 47.353'

Tree species that make up the Petrified Forest consist of coniferous trees, gingkoes, and tree ferns.

An assortment of petrified wood basks in the moonlight at Petrified Forest National Park.

THE ADVENTURE

Backpacking into the Petrified Forest National Wilderness Area is the best way to explore this International Dark Sky Park and enjoy its pristine night skies. This 5.1-mile adventure begins at the historic Painted Desert Inn and takes you through galleries of petrified wood, preserved

> The colors in petrified wood are created by impurities in the quartz, such as iron, manganese, and carbon.

from the Triassic period, 200 million years ago. Now composed of quartz crystals, the petrified wood laid out around Petrified Forest once stood tall in riparian areas teeming with dinosaurs and other prehistoric life. By camping in the park's backcountry, you can experience the paleontological wonders of the ancient forest and see the night sky nearly as dark as it was 200 million years ago. Start your adventure by obtaining a backcountry permit and making your way into the wilderness from the historic Painted Desert Inn.

This adventure will lead you to a couple of areas with lots of petrified wood and a camping area with plentiful campsites. Begin from the trailhead northward down steep switchbacks for 0.25 mile then head north for another 0.5 mile, following small washes and faint user tracks. At 0.75 mile you will reach the end of a small hill overlooking some interesting rock formations, below which you will head downhill and continue north

> **LOOK UP**
> At a speed of 514,000 miles per hour, it takes 230 million years for the solar system to orbit the Milky Way's core.

to Lithodendron Wash. At 1.45 miles you reach Lithodendron Wash, where you will follow the wash east then north for 1.05 miles. As you hike through the large wash, you will find pieces of petrified wood that have been washed down

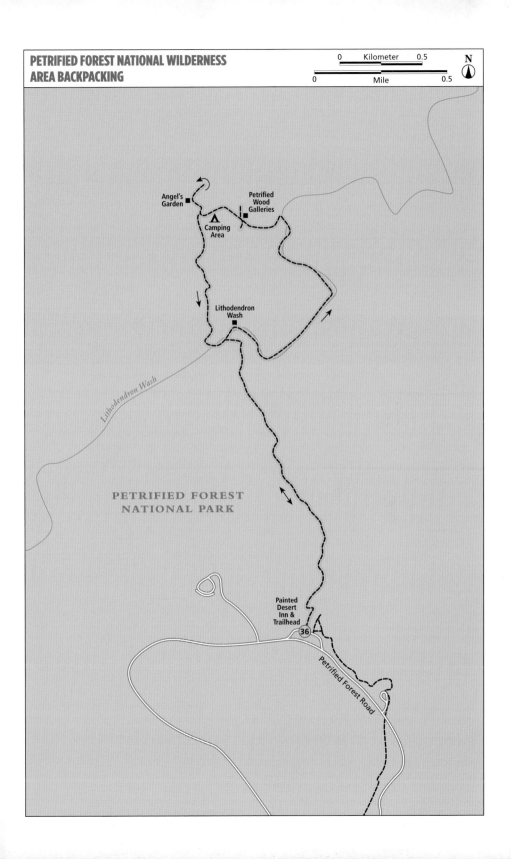

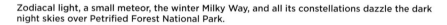

Zodiacal light, a small meteor, the winter Milky Way, and all its constellations dazzle the dark night skies over Petrified Forest National Park.

from the surrounding hills. Thousands of years of mineral replacement underground transformed the wood into giant logs of quartz crystals, seen today at Petrified Forest National Park.

Just before Lithodendron Wash turns east again, look for a small side canyon to the west; this is your gateway to the first gallery of petrified wood. Head westward into the small side canyon for 0.15 mile, and climb up the wash over chunks of petrified wood until you top out on a small mesa. To the north and south are fantastic galleries of petrified wood that are fun to explore. Travel through the small gullies around the petrified wood to protect the delicate soils of the park. Another 0.15 mile west of the petrified wood galleries is a moonscape of white soils and small rounded hills topped with reddish soil. This beautiful area offers solitude and also features many flat areas perfect for camping and a night of stargazing—try to set up camp here.

Enjoy a beautiful sunset over the Painted Desert from camp, and take in the views of the surrounding valleys as the sky transitions from twilight to night. The night sky over Petrified Forest National Park is one of the best in Arizona, with thousands of stars lighting the landscape with starlight. Take time to appreciate this area at night, and make your way through the otherworldly landscape toward the petrified wood galleries to the east of the camp area. The true darkness of the area combined with its barren landscape will make you feel as though you are on another planet. Once you've taken in your fill of the night sky, head back to camp and turn in for the night.

In the morning, descend the washes 0.1 mile to the northwest to see another amazing gallery of petrified wood at Angel's Garden. At Angel's Garden you'll see more giant crystalline trees buried in the Painted Desert and scattered throughout washes. Once ready to return to the trailhead, pack up your gear and head south, following closely along the western side of small white hills for 0.25 mile. Next, hike down an unnamed wash that meanders south for 0.4 mile toward Lithodendron Wash. From Lithodendron Wash, retrace your steps south toward the Painted Desert Inn, which can be seen on top of a hill 1.45 miles ahead. Ascend the steep switchbacks and return to the Painted Desert Inn Trailhead to finish your backpacking trip.

> **LOOK UP**
> Erosion has exposed the logs of petrified wood to a totally different night sky than the trees saw when they stood millions of years ago. As Earth has moved through the Milky Way over the last 200 million years, the night skies have changed, with stars exploding, forming, disappearing, or changing positions.

MILES AND DIRECTIONS

0.0   Start from the trailhead at the Painted Desert Inn and head north for 1.45 miles to Lithodendron Wash.

1.45   Reach Lithodendron Wash and start hiking east then north up the wash for 1.05 miles.

2.5   Exit Lithodendron Wash just before the wash turns east again, and head up a small side canyon toward the west for 0.15 mile.

2.65   Reach the top of a mesa with petrified wood scattered to the north and south. Continue west toward a camping area for 0.15 mile.

2.8   Arrive at a wide camping area marked by white soils and hills topped with reddish soils.

3.0   Explore Angel's Garden, 0.1 mile to the northwest of the camping area. To leave the camping area, travel south along the western side of the white cliffs for 0.25 mile.

3.25   Reach a small wash and hike through the wash, meandering southward toward Lithodendron Wash for 0.4 mile.

3.65   Intersect Lithodendron Wash and head south for 1.45 miles, retracing your steps toward the Painted Desert Inn trailhead on top of a long mesa to the south.

5.1   Arrive back at the trailhead.

37 CAVE CREEK CANYON— SUNNY FLAT CAMPGROUND CAR CAMPING

Camp around a grassy meadow at Sunny Flat Campground under the sharp cliffs of Cave Creek Canyon. A popular place for birders, this hidden gem in Arizona's Chiricahua Mountains also features a creek and one of the best night skies in Arizona.

Activity: Car camping
Location: Sunny Flat Campground; GPS: N31 53.101' / W109 10.576'
Difficulty: Easy
Seasons/schedule: Open year-round; best in spring, summer, and fall
Timing: No moon to a quarter moon
Fees and permits: Nightly camping fees required; see pay station at the campground or call the USDA Forest Service for current rates.
Campground contacts: Coronado National Forest, Douglas Ranger District, 1192 West Saddleview Rd., Douglas 85607; (520) 364-3468; fs.usda.gov/recarea/coronado/recarea/?recid=25428
Dog-friendly: Yes, leashed and under control
Land status: National forest
Nearest town: Portal, Arizona
Suitable camp setups: Tents, cars, SUVs, vans, small RVs, small trailers limited to 28 feet in length
Maps: USDA National Forest map available online at fs.usda.gov/recarea/coronado/recarea/?recid=25428

Facilities: Fire rings, picnic tables, bear boxes, tent pads; drinking water spigot; pit toilets; self-pay station; campground host
Water availability: Yes; drinking water spigot, and water is available in the creek (be sure to treat before using).
Special considerations: Campsites are offered on a first-come, first-served basis with no reservations. There is a 14-day stay limit. If the weather forecast indicates rainfall of 1.5 inches or greater, the campground will be evacuated due to flood danger. Black bears, mountain lions, squirrels, skunks, snakes, and deer inhabit the area. Store food properly in the provided bear boxes or inside vehicles. Wildfires and smoke are a danger throughout the fire season. Fire restrictions may be in place; check before you have a fire. Paved roads are available all the way to the campground.

FINDING THE CAMPGROUND
From Portal, take Portal Road west for 0.6 mile; turn left onto FR 42 and head south for 2.9 miles. Following the sign for Sunny Flat Campground, turn right onto Sunny Flat Road; cross a bridge and enter the campground. Campground GPS: N31 53.101' / W109 10.576'

THE ADVENTURE
Known to some as Arizona's Yosemite, Cave Creek Canyon lives up to its nickname by virtue of its huge rocky cliffs, forested creek, and amazing dark skies. The clear waters of Cave Creek support a lush riparian corridor where many unique bird species take refuge at this oasis in the Chihuahuan Desert. Located on the eastern side of the Chiricahua

CAVE CREEK CANYON—SUNNY FLAT CAMPGROUND CAR CAMPING

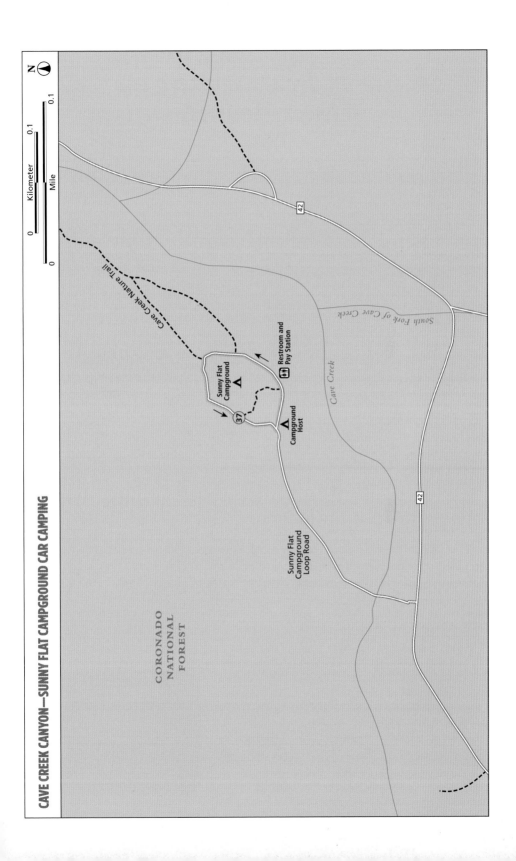

The core of the Milky Way rises over a moonlit skyline at Cave Creek Canyon.

Mountains, the canyon is sheltered from light pollution in every direction by cliff walls. Nights are peacefully dark, and astrophotographers will love capturing the unique rock formations that tower over the canyon. Sunny Flat Campground is in the heart of it all, making it an ideal place to take in everything Cave Creek Canyon has to offer.

FR 42 will lead you south into Cave Creek Canyon on a pleasant drive shaded by oak and picturesque sycamore trees. Cross a small bridge over Cave Creek to enter Sunny Flat Campground, and drive toward the northern side of the campground to the pay station. The best spots for stargazing are found around the Sunny Flat meadow at the northern side of the campground, so try to secure one of those sites. After finding your site, set up camp and admire the dramatic cliffs surrounding Sunny Flat, or go on a short walk to the creek just east of the campground. Take in the sights and smells of Cave Creek, keeping an eye out for coati families and the beautiful birds that call this place home.

As day transitions to night, let your eyes become adjusted to the dark skies that preside over the canyon. An unbelievable number of stars will take up residence in the sky, giving you plenty for your eyes to see. Take a walk around Sunny Flat on the campground loop road to get a 360-degree view of the sky. Although the canyon walls obscure some of your view of the horizon, you will be able to see the clearest and darkest parts of the night sky. Astrophotographers should take advantage of this unique location and photograph the sharp cliffs set against the Milky Way or their favorite constellations and asterisms. Once you have fully enjoyed the stars, head back to your campsite, enjoy a good night's rest, and consider waking up at another time of the night to see how the stars have changed.

LOOK UP

We don't see stars in every direction of the universe because the light has not reached us yet, even after more than 13.8 billion years!

38 MOUNT GRAHAM—HOSPITAL FLAT AND TREASURE PARK CAMPGROUNDS CAR CAMPING

Treat yourself to a night in the forests of Mount Graham at Hospital Flat or Treasure Park Campground. Located less than 0.5 mile apart, these campgrounds sit next to lush alpine meadows with wide-open views of the dark skies over the Pinaleño Mountains.

Activity: Car camping
Location: Hospital Flat Campground; GPS: N32 39.964' / W109 52.505'; Treasure Park Group Campground; GPS: N32 39.684' / W109 52.252'
Difficulty: Easy
Seasons/schedule: Open mid-Apr to mid-Nov, weather permitting; best in late spring, summer, and early fall
Timing: No moon to a quarter moon
Fees and permits: Per-night camping fees required at Hospital Flat and Treasure Park, plus extra-vehicle fee at Treasure Park. Treasure Park North and East group sites can be reserved online at recreation.gov.
Campground contacts: Coronado National Forest, Safford Ranger District, 711 14th Ave., Ste. D, Safford 85546; (928) 428-4150; fs.usda .gov/detail/coronado/about-forest/ districts/?cid=fswdev7_018660
Dog-friendly: Yes, leashed and under control
Land status: National forest
Nearest town: Safford, Arizona
Suitable camp setups: Tents only at Hospital Flat Campground; cars, trucks, SUVs, tents, and very small trailers at Treasure Park group campgrounds
Maps: USDA Forest Service map available online at fs .usda.gov/recarea/coronado/ recarea/?recid=80170

Facilities: Hospital Flat: Pay station; fire rings, grills, picnic tables; trash services, pit toilets; bear boxes for food storage. Treasure Park: Pay station; fire rings, picnic tables; drinking water spigot; bear boxes.
Water availability: Yes; there is a drinking water spigot on the north side of Treasure Park. Water is seasonably available in streams at Hospital Flat and Treasure Park.
Special considerations: Travel and camp on durable surfaces, especially when walking through the fragile mountain meadows. Black bears, mountain lions, bobcats, squirrels, and deer inhabit the area. Store food properly inside provided bear boxes or in vehicles. Located around 9,000 feet in elevation, nights will be very cold in all seasons. Summer monsoon storms can produce intense rain, lightning, and damaging winds. Wildfires and smoke are a threat throughout the fire season. Fire restrictions may be in place; check with the Forest Service before you have a fire. The Treasure Park group sites are normally reserved on weekends; check recreation.gov before you go. The roads looping through the campgrounds are dirt and may be impassable in wet weather.

FINDING THE CAMPGROUNDS
From Safford, take US 191 south for 7.3 miles. Turn right on AZ 366 and head southwest then northwest for 22.7 miles up Mount Graham. Travel west on the dirt part of AZ 366 for less than 1 mile and turn left into the Treasure Park Campground. For Hospital Flat, continue 0.3

Mount Graham is known to the Apache people as *Dził Nchaa Sí'an*, which means "Big Seated Mountain."

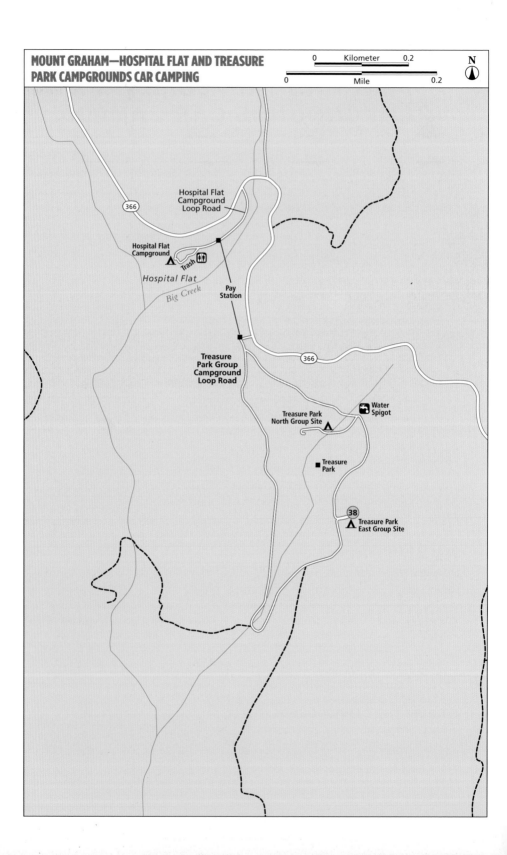

0   Kilometer   0.2

0   Mile   0.2

N

Hospital Flat
Campground
Loop Road

366

Hospital Flat
Campground

Trash

Hospital Flat

Big Creek

Pay
Station

Treasure
Park Group
Campground
Loop Road

366

Water
Spigot

Treasure Park
North Group Site

Treasure
Park

38

Treasure Park
East Group Site

A pair of ponderosa pines watch the Milky Way slide across the night sky over Hospital Flat in the Pinaleño Mountains.

mile past the Treasure Park turnoff on AZ 366; turn left into the Hospital Flat Campground. Campground GPS (Hospital Flat Campground): N32 39.964' / W109 52.505'; (Treasure Park group campground): N32 39.684' / W109 52.252'

THE ADVENTURE

Healing and trickery mark the past at Hospital Flat and Treasure Park, two similar but unique campgrounds that neighbor each other in Arizona's Pinaleño Mountains. Hospital Flat once served as a medical camp in the 1880s for ailing soldiers from Fort Grant and a summer retreat for officers and their families. As legend has it, a band of outlaws buried stolen gold and silver in Treasure Park and marked the site with colored stones. One day a man found the marker stones and dug down to bedrock but found nothing. Both Hospital Flat and Treasure Park feature their own campgrounds set next to gorgeous mountain meadows rich with summer wildflowers during the monsoon season. After dark, campers can enjoy an exceptional night sky shimmering over the open meadows.

The curvy drive up AZ 366, also known as the Swift Trail, is incredibly

LOOK UP
To the Apache people, the three stars of Orion's Belt are known as the "Three Vertebrae" and the Milky Way is known as the "Scattered Stars."

A row of trees stand in front of the Milky Way galaxy's core at Hospital Flat.

scenic all the way to Treasure Park and Hospital Flat. From desert to dense forest, the drive climbs more than 5,500 feet to the alpine meadows high in the Pinaleños. Step out of your vehicle, feel the cool mountain air at your campground of choice, and look to the south across the fields. Take a walk toward the fields, smell the wild-

> Fort Grant closed in 1905 and is now an Arizona state prison.

flowers, and enjoy an open view of the sky framed by tall trees. Set up your camp on a durable surface and enjoy daytime activities like a hike, mountain bike ride, or a drive further west on AZ 366 to Riggs Lake, a popular fishing lake.

A purple hue to the west will grace the skies at twilight before the darkness of night sets in. About an hour and a half after sunset, journey out to the meadow at Hospital Flat or Treasure Park and take in the full night sky. With your lights off, test the darkness of this place by moving one hand in front of the other and looking for a shadow. Only in the darkest of skies like these can you see faint shadows from bright stars or dense collections of stars like the Milky Way. When you've stood out in the cold long enough, crawl into your sleeping bag and enjoy a warm night's rest.

39 GILA BOX RIPARIAN NATIONAL CONSERVATION AREA CAR CAMPING

Camp near the wild and scenic Gila River as it carves through the canyons of Gila Box Riparian National Conservation Area.

Activity: Car camping
Location: Gila Box Riparian National Conservation Area, Riverview Campground; GPS: N32 53.236' / W109 28.742'
Difficulty: Easy; narrow paved road most of the way to the campground
Seasons/schedule: Open year-round; best in fall, winter, and spring
Timing: No moon to a new moon
Fees and permits: Nightly camping fees required; first-come, first-served. For current rates call the BLM Safford Field Office at (928) 348-4400.
Campground contacts: Bureau of Land Management, Safford Field Office, 711 South 14th Ave., Safford 85546; (928) 348-4400; blm.gov/visit/riverview-campground
Dog-friendly: Yes, leashed and under control
Land status: National conservation area
Nearest town: Solomon, Arizona

Suitable camp setups: Cars, trucks, UTVs, motorcycles, vans, small RVs, small fifth wheels
Maps: BLM maps available online at blm.gov/visit/riverview-campground
Facilities: Grills, fire rings, shaded picnic tables; drinking water, pit toilets, ramadas; informational kiosks; small watercraft takeout areas
Water availability: Yes
Special considerations: Daytime temperatures in summer will be very hot and may be freezing overnight in winter. Venomous reptiles and insects, javelinas, mountain lions, and black bears inhabit the area. Around 90 percent of the road to the Riverview Campground is paved; however, it is narrow and steep between the western entrance kiosk and the campground. The campground contains 13 first-come, first-served campsites and does not take reservations. Not all campsites are suitable for long trailers.

FINDING THE CAMPGROUND
From Safford, take US 191/US 70 to the east toward Solomon for 4.9 miles. Turn left onto Sanchez Road and continue for 8.1 miles. After a brief section of dirt road, turn left and head northeast on Bonita Creek Road for 3.8 miles along a narrow, winding paved road that eventually becomes a dirt road. Just past a cattle guard, turn right and head east onto Bull Gap Road for 0.6 mile. At the next fork in the road, follow signs to the Riverview Campground and turn right onto Buena Vista Aqueduct Road for 0.25 mile into the campground. Campground GPS: N32 53.236' / W109 28.742'

THE ADVENTURE
Just outside Safford, four perennial waterways cut deep box canyons in Gila Box Riparian National Conservation Area. The Gila and San Francisco Rivers, along with Eagle and Bonita Creeks, form lush bands of vegetation throughout

LOOK UP
The sun's mass accounts for 99.86 percent of the total mass in the solar system.

Left: The Gila River flows under a canopy of stars and riparian trees through Gila Box Riparian National Conservation Area.
Right: The outstretched branches of an ocotillo spread into the night sky high above the Gila River at Gila Box Riparian National Conservation Area.

the conservation area, hosting a variety of wildlife. Numerous bird species, amphibians, and even bears depend on these important desert riparian habitats. After dark, bats and moths take to the brilliant night skies, silhouetting themselves against a canopy of stars. The Riverview Campground provides a wonderful place to car camp near the river for daytime fun near the water and nighttime views of the stars.

> Saffordite, a black translucent rock popular with rock collectors, is scattered across the Gila Box RNCA landscape.

Load up your camping gear and start your dark sky adventure by heading about 30 minutes east of Safford.

Take your pick of campsites at the Riverview Campground, where all thirteen sites are first-come, first-served and self-paid. Each campsite is well-spaced from the others, offering fire rings, grills, and shaded picnic tables. Other amenities include potable water spigots, pit-toilet restrooms, and a seasonal campground host. Once you have paid for and set up your site, do some exploring at the nearby day-use areas. Around 0.5 mile to the north is the Bonito Creek Watchable Wildlife Area, where you can sit comfortably on a

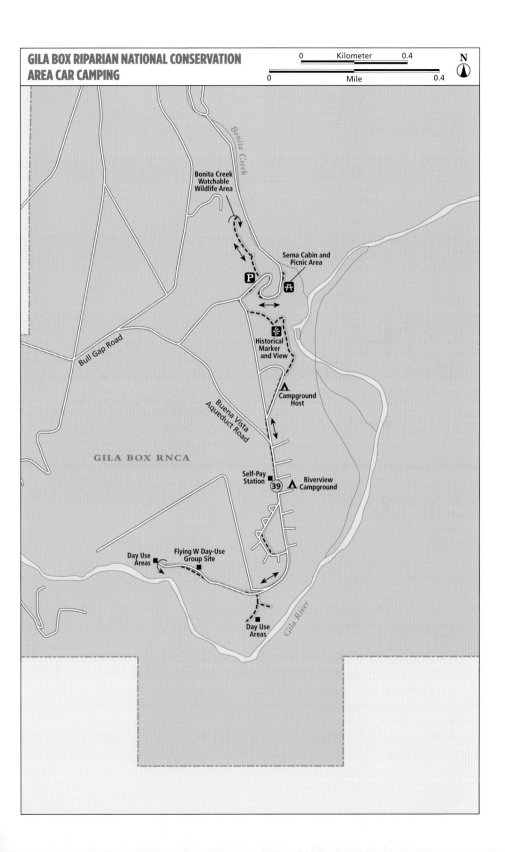

GILA BOX RIPARIAN NATIONAL CONSERVATION
AREA CAR CAMPING

0   Kilometer   0.4

0   Mile   0.4

N

Bonita Creek

Bonita Creek
Watchable
Wildlife Area

Serna Cabin and
Picnic Area

P

Historical
Marker
and View

Bull Gap Road

Campground
Host

Buena Vista
Aqueduct Road

GILA BOX RNCA

Self-Pay
Station

39

Riverview
Campground

Day Use
Areas

Flying W Day-Use
Group Site

Day Use
Areas

Gila River

The core of the Milky Way rises over the mountains of Gila Box Riparian National Conservation Area.

bench high above a forest of cottonwoods and watch wildlife thrive. To the south of the campground are the Flying W group day-use site and other day-use sites less than 0.5 mile away, with access to the Gila River for water-play activities.

LOOK UP
Arcturus, a red-giant star 37 light-years away in the Boötes constellation, is the fourth-brightest star in the night sky.

After enjoying some day-use activities, prepare some dinner before sunset and wait for the night show to begin. Around an hour after sunset, watch the stars dominate the skies above Gila Box, with views of the night sky available in all directions. In late spring and early summer, watch as the gigantic core of the Milky Way begins its reign over the night sky to the east. Over winter, enjoy fantastic views of Orion, Taurus, and Auriga as they dazzle the chilly night skies with their bright stars. Hear the sounds of the Gila River in the distance and agile bats softly chirping their way through the lovely night sky.

A good night's rest will be followed by the pleasant notes of songbirds echoing throughout Gila Box's canyons in the morning. Hopefully you will take in more days and nights of connecting with the night sky. Try enjoying different activities, such as walking through the campground at night or listening to nocturnal wildlife and frogs at nearby day-use areas like the Bonito Creek Watchable Wildlife Area. When you are ready to depart the Riverview Campground, clean your campsite and try to leave it better than how you found it.

40 ROPER LAKE STATE PARK STARGAZING

Watch the sunset behind Mount Graham and stargaze under a dark sky near the gently rippling waters of Roper Lake State Park south of Safford.

Activity: Stargazing
Location: Roper Lake State Park, 101 East Roper Lake Rd., Safford
Difficulty: Easy due to proximity to Safford and paved access roads
Adventure time: About 1 hour
Seasons/schedule: Open year-round except Christmas Day from 6 a.m. to 8 p.m., with the gate closing at 9 p.m.; great in any season
Timing: No moon to a crescent moon
Fees and permits: Park entrance fees required; see azstateparks.com/roper-lake for current fees.
Trail contacts: Roper Lake State Park, 101 East Roper Lake Rd., Safford 85546; (928) 428-6760; azstateparks.com/roper-lake
Dog-friendly: Yes, leashed and under control
Trail surface: Pavement and dirt
Land status: State park

Nearest town: Safford, Arizona
Other users: Children, anglers, kayakers, walkers, campers, photographers
Maps: State park maps available online at azstateparks.com/roper-lake/explore/maps
Water availability: Yes
Special considerations: In summer, the park closes soon after the sun sets. Summer monsoon storms can produce lightning, torrential rain, and damaging winds. Cloud cover in the monsoon season and during winter storms may hamper stargazing at the park. Venomous snakes and spiders inhabit the area; use caution. Fires allowed only in designated fire rings. Swimming beaches may be closed due to low water. The hot tub is permanently closed.
Other: Campsites and cabins are available for reservation

FINDING THE PARK

From Safford, drive south on US 191 for 5.3 miles; turn left onto East Roper Lake Road and head east for 0.5 mile. Follow signs for Roper Lake State Park, and turn right into the park to pay fees at the entrance station. Picnic tables, fishing piers, and parking lots around the park are great stargazing locations. Park GPS: N32 45.432' / W109 42.304'

THE ADVENTURE

Intended as a recreational lake from the start, Roper Lake State Park is positioned at the base of the scenic Pinaleño Mountains. Mount Graham towers over the western shores of this 32-acre reservoir lined with trees and cattails. Conveniently located just 6 miles south of Saf-

> Mount Graham is 10,724 feet tall and has a prominence of 6,320 feet over the valley floor, the most in all of Arizona.

ford, Roper Lake is a popular oasis in the desert featuring activities such as fishing, camping, and stargazing. As night sweeps over the pond, hundreds of bright stars pierce the skies and reflect in the calm waters of Roper Lake. For this adventure, come to the water's edge and enjoy a peaceful night sky over the park.

ROPER LAKE STATE PARK STARGAZING

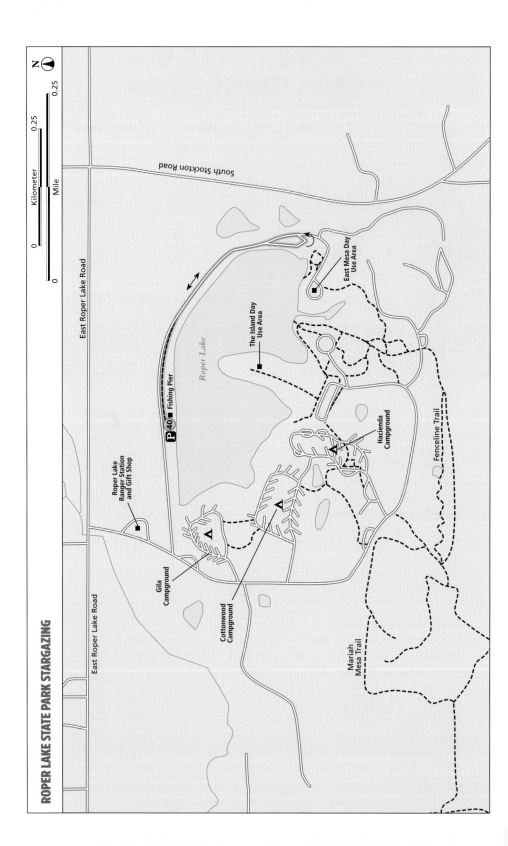

Reeds poke out of Roper Lake, with the Milky Way's core hanging over Mount Graham.

Whether you're staying nearby in Safford or camping in the park, make your way to the lakeshore around sunset to begin this adventure. Experience stunning views of the sun's rays radiating over Mount Graham as the sun sets behind the giant mountain. Note how the direction of the wind changes after sunset and how the lake becomes calmer. For anglers new and old, this would be a good time to cast a line into the lake for a fish! Watch as gradients of blue and magenta appear as the Belt of Venus graces the eastern skies over Roper Lake. As nature signals that night is coming, start looking for the brightest stars and planets making their appearance in the twilight.

LOOK UP

Sunsets on Mars are blue because fine dust particles in the Martian atmosphere allow blue light to pass through more than other colors like the reds, oranges, and yellows we see on Earth.

It all starts with one; then hundreds of stars begin to appear over Roper Lake for your stargazing pleasure. Light pollution from Safford to the north and Mount Graham's tall skyline to the west will be your only obstacles to seeing the stars in this dark sky area. On windless nights, the long ellipses of bright stars and park lights make candle-like reflections on the water's surface. For those with cameras, capture the moment with a few long exposures of the night sky. Bring out the telescope or the binoculars to see distant planets or nebulae deep in the starry skies. When it's closing time at the park or your bedtime, head out of the park or into the comfort of your bedroll at camp.

A mitten-shaped mountain paws at the night skies over Kofa National Wildlife Refuge in Western Arizona.

WESTERN ARIZONA

WESTERN ARIZONA IS A LOT LIKE IT WAS DURING THE DAYS of the Wild West: hot, dry, and sprinkled with hidden gems. Nicknamed Arizona's west coast, the Colorado River cuts canyons through striking desert landscape to feed large reservoirs like Lake Mohave and Lake Havasu. Sparse population across the region means little to no light pollution will mar its awesome night skies where saguaros reach for the stars. Native tribes such as the Mohave and the Chemehuevi have long inhabited the Colorado River Valley, where they weaved baskets from the reeds and farmed the fertile floodplains. The Wild West qualities of Western Arizona are perfect for anyone seeking the solitude of a clear desert night.

Dominated by the Mojave and Sonoran Deserts, Western Arizona is notorious for being brown and extremely hot in the summer, with temperatures exceeding 115°F. This place is way more than just brown; it's green and spiky, like the world's most pristine Joshua tree forest in the Mojave Desert of northwestern Arizona. The Sonoran Desert of Western Arizona features stands of rugged ironwood trees and stately saguaro ornamented with white blooms in late spring. The sparkling blue reservoirs of Lake Mead, Lake Mohave, and Lake Havasu lap at Arizona's west coast, creating unparalleled desert-boating opportunities. Not every wash is a dry rock collection, with perennial streams like Burro Creek creating lush riparian habitat for fish and migratory birds. Most animals have learned to live their lives after dark to escape the region's brutal daytime summer temperatures.

Stargazing is a perfect activity for Western Arizona because the night offers the perfect escape from the heat of the day. Winter is a great time to stargaze in this region due to temperate daytime temperatures, cold nights suitable for camping, and of course the beauty of winter constellations. Light pollution is low across Western Arizona thanks to its small population and places like Lake Havasu City being intentionally designed with few street lights to limit light pollution. A network of paved and dirt roads across the region's public lands gives access to dark skies over remote places like Kofa National Wildlife Refuge. Desert lakes provide a fun way to cool off and stargaze in summer, and the Arizona Hot Springs are a great place to heat up under the stars in winter.

For generations the Colorado River has been a lifeline for people living in Western Arizona and, today, 40 million people across the southwestern United States. The river basin was once inhabited by much smaller populations of Native Americans like the Mohave and Chemehuevi peoples, who lived on a wild Colorado River. As the West has been settled over the past 150 years, demands for water and needs for flood control resulted in the creation of major dams and reservoirs on the Colorado, such as Hoover Dam and Lake Mead. The fabulous winter weather of Western Arizona has attracted many seasonal residents seeking refuge from cold snowy winters, moving to towns like Yuma and Lake Havasu City. Booming population growth in the Southwest is

Courthouse Rock and the Eagletail Mountain Wilderness bathe in moonlight.

also threatening the survival of the Colorado River, arguably Arizona's most important resource.

Ideal stargazing conditions and diverse recreational opportunities make Western Arizona a special place to have an adventure under the night sky. The region's predominantly dry desert environment means you can stargaze almost any night of the year. Clear desert skies with little light pollution are perfect for seeing the Milky Way in all its glory. Reservoirs created by dams along the Colorado are great places to recreate under the stars in new and fun ways. In this chapter, saddle up and come out to Western Arizona for a starry sky adventure across ten beautiful locations in the desert, on the water, and even in the cool pines.

41 ARIZONA JOSHUA TREE FOREST STARGAZING

Stargaze under prime darkness in the Arizona Joshua Tree Forest, the most pristine forest of its kind in the world. This adventure features an easy walk along an interpretive path through the Mojave Desert, far from sources of light pollution.

Activity: Walking and stargazing
Location: Grapevine Mesa National Natural Landmark; GPS: N35 51.722' / W114 04.913'
Start: Arizona Joshua Tree Forest Interpretive Trailhead; GPS: N35 51.722' / W114 04.913'
Elevation gain: 0 feet
Distance: 0.1-mile loop
Difficulty: Easy; flat dirt trail
Hiking time: About 5 minutes
Seasons/schedule: All seasons
Timing: No moon to a quarter moon
Fees and permits: None
Trail contacts: Bureau of Land Management, Kingman Field Office, 755 Mission Blvd., Kingman 86401; (928) 718-3700; blm.gov/office/kingman-field-office
Dog-friendly: Yes, leashed and under control
Trail surface: Dirt

Land status: National natural landmark
Nearest town: Meadview, Arizona
Other trail users: Walkers, photographers
Maps: CalTopo map of the trail area available at caltopo.com/map.html#ll=35.86188,-114.08188&z=18&b=imagery
Water availability: None
Special considerations: In summer, daytime temperatures in the Mojave Desert can be extremely hot; in winter, freezing temperatures are common at night.
Other: "Arizona Joshua Tree Forest" and the "Grapevine Mesa Joshua Tree Forest" are two names for the same location. This site is located 19.5 miles southwest from Grand Canyon West.

FINDING THE TRAILHEAD

From US 93, exit onto Pierce Ferry Road, heading northeast toward Dolan Springs. Continue on Pierce Ferry Road for 28.8 miles; pass through Dolan Springs, and turn right onto Diamond Bar Road. Park at the paved parking lot on the right, about 250 feet from the turnoff. The Arizona Joshua Tree Forest interpretive loop trail begins after crossing a footbridge at the western side of the parking lot. Trailhead GPS: N35 51.722' / W114 04.913'

THE ADVENTURE

The Arizona Joshua Tree Forest near Grand Canyon West is the best example of a healthy Joshua tree forest in the United States. The National Park Service calls this area the Grapevine Mesa Joshua Tree Forest National Natural Landmark. National natural landmarks conserve the natural heritage of the United States by recognizing areas for their pristine condition and biological value. By day you can see thousands of Joshua trees reaching for the sky, while at night you can see them almost touching the stars under a very dark sky. For this adventure, gaze at thousands of stars and learn about the Mojave Desert on a walk along a short, easy interpretive loop.

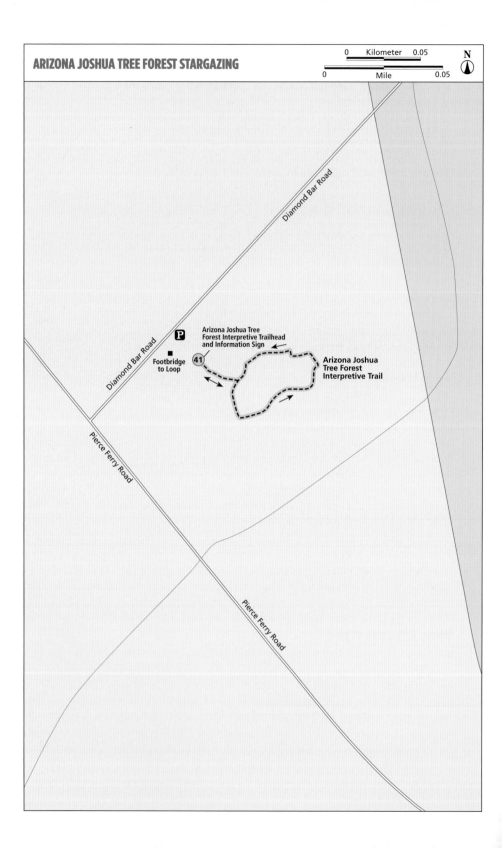

ARIZONA JOSHUA TREE FOREST STARGAZING

0   Kilometer   0.05

0   Mile   0.05

N

Diamond Bar Road

Diamond Bar Road

P

Footbridge
to Loop

41

Arizona Joshua Tree
Forest Interpretive Trailhead
and Information Sign

Arizona Joshua
Tree Forest
Interpretive Trail

Pierce Ferry Road

Pierce Ferry Road

Orion and his winter sky shine bright over the Joshua trees of Grapevine Mesa.

Begin your experience by crossing a small footbridge from a paved parking lot near the intersection of Pierce Ferry and Diamond Bar Roads toward a large interpretive sign. Give your eyes the chance to get adjusted to the darkness by using a red-bulb flashlight to read the sign, learning about the Joshua tree forest around you. Slip through the entrance to the dirt path and start your walk around the loop in either direction once you reach the fork. The loop meanders for 0.1 mile around mature Joshua trees on a flat course with a cable fence keeping you on the path at all times and off the vegetation. More interpretive signs are present throughout the loop, describing the human history and facts about the ecosystem.

> **LOOK UP**
> The names of the three major stars of Orion's Belt are, from left to right, Alnitak, Alnilam, and Mintaka. Focus on Orion's sword just below Alnitak to see the fuzzy, reddish Orion Nebula.

On a clear, moonless night, the stars at this location are simply dazzling. Very little light pollution, clean air, and the silhouettes of gangly Joshua trees combine to create ideal conditions for stargazing. While walking along the loop, you will be able to see stars above the low mountains on every horizon and the glow of the distant lights of Las Vegas to the northwest. The darkness at this location allows you to spot faint nebulae, dark galactic dust lanes, and dense star clusters. The night sky at Arizona Joshua Tree Forest is ideal for using star charts to spot your favorite constellations and learn new ones. Once your eyes have had their fill of the universe, simply finish the loop, slip through the entrance once more, and cross the footbridge to the parking lot.

The Arizona Joshua Tree Forest offers some of the darkest skies in the state and a fine example of the Mojave Desert. Whether you stop by on the way from Grand Canyon West or make it your only destination, it's worth seeing the stars shine over this pristine area.

MILES AND DIRECTIONS

0.0   Start by crossing the footbridge from the west side of the paved parking lot located near Pierce Ferry and Diamond Bar Roads. The loop begins just past a large interpretive sign on the other side of the footbridge. Walk the loop in either direction.

0.1   Arrive back at the trailhead.

42 PAINTED ROCK PETROGLYPH SITE STARGAZING AND ASTROPHOTOGRAPHY

Discover the largest and most dense collection of petroglyphs in Arizona at the Painted Rock Petroglyph Site. Take an easy walk under the stars and use your flashlight to spot some of the 3,800 petroglyphs etched into boulders. Create unique night images of the petroglyphs scribbled in the foreground under very dark skies.

Activity: Astrophotography and stargazing
Location: Painted Rock Petroglyph Site and Campground, 46101 Rocky Point Road, Gila Bend
Start: Painted Rock Petroglyph Site day-use parking lot; GPS: N33 01.384' / W113 02.845'
Elevation gain: 0 feet
Distance: 0.25-mile loop
Difficulty: Easy; flat trail
Hiking time: About 10 minutes
Seasons/schedule: Any season; open 24 hours per day
Timing: Any time of the month
Fees and permits: Yes; small entrance fee required upon arrival at the site
Trail contacts: Bureau of Land Management, Lower Sonoran Field Office, 21605 North 7th Ave., Phoenix 85027-2929; (623) 580-5500; blm .gov/visit/painted-rock-petroglyph-campground
Dog-friendly: No on the trail around the petroglyphs; dogs allowed at the adjacent Painted Rocks Campground

Trail surface: Dirt
Land status: BLM lands and National Register of Historic Places
Nearest town: Gila Bend, Arizona
Other trail users: Photographers, walkers
Maps: BLM map available online at blm.gov/visit/painted-rock-petroglyph-campground
Water availability: None
Special considerations: Do not climb over the small barrier and walk off-trail to get a closer look at the petroglyphs. Daytime temperatures are extreme in summer and can be freezing at night in winter. Venomous reptiles are present in the area.
Other: A majority of the roads to the Painted Rock Petroglyph Site are completely paved except for a 0.1-mile dirt section of gravel road just before the trailhead parking lot. You can stay at the campground next to the petroglyph site for a fee.

FINDING THE TRAILHEAD

From I-8, take the Painted Rock Road/Citrus Valley Road exit and head north on Painted Rock Road for 10.8 miles. Painted Rock Road eventually becomes Painted Rock Dam Road and heads northwest then west. At 10.8 miles from I-8, where you see a sign for Painted Rock Petroglyph Site and Campground, turn left at the fork, heading west

Grinding bowls can be observed in the boulders at the Painted Rock Petroglyph Site and are thought to have been used for grinding pigments.

on Rocky Point Road Drive for 0.5 mile. At a second fork on Rocky Point Road, turn left onto the dirt road, following the sign for Painted Rock Petroglyph Site and Campground. Continue on the dirt road for 0.1 mile southwest and turn right to the Painted Rock Petroglyph Site day-use parking lot. Trailhead GPS: N33 01.384' / W113 02.845'

Left: Petroglyphs adorn moonlit rocks at Painted Rocks Petroglyph Site.
Right: Hundreds of petroglyphs bask in the moonlight at Painted Rocks Petroglyph Site.

THE ADVENTURE

Arizona is known for its rich Native American cultural and archaeological history. The 3,800 petroglyphs at the Painted Rock Petroglyph Site are prime examples of the artistic and storytelling ability of the prehistoric Patayan and Hohokam peoples. Archaeologists suspect that some of the petroglyphs have archaeoastronomical significance, with shadows and light daggers falling over the petroglyphs in a peculiar way during solstice events. Today, a pleasant 0.25-mile trail wraps around a pile of desert-varnished boulders covered in petroglyphs for visitors to enjoy. Dark skies and rich history combine to create a wonderful place for astrophotography and discovery at the Painted Rock Petroglyph Site.

Start your adventure by showing up at night and walking west from the day-use parking lot toward a dark pile of boulders. A half circle of interpretive signs will educate you on the history and cultural importance of this site just steps from the petroglyphs. Begin your walk on the dirt loop by heading either direction at the fork; use your flashlight to spot petroglyphs of lizards, people, and mysterious shapes. The stars at this location are also gorgeous, and with the help of the moon, you should be able to see petroglyphs without a flashlight. As you walk around the loop, imagine all the people who have visited this site over thousands of years and gazed at the same stars you are seeing.

The Painted Rock Petroglyph Site likely received its name because the petroglyphs may have been painted by Native Americans.

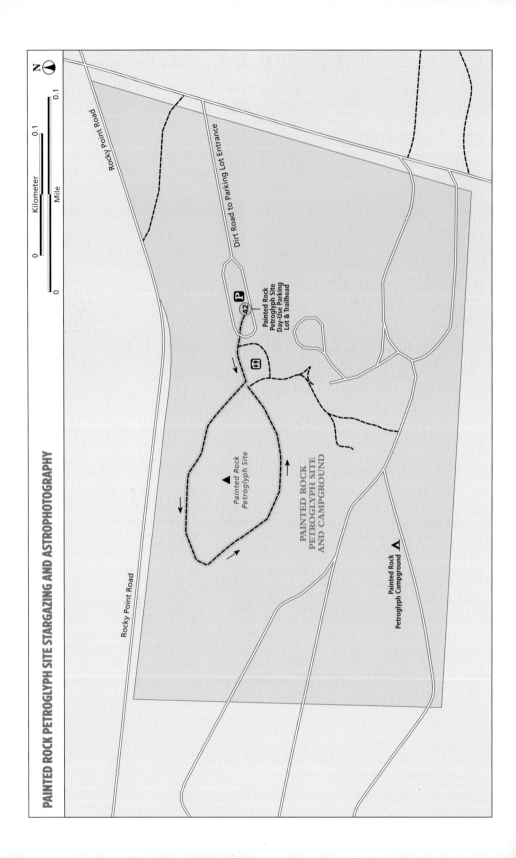

PAINTED ROCK PETROGLYPH SITE STARGAZING AND ASTROPHOTOGRAPHY

N

Kilometer

0   0.1   0.1

0   0.1

Mile

Rocky Point Road

Rocky Point Road

Dirt Road to Parking Lot Entrance

P

42

**Painted Rock
Petroglyph Site
Day-Use Parking
Lot & Trailhead**

Painted Rock
Petroglyph Site

**PAINTED ROCK
PETROGLYPH SITE
AND CAMPGROUND**

**Painted Rock
Petroglyph Campground**

A pile of rocks covered in petroglyphs sits out in the Sonoran Desert at Painted Rock Petroglyph Site.

Capture your moment in time at the Painted Rock petroglyphs against a deep night sky by using your camera of choice on a steady tripod. To gain sharper images of the petroglyphs, shine your flashlight on the petroglyphs and use manual focus on your camera to get your favorite petroglyphs in the image tack sharp. Between photos, make sure you're also living in the moment and appreciating the ancient night sky above and the petroglyphs around you. Notice the rock markings of passing travelers from the nineteenth and twentieth centuries and the unfortunate vandalism from modern times. Respect the people who created these symbols, and be sure to stay outside the short perimeter fence around the rocks.

Complete the 0.25-mile loop around the petroglyphs as many times as desired to find more amazing petroglyphs. When ready to leave, simply take the path east to the parking lot from the half circle of signs. On the way home, sit in the humility of being one of many people who have come to the Painted Rock petroglyphs for millennia.

MILES AND DIRECTIONS

0.0 Start from the Painted Rock Petroglyph Site day-use parking lot and head west toward a dark pile of boulders.

0.03 At the semicircle of informational signs, start either west or north on the looped petroglyph viewing trail.

0.25 Complete a loop around the petroglyph viewing trail and return to the parking lot to the east, arriving back at the trailhead.

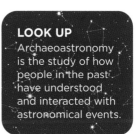

LOOK UP
Archaeoastronomy is the study of how people in the past have understood and interacted with astronomical events.

43 EAGLETAIL MOUNTAINS STARGAZING AND ASTROPHOTOGRAPHY

Journey on roads less traveled and experience starry skies over Courthouse Rock in the Eagletail Mountains. Break out your camera, tripod, and imagination to create amazing images in this seldom-photographed landscape.

Activity: Stargazing and astrophotography
Location: Eagletail Mountains Wilderness; GPS: N33 24.431' / W113 23.404'
Start: Harquahala Valley and Centennial Roads; GPS: N33 27.874' / W113 09.716'
Elevation gain: 463 feet
Distance: 25.16 miles out and back
Difficulty: Moderate, rough and sandy dirt roads
Driving time: About 45 minutes
Seasons/schedule: Open year-round; best in late fall, winter, and spring
Timing: Any time of the month; best with less than a quarter moon
Fees and permits: None
Trail contacts: Bureau of Land Management, Yuma Field Office, 2555 East Gila Ridge Rd., Yuma 85364; (928) 317-3200; blm.gov/visit/eagletail-mountains-wilderness
Dog-friendly: Yes, under control
Trail surface: Dirt and sand
Land status: Federally designated wilderness and BLM lands

Nearest town: Tonopah, Arizona
Other trail users: Equestrians, rock climbers, hunters, backpackers
Maps: BLM map available online at blm.gov/visit/eagletail-mountains-wilderness
Water availability: None
Special considerations: There is private land along Courthouse Rock Road/Centennial Road, so be cautious of where you park your vehicle if riding a bike to the Eagletail Mountains Wilderness. Temperatures can reach 115°F during summer days and be below freezing at night in winter. Mountain lions and venomous reptiles and insects are present in this area. Roads to Eagletail Mountains Wilderness are rough and sandy in areas, requiring high-clearance, four-wheel-drive vehicles. Flash flooding can occur at any time of the year in this area, especially during the summer monsoon season.

FINDING THE TRAILHEAD
From I-10, take the Salome Road exit and head south toward Harquahala Valley Road. Turn right and head west then south on Harquahala Valley Road for 5.5 miles. Turn right and drive west on Centennial Road to begin the drive or the bike ride toward the Eagletail Mountains Wilderness. Trailhead GPS: N33 27.874' / W113 09.716'

THE ADVENTURE
Little known by most people, the Eagletail Mountains Wilderness appears as a skyline of dramatic desert peaks on the southern horizon from I-10 west of Phoenix. This Sonoran Desert wilderness in Western Arizona harbors a rugged

The Eagletail Mountains Wilderness contains prehistoric cultural and ceremonial sites dating back to around 1500 BCE.

A tall saguaro stands among the stars and Courthouse Rock.

landscape featuring saguaro cacti, archaeological sites, and star-filled skies. Landmarks like the hulking Courthouse Rock and the dual peaks of Eagletail Mountain make exciting subjects for astrophotography. Peaceful solitude is a guarantee in the Eagletail Mountains, along with remarkably dark skies. Getting to the Eagletail Mountains Wilderness requires a journey down long, sandy, four-wheel-drive dirt roads.

Start the journey by taking the Salome Road exit from I-10 and head south on Harquahala Valley Road for 5.5 miles. Once you reach Centennial Road, head west toward Courthouse Rock for about 7 miles to the El Paso Gas Pipeline Road, passing vast agricultural fields and huge ironwood trees. Head northwest on the gas pipeline road for 4 miles through hilly desert terrain until you reach a turnoff to the southwest for Eagletail Mountains Wilderness, marked by a large sign. Continue southwest on the unnamed doubletrack road for 1.58 miles; however, beware of a very rugged section around 1.17 miles down the road next to a small mountain. At the end of the road is a parking area with an informational kiosk and the entrance to the Eagletail Mountains Wilderness.

At the trailhead, get your first look at the clear skies over Courthouse Rock. Very dark skies dominate the Eagletail Mountains, providing magical views of constellations and the dust lanes of the Milky Way. The trailhead area provides many opportunities for stargazing and astrophotography featuring subjects like Courthouse Rock to the south, large saguaros, and ocotillos. Time your adventure to watch moonrise light up the landscape, or visit during a meteor shower to capture meteors streaking across the sky. If you wish to add more adventure, take the Ben Avery Trail 3.5 miles south into the Eagletail Mountains Wilderness, crossing desert washes to Indian Spring.

LOOK UP
In Greek legend, the Canis Major constellation represents Sirius, the dog of the hunter Orion.

EAGLETAIL MOUNTAINS STARGAZING AND ASTROPHOTOGRAPHY

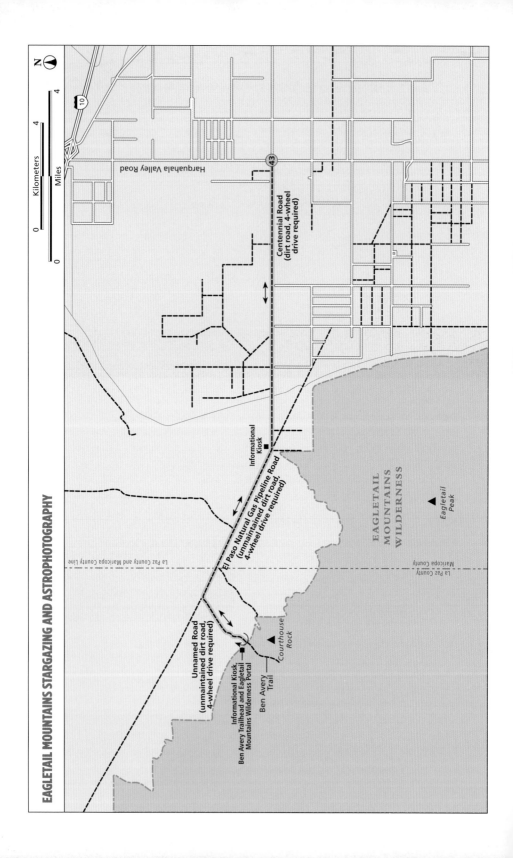

N

Kilometers
0   4   4

Miles
0   4

Harquahala Valley Road

Centennial Road
(dirt road, 4-wheel
drive required)

Informational
Kiosk

El Paso Natural Gas Pipeline Road
(unmaintained dirt road,
4-wheel drive required)

La Paz County and Maricopa County Line

Maricopa County
La Paz County

EAGLETAIL
MOUNTAINS
WILDERNESS

Eagletail
Peak

Unnamed Road
(unmaintained dirt road,
4-wheel drive required)

Informational Kiosk,
Ben Avery Trailhead and Eagletail
Mountains Wilderness Portal

Ben Avery
Trail

Courthouse
Rock

Moonlight breaks across the desert, lighting up Courthouse Rock under thousands of stars.

The quiet of the Eagletail Mountains provides a peaceful and pristine night sky experience and a fun adventure on roads less traveled. Once you are satisfied with your stargazing and photographs, head back the same way you came to the Eagletail Mountains. If riding a mountain bike on the roads to the Eagletail Mountains, you will be delighted by a mostly downhill cruise to Harquahala Valley Road.

MILES AND DIRECTIONS

0.0   Start from the intersection of Harquahala Valley and Centennial Roads and head west on Centennial Road for 7.0 miles.

7.0   Turn northwest onto El Paso Gas Pipeline Road and head northwest for 4.0 miles.

11.0   Turn southwest onto an unnamed dirt road marked by a large sign for the Eagletail Mountains Wilderness. Head southwest for 1.58 miles on the unnamed road, and beware of a very rugged section of the road 1.17 miles from the turnoff.

12.58   Arrive at the Eagletail Mountains Wilderness boundary and the trailhead for the Ben Avery Trail, marked by an informational kiosk. (The Ben Avery Trail is optional.) Return the way you came to the intersection of Harquahala Valley and Centennial Roads.

25.16   Arrive back at the trailhead.

> **LOOK UP**
> There are more than 800 stars in the Pleiades open star cluster, located in the constellation Taurus.

44 KOFA NATIONAL WILDLIFE REFUGE 4×4 CAMPING

Fuel up for a four-wheel-drive adventure to the striking Kofa National Wildlife Refuge in Western Arizona. Watch a sunset paint the jagged mountains red, then witness the rise of thousands of stars in a very dark sky.

Activity: Car camping
Location: Kofa National Wildlife Refuge; GPS: N33 22.299' / W114 09.856'
Difficulty: Moderate for a narrow and rocky 4×4 track
Seasons/schedule: Open year-round; best in late fall, winter, and early spring
Timing: No moon to a quarter moon
Fees and permits: None
Campground contacts: Kofa National Wildlife Refuge, 9300 East 28th St., Yuma 85365; (928) 783-7861; fws.gov/refuge/Kofa/
Dog-friendly: Yes, leashed and under control
Land status: National wildlife refuge and federally designated wilderness
Nearest town: Quartzite, Arizona
Suitable camp setups: Jeeps, pickup trucks, UTVs, dirt bikes/ADV bikes, SUVs, small fifth wheels
Maps: Kofa National Wildlife Refuge map available online at fws.gov/refuge/Kofa/map.html; Wilderness Connect map available at wilderness.net/visit-wilderness/maps.php

Facilities: None
Water availability: No water is available; bring 1 gallon per person, per day. This area receives an average of 2 to 4 inches of rain per year, and water is very scarce.
Special considerations: Summer temperatures can reach 115°F during the day, and winter temperatures can be below freezing. Mountain lions and venomous reptiles and insects are present in this area. Kofa National Wildlife refuge has both maintained dirt roads and rough unmaintained roads. Check with the US Fish & Wildlife Service on current road conditions. Kofa Queen Canyon Road is a narrow four-wheel-drive road requiring high clearance. Flash flooding can occur at any time of year in this area, especially during the summer monsoon season. Camping is limited to 14 days in any 12-month period. Vehicles must remain within 100 feet of designated roads and are prohibited within 0.25 mile of any water sources.

FINDING THE CAMPGROUND
From US 95, take Palm Canyon Road, a graded dirt road, for 3.4 miles to the Kofa Queen Canyon Road turnoff near an informational kiosk. Take Kofa Queen Canyon Road northwest then east for 4.5 miles up a gentle grade. Kofa Queen Canyon Road is rough, unmaintained, rocky, and should only be driven by four-wheel-drive vehicles. Multiple car camping sites are located along the drive to the mouth of Kofa Queen Canyon. Some of the most picturesque campsites are located 4.5 miles from the turn-off at Palm Canyon Road. Campground GPS: N33 23.096' / W114 06.142'

THE ADVENTURE
The rugged landscape of Kofa National Wildlife Refuge is a haven for many animals and a very dark night sky. The elements have whittled the volcanic rock into a serrated skyline, providing ideal habitat for desert bighorn sheep. Situated hours away from big

The picturesque mountains near Kofa Queen Canyon meet thousands of stars in the sky.

cities, Kofa's night skies make it possible to see your favorite constellations and deep sky objects in detail. Rough four-wheel-drive roads crisscross the refuge, allowing access and many camping opportunities in this desert wilderness. Kofa Queen Canyon

> "Kofa" is actually a contraction for a historic gold mine on the refuge called the King of Arizona Mine.

is one of the most beautiful areas in this wilderness, and luckily you can drive right to it.

Start this adventure by taking Palm Canyon Road eastward from US 95 for 3.4 miles and then turn northwest onto Kofa Queen Canyon Road. Follow this rough 4×4 road northwest and then east for 4.5 miles, with the Kofa Wilderness surrounding you on each side. Teddy bear cholla, saguaro, and ocotillo line the road all the way on your drive to a group of striking rock formations at the mouth of Kofa Queen Canyon. Find an existing roadside campsite between 4 and 4.5 miles down Kofa Queen Canyon Road and prepare your space for an incredible night of stargazing. Kick back in your camp and watch as the setting sun lights up the landscape with sweet red light.

As the gentle twilight fades from the sky, take some time to explore the area around your campsite on foot, being mindful of cholla balls and venomous reptiles and insects. Peer through the flimsy ocotillo branches at a gorgeous skyline of sharp peaks set against a truly dark sky. Getting away from the campfire and artificial lights of camp will let your eyes fully adjust to the dark, revealing faint and extremely distant objects. From Kofa you can appreciate almost every star in the constellations and the true size of deep sky objects like the Andromeda galaxy. The sky

LOOK UP
At 2.5 million light-years away, the Andromeda galaxy is the most distant object humans can see with the naked eye.

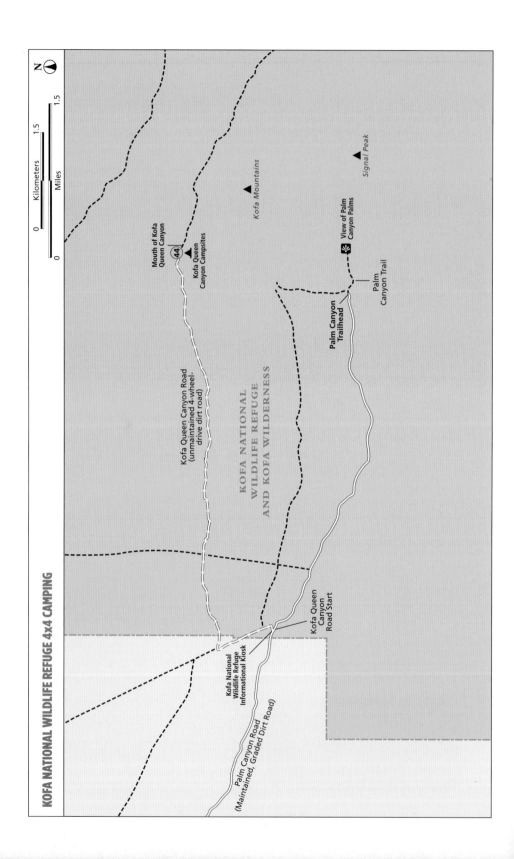

KOFA NATIONAL WILDLIFE REFUGE 4x4 CAMPING

N

0   Kilometers   1.5

0   Miles   1.5

Mouth of Kofa
Queen Canyon

44

Kofa Queen
Canyon Campsites

Kofa Mountains

Signal Peak

View of Palm
Canyon Palms

Palm Canyon
Trailhead

Palm
Canyon Trail

Kofa Queen Canyon Road
(unmaintained 4-wheel-
drive dirt road)

KOFA NATIONAL
WILDLIFE REFUGE
AND KOFA WILDERNESS

Kofa Queen
Canyon Road Start

Kofa National
Wildlife Refuge
Informational Kiosk

Palm Canyon Road
(Maintained, Graded Dirt Road)

Ice-cold moonlight illuminates a family of teddy bear cholla in the Kofa Mountains.

will continue to rotate overhead, revealing more star patterns and shifting the galactic plane into breathtaking arcs of starlight.

The rare Sonoran pronghorn were reintroduced to Kofa National Wildlife Refuge in 2011.

Take advantage of the wonderful dark skies at Kofa, and enhance your viewing experience by using technology. Break out your favorite stargazing app, a pair of binoculars, or your telescope, and be amazed by the discoveries you make. Astrophotography is simply a joy at Kofa due to the dark skies and the many different compositions that are possible with cholla, ocotillo, and the iconic Kofa Mountains. Stay up stargazing for as long as you want, and remember to leave your campsite better than you found it once you're ready to leave. To exit, simply drive southwest on Kofa Queen Canyon Road the same way you came and head west on Palm Canyon Road to US 95.

Side-Hike: The 0.7-mile Palm Canyon Trail, located at the end of Palm Canyon Road, offers a view of rare native California fan palms in a dramatic landscape.

45 ALAMO LAKE STATE PARK CAR CAMPING

Prime dark skies, the blue waters of Alamo Lake, and fuzzy burros browsing the desert make wonderful scenery for car camping at Alamo Lake State Park. Alamo Lake is a hidden gem tucked deep into the heart of Western Arizona's desert backcountry.

Activity: Car camping
Location: Alamo Lake State Park; GPS: N34 13.825' / W113 34.711'
Difficulty: Easy
Seasons/schedule: Open year-round; best in fall, winter, and spring
Timing: No moon to a quarter moon
Fees and permits: Nightly camping fees required; see azstateparks.com/alamo-lake/camping-and-cabins/rv-and-tent-camping for current fees.
Campground contacts: Alamo Lake State Park, PO Box 38, Wenden 85357; (928) 669-2088; azstateparks.com/alamo-lake
Dog-friendly: Yes
Land status: State park
Nearest town: Wenden, Arizona
Suitable camp setups: RVs, trailers, trucks, SUVs, cars, vans, fifth wheels, tents

Maps: Alamo State Park maps available online at azstateparks.com/alamo-lake/explore/maps
Facilities: Picnic tables, fire rings, tent pads, grills; ramadas; pit toilets, flush toilets, running water; water and electrical hookups, blackwater dump station; boat launch ramps
Water availability: Yes
Special considerations: Temperatures can exceed 115°F in summer and be below freezing in winter at night. Venomous reptiles and insects inhabit the area. Campsites are available by reservation or, in some situations, first-come, first-served. Cabins are also available for rent.

FINDING THE CAMPGROUND

From US 60 in Wenden, head north on 2nd Street/Alamo Road for 34 miles. Alamo Road is paved all the way to Alamo Lake State Park. Follow the signs to turn into one of the campground loop roads as you drive down Alamo Road into the park. Campground GPS (visitor center and campground check-in station): N34 13.825' / W113 34.711'

THE ADVENTURE

Alamo Lake can be described as "the middle of nowhere"; however, it's definitely "somewhere" for the stars to shine bright in the sky. Tucked away in the mountains of Western Arizona, Alamo Lake State Park offers boating, fishing, camping, hiking, and premier stargazing opportunities in the darkest sky state park in Arizona. Pitch your tent or park your RV in one of the dozens of beautiful campsites in the saguaro-studded hills overlooking the lake. Some sites offer full RV hookups for electricity and water, but all campsites in the park offer unobstructed views of the dark night sky. Start your adventure from the little Arizona town of Wenden.

From Wenden, head north on 2nd Street/Alamo Road from US 60 for 34 miles through a harsh desert environment of sand and desolate mountains. Alamo Lake will

ALAMO LAKE STATE PARK CAR CAMPING

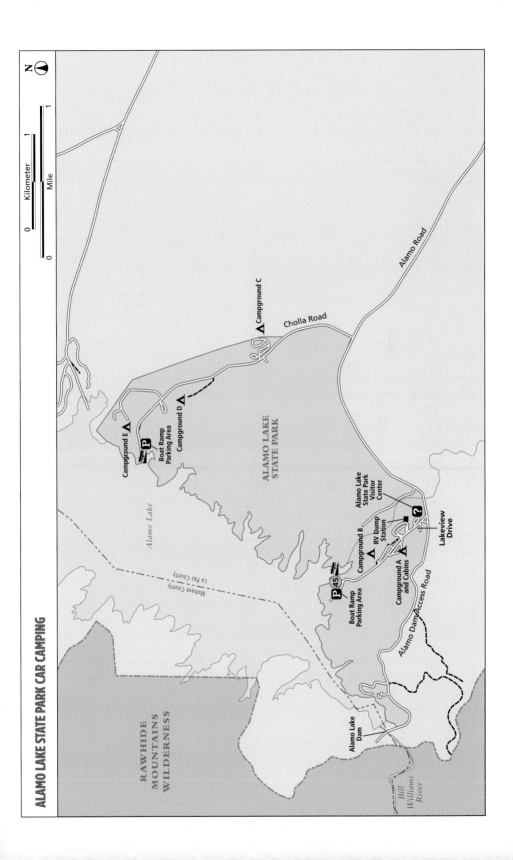

A stargazer looks at the stars of the Orion and Taurus constellations as they set over Alamo Lake.

first appear as a distant patch of blue in a sea of desert. As you approach closer, your view of the lake will grow in the windshield to a large desert oasis for many species of wildlife. The scenic drive through Alamo Lake State Park includes rolling desert hills, desert-grazing burros, and long views across the lake toward Artillery Peak. Follow the signs along Alamo Road to the visitor center to check in for your campsite, and then head to one of several campgrounds in the park.

After setting up camp, take some time to appreciate the landscape around you. Alamo Lake was created as a flood-control project on the Bill Williams River by the US Army Corps of Engineers in 1968. The wild burros that roam the park are descendants of domesticated burros that were used as work animals for miners in the 1800s. As day turns to night at Alamo Lake, you will be treated to skies that have measured "2" on the Bortle scale, the second-darkest skies available in the world. The collection of stars in the sky above Alamo Lake are so bright that details of the Milky Way and deep sky objects are easily visible.

Branches of a bony white plant break the surface of Alamo Lake as thousands of stars hang overhead.

The depth of the dark sky at Alamo Lake is unforgettable and is best enjoyed on a night with no moon. Once your eyes have become fully adjusted to the night sky, notice how the stars over Alamo Lake cast faint shadows on the ground. If you're feeling adventurous, journey down to the boat piers, take a walk along a trail, or walk through the campground loops to see the night sky from different perspectives. Other night activities to enjoy include listening for bats, night fishing, or pointing your telescope at the multitude of astronomical objects above. Enjoy your days camping at Alamo Lake, and be sure to leave your campsite better than you found it.

46 **BURRO CREEK CAMPGROUND CAR CAMPING**

Camp peacefully under dark skies at Burro Creek Campground, a quiet developed campground in Western Arizona's Sonoran Desert featuring the clear perennial waters of Burro Creek.

Activity: Car and RV camping
Location: Burro Creek Campground; GPS: N34 32.300' / W113 26.941'
Difficulty: Easy due to a paved entrance road located near US 93
Seasons/schedule: Open year-round; best in fall, winter, and spring
Timing: Any time; best during no moon to a quarter moon
Fees and permits: Nightly fees required, and some sites are reservable; see blm.gov/visit/burro-creek-campground for current rates.
Campground contacts: Bureau of Land Management, Kingman Field Office, 2755 Mission Blvd., Kingman 86401; (928) 718-3700; blm.gov/office/kingman-field-office
Dog-friendly: Yes, leashed and under control
Land status: Bureau of Land Management lands
Nearest town: Wikieup, Arizona
Suitable camp setups: Class A RVs, fifth wheels, cars, trucks, tents

Maps: BLM map available online at blm.gov/visit/burro-creek-campground
Facilities: Fire rings, grills, shaded tables at campsites; flush toilets, drinking water stations (no water hookups), trash cans; RV sewage dump station; fee pay station
Water availability: Yes; drinking water available at the campground
Special considerations: Winter overnight temperatures can be below freezing, and summer daytime temperatures can exceed 115°F. Flash flooding can occur at any time of the year on Burro Creek. Wildlife to be cautious of include bees, venomous reptiles and insects, cattle, wild burros, wild horses, and raccoons. Campers with large RVs should reach out to the Kingman Field Office about recommended campsites.
Other: Some campsites are offered on a first-come, first-served basis; others are reservable.

FINDING THE CAMPGROUND

From US 93, near milepost 140, take Burro Creek Campground Road for 1.25 miles to the campground, on the right just before a bridge. Campground GPS: N34 32.300' / W113 26.941'

THE ADVENTURE

Easy to miss but hard to forget, Burro Creek Campground provides campers with fantastic views of the stars at night and a place to cool off during the day. Located halfway between Phoenix and Las Vegas, Burro Creek is a perennial stream that cuts deep through canyons of volcanic rock, creating swimming holes and a refuge for wildlife. The remote nature of Burro Creek Campground makes it an ideal place to camp and stargaze with skies untainted by light pollution. Nocturnal wildlife viewing for bats, owls, and frogs will also keep you entertained as you spend the night at camp. Start your campground adventure by taking the Burro Creek Campground Road exit off US 93.

Follow Burro Creek Campground Road 1.25 miles to the Burro Creek Campground, marked by a large BLM sign. Proceed to your reserved campsite or first-come,

Moonlight bathes Joshua trees and saguaros at the desert garden of Burro Creek Campground.

DESERT GARDEN

first-served site and find what works for your camping setup. Once you are settled in and have taken care of any camping fees, be sure to explore the wonderful area around the campground. Near the campground entrance is the day-use area, with access to Burro

LOOK UP
Find the handle of the Big Dipper and look closely at the second star from the end, Mizar, to find its visual double Alcor. Ancient cultures used this visual double as an eye test.

BURRO CREEK CAMPGROUND CAR CAMPING

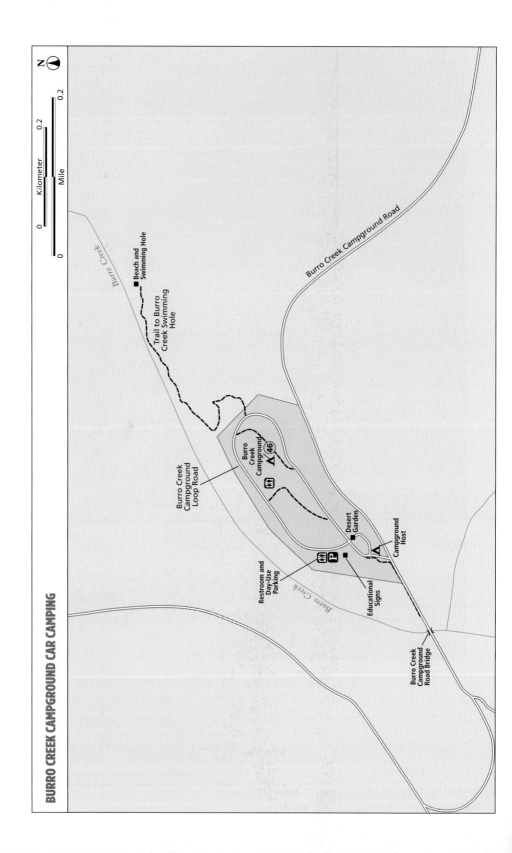

Burro Creek Bridge spans a deep canyon, and stars reflect in a calm pool on the banks of Burro Creek.

Creek, educational signs, the desert garden, and a bridge with great views of the Burro Creek canyon.

On the northeastern side of the campground is a short trail leading down to the flood banks of the creek, where many rounded river rocks can be found. Continuing east along the creek bed for 0.2 mile will eventually bring you to a small beach with a fantastic view of the Burro Creek bridge and a small swimming hole. During the day, many species of birds can be found around the campground, such as great blue herons and agile swifts darting through the air to catch bugs. As the sun sets on the area, keep an eye out for bats and owls taking to the skies.

Night will introduce itself slowly at Burro Creek, starting with one star and expanding to thousands more within an hour of sunset. The campground is situated in an open area, so opportunities for observing the starry night sky are plentiful. Enhance your experience by taking a peaceful walk around the 0.5-mile campground loop road, relaxing at the desert garden, visiting the creek banks, or stargazing from the small bridge near the campground entrance. While night hiking, listen for nocturnal crickets and frogs along the banks of the creek, and remember that you are just a visitor to their home. Finish up your night with a nice meal by the campfire, and be sure to leave your campsite better than you found it when it's time to go home.

LOOK UP

Navajo legend says that Polaris represents a fire in a hogan, a traditional Navajo dwelling.

Southwestern Native American tribes have a legend that the black pinacate beetle/stink bug was responsible for placing all the stars in the heavens. The beetle spilled the stars across the sky, forming the Milky Way, and ever since it has ducked its head in shame whenever a person or animal gets close.

47 ARIZONA HOT SPRINGS SOAK AND NIGHT HIKE

Take a hike through a dramatic canyon to the Arizona Hot Springs, where you can soak in the Earth's heat and enjoy views of the cool night sky.

Activity: Night hiking and hot spring soaking
Location: Arizona Hot Springs; GPS: N35 57.634' / W114 43.556'
Start: Arizona Hot Springs Trailhead; GPS: N35 58.808' / W114 41.864'
Elevation gain: 894 feet
Distance: 6.8 miles out and back
Difficulty: Moderate due to short, rocky scrambles and a ladder climb
Hiking time: About 4 hours
Seasons/schedule: Best in winter, open generally from Oct to May
Timing: No moon to a quarter moon
Fees and permits: None
Trail contacts: Lake Mead National Recreation Area, 601 Nevada Way, Boulder City, NV 89005; (702) 293-8990; nps.gov/lake/index.htm
Dog-friendly: No, due to rock scrambles and a ladder climb
Trail surface: Dirt and rock
Land status: National recreation area
Nearest town: Boulder City, Nevada
Other trail users: Backpackers, photographers, trail runners
Maps: Lake Mead National Recreation Area maps available online at nps.gov/lake/planyourvisit/maps.htm
Water availability: Water available in the Colorado River; however, it should be filtered before using.
Special considerations: The hot springs become increasingly hot as you move up through the series of four pools. Naegleria fowleri, a rare, potentially lethal amoeba, may be present in the hot springs. However, it can only enter the body through the nose, so keep your head above water. Late springtime temperatures can exceed 100°F on this hike, so be very cautious if hiking while temperatures are high. The hot springs trail is closed generally May through Sept due to extreme heat, and it is a felony to trespass onto the trail during these months. Spiders, scorpions, and venomous reptiles may be present along the hike. Storms can cause flash flooding at any time in both Arizona Hot Springs Canyon and White Rock Canyon. Clothing is optional at the hot springs.
Other: Camping is available for kayakers and backpackers along the Colorado River near the mouth of White Rock and Arizona Hot Springs Canyons. A pair of pit toilets are available at the end of the Arizona Hot Springs Canyon wash, about 1,000 feet from the springs. Another way to get to the hot springs is the Arizona Hot Springs Trail, which approaches the hot springs from upstream.

FINDING THE TRAILHEAD
From US 93, about 4.2 miles south of Hoover Dam, take the exit for the White Rock Canyon/Arizona Hot Springs Trailhead toward the east. The Arizona Hot Springs Trail begins on the eastern side of the parking lot, near an informational kiosk with a map. Trailhead GPS: N35 58.808' / W114 41.864'

LOOK UP
Sirius, 8.6 light-years away, is twice the mass of the sun and is the brightest star in the night sky.

View of the warm water and the Pleiades through the Arizona Hot Springs slot canyon.

The mineral-rich waters of the Arizona Hot Springs are heated by the internal heat of the Earth to 111°F and flow at 30 gallons per minute through faults in the slot canyon.

The heat and high mineral content of hot springs can soothe muscles and add minerals to the body through absorption.

ARIZONA HOT SPRINGS SOAK AND NIGHT HIKE

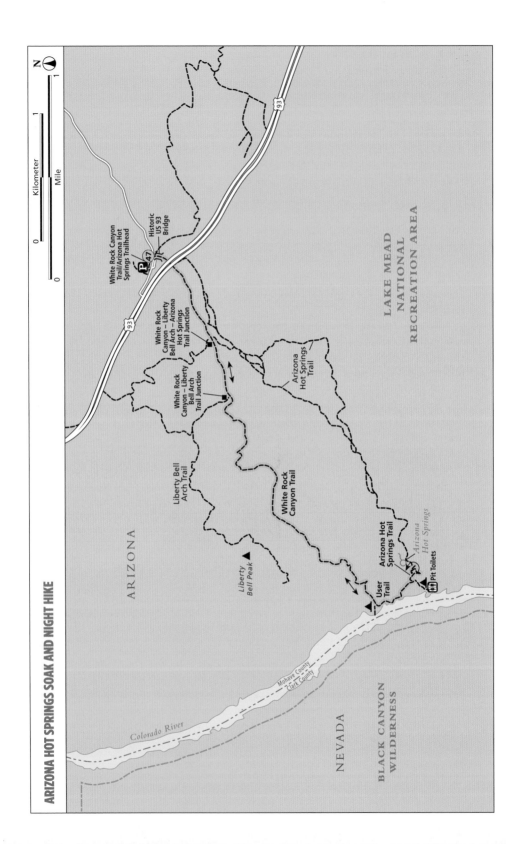

THE ADVENTURE

The Arizona Hot Springs are one of the most striking hot springs to visit in Arizona. Located in a slot canyon just 1,000 feet from the Colorado River, the hot springs have a constant supply of water at a temperature of 111°F. Getting to the Arizona Hot Springs includes a hike through a canyon with imposing cliff walls, followed by a scramble along the rocky shores of the Colorado River, and finally a short slot canyon hike topped off with a ladder climb to the springs. At night the stars have a chance to shine despite light pollution from Las Vegas, 15 miles away. Combine the beauty of the night sky and the warmth of the hot springs by starting your adventure on the White Rock Canyon Trail.

One great way to experience the adventure to the Arizona Hot Springs is by starting an hour or two before sunset to see the terrain before it gets dark. From the Arizona Hot Springs Trailhead, start your hike westward on the White Rock Canyon Trail by going under the US 93 highway bridge. Continue down the wash for about 0.55 mile until you reach a trail junction for the Liberty Bell Arch and Arizona Hot Springs Trails. Head west to continue the White Rock Canyon Trail down the wash into a low canyon. Continue west for 2.45 miles, snaking through a deep canyon all the way to the Colorado River.

White Rock Canyon will open up to the clear, cold waters of the Colorado River, marking the end of the White Rock Canyon Trail. Take a sharp left, following a small user trail for 0.25 mile south, up and down some rocky outcrops along the Colorado River. Views of the Black Canyon along this short user trail are gorgeous, but watch your footing around the sharp drop-offs. Multiple user trails exist in this area, making navigation challenging at times, but try to follow yellow painted arrows in the rocky sections. Once you reach a small brown trail arrow sign at the top of a steep hill, about 0.25 mile from White Rock Canyon, take the steep trail down the eastern side of the hill for 200 feet into Arizona Hot Springs Canyon.

At the bottom of the steep trail, turn left (north) at the beginning of the trail to the Arizona Hot Springs and start hiking through the tight wash. Water may be flowing in the small slot canyon as you hike roughly 600 feet east, curving around reddish-purple rocks and climbing small waterfalls. At the end of the wash, you will reach a ladder anchored into a waterfall of warm water; this is your ticket to the Arizona Hot Springs. At the foot of the ladder, you will have plenty of space to change shoes or put on a bathing suit. Climb to the top of the ladder and feel the warm water falling over your hands and feet.

Dismount the ladder with care, and step into the relaxing heat of the first of four hot pools in a deep slot canyon. Hop over the sandbag dams to the upper pools for more heat if you can take it, and sit down in the thigh-deep water to just relax. Looking up through the slot canyon will reveal a limited selection of stars to watch as you soak. Take your time at this place; there is no rush to start the hike back to the car or your nearby camp. Once ready to depart, carefully make your way down the metal ladder and hike out through Arizona Hot Springs Canyon.

To see many more stars in the sky, make your way to the Colorado River by taking the same 0.25-mile user trail north you used to get to the hot spring wash. Looking south (downstream) on the Colorado will reveal a pretty dark sky, allowing you to see full constellations and enjoy the peaceful sounds of the river. To return to the trailhead, take the 3-mile hike eastward on the White Rock Canyon Trail on a gentle uphill grade to the east side of the US 93 bridge, where you will climb a hill to the parking lot.

A view of Black Canyon at night on the Colorado River, upstream of the Arizona Hot Springs

MILES AND DIRECTIONS

0.0   Start from the White Rock Canyon/Arizona Hot Springs Trailhead and hike down-hill following the wash west underneath the US 93 bridge for 0.55 mile.

0.55   Meet the Liberty Bell Arch Trail and Arizona Hot Springs Trail junction; continue west on the White Rock Canyon Trail for 2.45 miles to the Colorado River through a deep canyon.

3.0   Reach the Colorado River and take a small user trail south for 0.25 mile through some riparian vegetation and up and down some rocky hills.

3.25   Crest a small hill with a brown trail arrow sign, and descend the eastern side of the hill for 200 feet to the Arizona Hot Springs Canyon wash.

3.3   Turn left (north) and follow the Arizona Hot Springs Canyon wash for 600 feet.

3.4   Arrive at the ladder and climb up to the Arizona Hot Springs. After your soak, return to the White Rock Canyon/Arizona Hot Springs Canyon Trailhead the same way you came.

6.8   Arrive back at the trailhead.

48 LAKE MOHAVE KAYAK CAMPING

Paddle across Lake Mohave's crystal-clear waters and camp out on sandy beaches under quiet starry skies.

Activity: Kayak camping
Location: Lake Mohave; GPS: N35 29.863' / W114 40.654'
Put-in: Cottonwood Cove; GPS: N35 29.620' / W114 41.166'
Takeout: Cottonwood Cove Boat Ramp; GPS: N35 29.550' / W114 41.132'
Distance: 2.75-mile loop
Paddling time: About 2 hours
Difficulty: Easy due to flat water and easy access
Waterway type: Lake
Land status: National recreation area
Park contact: Lake Mead National Recreation Area, 601 Nevada Way, Boulder City, NV 89005; (702) 293-8990; nps.gov/lake/index.htm
Nearest town: Searchlight, Nevada
Seasons/schedule: Open year-round; best in fall, winter, and spring
Timing: No moon to a quarter moon
Fees and permits: Entrance fees required for Lake Mead National Recreation Area; see nps.gov/lake/planyourvisit/fees.htm for current fees.
Boats used: Kayaks, paddleboards, canoes
Maps: Lake Mohave maps available online at nps.gov/lake/planyourvisit/maps.htm

PUT-IN/TAKEOUT INFORMATION

To get to Cottonwood Cove, head east on Cottonwood Cove Road for 13.5 miles from Searchlight, Nevada. Turn left into the Cottonwood Cove boat ramp parking lot, and park your vehicle overnight. Put in your boat less than 50 feet east at the Cottonwood Cove boat ramp or on the sandy beach of Cottonwood Cove. Take out your boat from the lake on the Cottonwood Cove boat ramp or at the beach.

OVERVIEW

Surrounded by stark Mojave Desert, Lake Mohave is a sparkling blue oasis in Western Arizona. Created in 1951 by Davis Dam on the Colorado River near Laughlin and Bullhead City, this quiet desert lake features sandy coves, wild burros, and dark skies miles away from light pollution. Warm, clear water paired with soft sand make Lake Mohave an ideal place to swim in early fall and late spring. Little to no current creates a pleasant paddling experience for those wanting to try kayak camping for the first time. For this adventure, you will paddle out of Cottonwood Cove, Nevada, and cross Lake Mohave to the sandy shores on the Arizona side for camping.

Cottonwood Cove is a local favorite in southern Nevada, which means the cove will be busy on weekends, especially in the warm months. The Arizona side across from Cottonwood Cove is very quiet, and at night nearly all boats go away, allowing a wonderfully quiet lakeside camping experience. Arrive any time of day, and after prepping your boat, dip your paddles in and head eastward. Leave the swimmers behind and head north out of Cottonwood Cove, gliding through the still water along the western shore of the lake. About 0.7 mile up the western shore near a small peninsula, carefully cross Lake Mohave 0.45 mile eastward to the Arizona side of the lake.

The core of the Milky Way rises over the sandy shores of Lake Mohave.

On the Arizona side of the lake, cruise along the shore, heading south for 0.63 mile until you reach Williams Cove, directly across from Cottonwood Cove. Excellent sandy campsites are just uphill from the shore, north of a large tamarisk tree. Additional campsites are available further south on the Arizona side of the lake, so explore until you find one that suits you. After skidding to a halt on a shore of your choice, unload your gear and enjoy some daytime activities like swimming, fishing, or simply tanning in the sun. As night settles in over Lake Mohave, note how calm the water becomes and the distant sounds of burros braying in the distance.

Enjoy some stargazing at the water's edge, taking in the sounds of gentle wavelets lapping the shore as thousands of stars spread across the sky. Only a small light dome from Laughlin to the southeast and a distant light pollution bubble to the northwest over Las Vegas will slightly limit your views of the sky. Listen for bats skimming the skies for insects, and make sure to look all around for shooting stars. When it comes time to leave your campsite, pack up your gear and simply cross Lake Mohave westward for 0.97 mile to Cottonwood Cove. Return to the Cottonwood Cove boat ramp or the sandy beach you launched from to take out your boat.

> **LOOK UP**
> We can only see half of the Milky Way from Earth because of gas and dust blocking our view of the entire galaxy.

> **KAYAK CAMPING TIP**
> Pack the heaviest items to the center of the kayak to keep the boat balanced and tracking straight through the water.

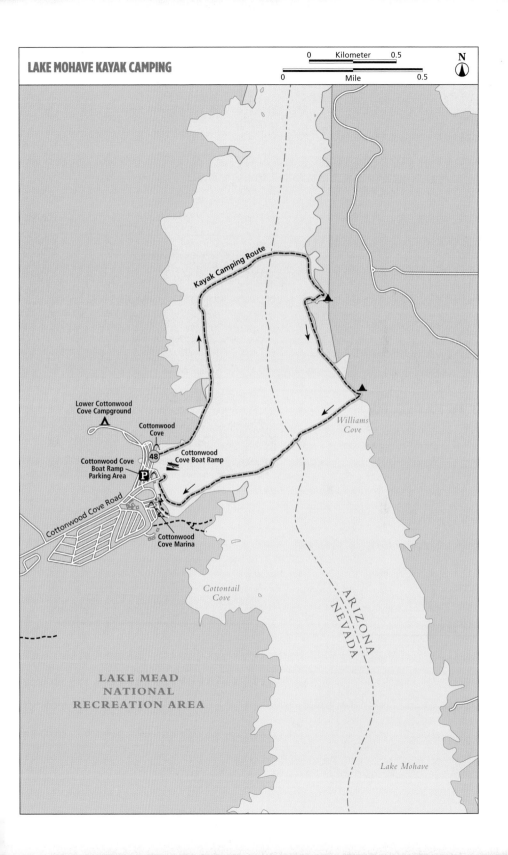

LAKE MOHAVE KAYAK CAMPING

N

0   Kilometer   0.5

0   Mile   0.5

Kayak Camping Route

Lower Cottonwood
Cove Campground

Cottonwood
Cove

Cottonwood Cove
Boat Ramp
Parking Area

48

Cottonwood
Cove Boat Ramp

P

Williams
Cove

Cottonwood Cove Road

Cottonwood
Cove Marina

Cottontail
Cove

ARIZONA
NEVADA

LAKE MEAD
NATIONAL
RECREATION AREA

Lake Mohave

Tamarisk branches reach into the starry skies over Western Arizona's Lake Mohave

THE PADDLING

Overall, when winds are calm, Lake Mohave is calm with small waves and pleasant paddling over extremely clear water. Boat traffic can be heavy across the lake, presenting the greatest hazard to boaters. When winds are active, they are channeled in a north or south direction across the lake, depending on the season. In windy conditions, Lake Mohave can become very wavy and dangerous to paddle across, with waves greater than 3 feet in height. Winds are most prevalent during spring and summer monsoon storms.

MILES AND DIRECTIONS

0.0 Start from Cottonwood Cove and exit the cove, heading north for 0.7 mile along the western side of Lake Mohave.

0.7 Near a peninsula, cross Lake Mohave heading east for 0.45 mile to the Arizona side of the lake.

1.15 Head south along the Arizona side of Lake Mohave for 0.63 mile and find a sandy cove or area to camp.

1.78 After you have finished camping, pack up and head westward for 0.97 mile toward the Cottonwood Cove boat ramp on the Nevada side of the lake.

2.75 Arrive at the takeout point.

> **LOOK UP**
> Most meteors become visible about 60 miles from the Earth's surface.

49 HUALAPAI MOUNTAIN PARK CAMPING

Snuggle up in a cabin, park the RV, or simply pop a tent in Western Arizona's highest mountains at Hualapai Mountain Park. Located a short 20-minute drive from downtown Kingman, the Hualapai Mountains are an easy getaway, allowing you to enjoy its starry skies and scenic forests.

Activity: Car camping or cabin rental

Location: Hualapai Mountain Park, 6250 Hualapai Mountain Rd., Kingman

Difficulty: Easy

Seasons/schedule: The park, cabins, and some tent campsites closer to the ranger station are open year-round. RV sites and campsites down dirt roads are open May 1–Oct 31. Best in spring, summer, and fall.

Timing: No moon to a quarter moon

Fees and permits: Nightly camping or cabin-rental fees required; see parks.mohave.gov/parks/hualapai-mountain-park/fees/?v=2 for current fees.

Campground contacts: Mohave County Parks, Hualapai Mountain Park, PO Box 7000, Kingman 86402; (928) 681-5700; parks.mohave.gov/parks/hualapai-mountain-park/

Dog-friendly: Yes, leashed and under control. Daily pet fees and rabies immunization are required; see "Frequently Asked Questions" page at parks.mohave.gov/parks/faq/.

Land status: County park

Nearest town: Kingman, Arizona

Suitable camp setups: RVs, cars, trucks, SUVs, trailers, tents, vans

Maps: Trail map available online at parks.mohave.gov/parks/hualapai-mountain-park/trails/

Facilities: Fire rings, grills, picnic tables; pit toilets, flush toilets, showers, drinking water, trash services; full RV hookups (water, electricity, and sewer); cabins; playgrounds

Water availability: Yes, for RV hookups; running sinks and drinking water spigots

Special considerations: Elk, bears, and mountain lions inhabit the Hualapai Mountains; be cautious. Some campsites are accessed by dirt roads, which may be impassable when wet or when snow is present. Many campsites are located in the trees, and some stargazers will need to find open space to stargaze. Store food responsibly, and avoid feeding wildlife like bears and squirrels. Lightning and wildfires are a danger in the forest during the fire season. Campfire restrictions may be in place, so call the ranger station to check current restrictions. Cell-phone coverage is limited at the park.

FINDING THE CAMPGROUND

From Kingman, head southeast on Hualapai Mountain Road for 11.4 miles. Check in at the Hualapai Mountain Park entrance and ranger station on the right. The ranger station is a large wooden two-story building. Campground GPS: N35 05.941' / W113 53.086'

"Hualapai" means "people of the tall pines," referring to ancestors of the modern-day Hualapai tribe who once inhabited these mountains.

The core of the Milky Way shines over the ridgeline of the Hualapai Mountains in Western Arizona.

THE ADVENTURE

The Hualapai Mountains, just southeast of Kingman, Arizona, are one of Western Arizona's best-kept secrets. Many people drive right past the Hualapai Mountains on I-40, just north of the range, but have no idea of the beauty of this sky island. Rocky peaks covered in a forest of ponderosa pine provide a scenic backdrop for huge vultures flying through the sky and graceful elk that browse the forest. The high-elevation nature of these mountains along with their distance from heavy light pollution make it an excellent place to stargaze in Western Arizona. Abundant camping opportunities can be found in the scenic heart of the mountains at Hualapai Mountain Park, including cabin rentals, full RV hookups, and tent camping.

The cruise up Hualapai Mountain Road from Kingman will make you wonder why you haven't come up before. After getting oriented at the ranger station, try to find a campsite that has open views of the sky for stargazing later on. The campsites on the northeastern and southwestern sides of the campground generally have better sky viewing. Upon arrival at your campsite or cabin, you'll notice it's at least 10 to 20 degrees cooler than the Mojave Desert down the mountain. Daytime activities you can enjoy include hiking the forest trails from the main trailhead, picnicking, birding, or simply hanging out in the cool mountain air.

Enjoy a spectacular sunset that silhouettes the trees against a purple sky. One by one, stars will break through the darkness, revealing Hualapai Mountain Park's other side. The disc of the Milky Way is so bright here, you can clearly see lanes of interstellar dust and the fainter stars of your favorite constellations. If you don't have a great view of the stars from camp, take a short walk down the campground roads until you find a nice spot to see the sky. A great place to see a sky full of stars is the OHV Trailhead parking lot, on the north side of the campground.

HUALAPAI MOUNTAIN PARK CAMPING

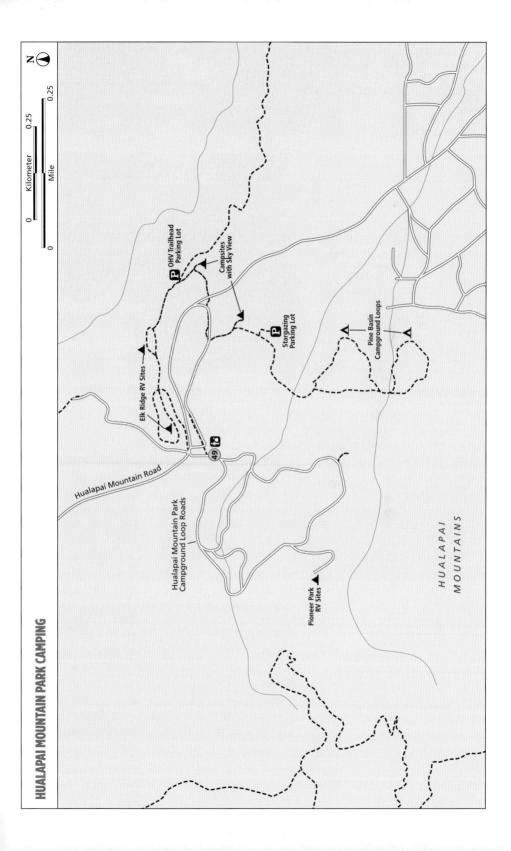

OHV Trailhead Parking Lot

Campsites with Sky View

Stargazing Parking Lot

Elk Ridge RV Sites

Pine Basin Campground Loops

Hualapai Mountain Road

Hualapai Mountain Park Campground Loop Roads

Pioneer Park RV Sites

HUALAPAI MOUNTAINS

N

Kilometer
0   0.25   0.25

Mile
0   0.25

A fully grown ponderosa pine touches the summer triangle asterism in the night skies over Hualapai Mountain Park.

Try waking up at least one different time of the night to see the changes to the night sky. Even a single night at Hualapai Mountain Park will be an unforgettable experience. In the morning, enjoy the crisp air and start another day in the Hualapai Mountains. Keep an eye out for wildlife in the morning, like hungry elk roaming the campground or woodpeckers chatting in a tree. Be sure to clean up your campsite and make sure your campfire is dead out before leaving this special place.

LOOK UP
Mars, the fourth planet from the sun, has a maximum recorded temperature of 86°F. A year on Mars is 687 Earth days long. Mars has only one-tenth of the mass of Earth, and if you were standing on Mars, you would experience 62.5 percent less gravity than on Earth.

50 TOPOCK GORGE MOONLIT KAYAKING

Under brilliant moonlight, kayak through Topock Gorge, a dramatic canyon on the Colorado River within Havasu National Wildlife Refuge. Experience nocturnal wildlife like bats and beavers while you paddle through waters so glassy, it feels like kayaking on a mirror.

Activity: Night kayaking

Location: Topock Gorge; GPS: N34 40.144' / W114 27.067'

Put-in: Moabi Regional Park Boat Launch, 100 Park Moabi Rd., Needles, California; GPS: N34 43.728' / W114 30.666'

Takeout: Castle Rock Bay; GPS: N34 33.904' / W114 23.564'

Distance: 16.45 miles point to point

Paddling time: 7–8 hours

Difficulty: Moderate to hard due to long miles of paddling, a slow current, and required nighttime navigation skills

Rapids: None

Waterway type: River and lake

Current: Slow to none in some areas

River gradient: 3 inches of descent per mile

Land status: Waters of the United States and national wildlife refuge

Park contacts: Havasu National Wildlife Refuge (NWR), 317 Mesquite Ave., Needles, CA 92363-2649; (760) 326-3853; fws.gov/refuge/havasu

Moabi Regional Park, 100 Park Moabi Rd., Needles, CA 92363; (760) 326-9000; parks.sbcounty.gov/park/moabi-regional-park/

Nearest towns: Needles, California; Lake Havasu City, Arizona

Seasons/schedule: Open year-round; best in warmer seasons

Timing: Kayak with a waxing quarter moon to a full moon to have plenty of moonlight. Start the kayaking trip at least 2 hours before sunset.

Fees and permits: Moabi Regional Park requires a day-use and overnight vehicle parking fee; see parks.sbcounty.gov/park/moabi-regional-park/ for current fees. No fees or permits required for Havasu NWR.

Boats used: Kayaks, canoes, paddleboards

Maps: Moabi Regional Park map available online at piratecoveresort .com/wp-content/uploads/2021/03/map-1.jpg. Havasu NWR map available at fws.gov/refuge/havasu/map.

PUT-IN/TAKEOUT INFORMATION

Start your kayaking adventure at the Moabi Regional Park boat launch (GPS: N34 43.728' / W114 30.666'). To get to Moabi Regional Park from Lake Havasu City, take AZ 95 North for 18 miles then head west on I-40 for 10.6 miles to the Park Moabi Road/Historic Route 66 exit. Take Park Moabi Road north for 0.6 mile; turn left into the park entrance to launch your boat at the boat ramp. Overnight vehicle parking at Moabi Regional Park must be at the overflow parking lot (GPS: N34 43.595' / W114 30.688'), located across from the visitor services desk. For the takeout at Castle Rock Bay, organize a pickup or stage a vehicle at the parking lot just 730 feet northeast of the shore (GPS: N34 33.944' / W114 23.553'). To get to Castle Rock Bay from Lake Havasu City, head north on AZ 95 for 6 miles and turn left onto London Bridge Road/Crystal Avenue. Head

> **LOOK UP**
> The moon is tidally locked to the Earth, meaning the same side of the moon, known as the near side, always faces the Earth.

southwest on London Bridge Road for 0.7 mile, then turn right and head west on Fathom Drive for 0.7 mile. Turn left and head south on Reef Drive for 0.1 mile; turn right onto Vista Drive and head west for 0.2 mile. Follow the sign for Castle Rock Bay; turn left onto Castle Rock Bay Road and travel southwest down the dirt road for 0.3 mile to the Castle Rock Bay parking lot. Shuttles and kayak rentals are available from Lake Havasu City by Western Arizona Canoe and Kayak Outfitters (WACKO). See their website at azwacko.com/services, or call (928) 855-6414.

OVERVIEW

Havasu National Wildlife Refuge shelters one of the last untouched sections of the Lower Colorado River at Topock Gorge, north of Lake Havasu. Here, jagged desert peaks cut into the skies over Arizona's wet border with California. During the day, Topock Gorge is a popular boating destination; however, at night you can have the whole place to yourself for a moonlit kayaking adventure. Enjoy the sights and sounds of nocturnal wildlife, like beavers swimming across sandy coves, bats circling the skies, and toads singing into the night sky. On this adventure, have Topock Gorge all to yourself for 16 miles of unforgettable adventure under the moon's magical light.

Begin your adventure on the California side of the river from Moabi Regional Park's boat launch 2 hours before sunset. Kayak east through the canal to the Colorado River

A moonlit sandy cove at Topock Gorge reflects the stars and an assortment of desert cliffs.

The Milky Way sets over Castle Rock Bay on Lake Havasu.

0.82 mile ahead, then turn right and head south on the Colorado River. At the river you'll notice a small difference in the current pushing you southward and waves from the boats cruising up and down the river. Follow the river another 1.4 miles south then east under the huge bridges for the train, freeway, and pipelines to reach a calm, no-wake zone of the river. Continue 0.7 mile past the bridges and follow the river south to begin a peaceful paddle through Topock Gorge.

Dramatic desert peaks lit by the sunset frame the river as you kayak south for 3.55 miles into Havasu National Wildlife Refuge. The sun's influence on the sky wanes with fading twilight as the moon begins to dominate, adding a magical blue-white glow to the landscape. Take a break at one of the sandy coves and take in the mysterious landscape, silently bathed in moonlight under a sky full of stars. After feeling rippled sand under your toes, continue south for 0.9 mile to curve around the Devil's Elbow, a bend in the river surrounded by tall red cliffs. Once you pass through Devil's Elbow, continue paddling in the moonlight south for 4.7 miles and enjoy the sounds of nocturnal toads croaking in the marshes. A calm night will render a smooth, mirrorlike surface on the river that will feel like you're floating through space.

On approach to Blankenship Bend, you'll come across a large, shallow sandbar illuminated by moonlight. Navigate cautiously around the sandbar, avoiding dead trees and driftwood, and then follow Blankenship Bend west to southeast for 0.87 mile. After going around the final bend, stick to the left and follow the eastern shore of the river south for 2.6 miles to a canal that will connect you to Castle Rock Bay. A small island

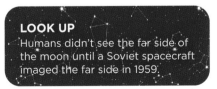

LOOK UP
Humans didn't see the far side of the moon until a Soviet spacecraft imaged the far side in 1959.

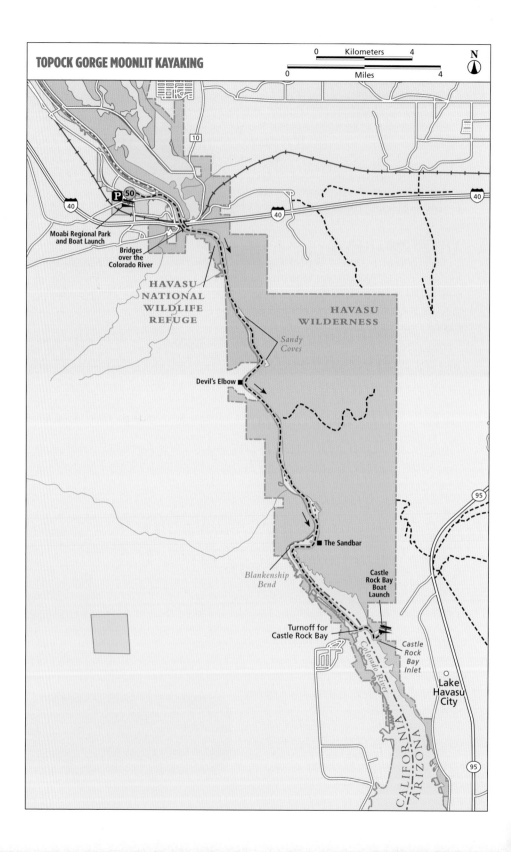

TOPOCK GORGE MOONLIT KAYAKING

0 Kilometers 4

0 Miles 4

N

Moabi Regional Park
and Boat Launch

Bridges
over the
Colorado River

HAVASU
NATIONAL
WILDLIFE
REFUGE

HAVASU
WILDERNESS

Sandy
Coves

Devil's Elbow

The Sandbar

Blankenship
Bend

Castle
Rock Bay
Boat
Launch

Turnoff for
Castle Rock Bay

Castle
Rock
Bay
Inlet

Lake
Havasu
City

Colorado River

CALIFORNIA
ARIZONA

on the east side of the river with a sign posted on top marks the fork in the river where you turn left and head down the channel toward Castle Rock Bay for 0.5 mile. With your headlamp, stick to the east (left) side of the channel and look closely for a small, 6-foot-wide inlet with a clear watery path in the reeds east to Castle Rock Bay. Paddle your way east through the reeds for 0.2 mile to reach wide-open Castle Rock Bay, where you'll head straight east for 0.21 mile to the shoreline under Castle Rock. Complete your adventure under the moon with a final skid to the shore and a 730-foot portage of your boat northeast around Castle Rock to the parking lot and your vehicle.

THE PADDLING

Paddlers will start north of Topock Gorge and head south, following the Colorado River's slow current. As you get closer to Lake Havasu, the current slows significantly and you will be doing most of the work to move your watercraft. Bring a strong headlamp so you can see potential hazards in the river and especially for locating the turns you need to make into Castle Rock Bay.

MILES AND DIRECTIONS

0.0   Start from the Moabi Regional Park boat launch and head east through the channel for 0.82 mile to the Colorado River main channel.

0.82   Turn right into the main channel of the Colorado River and follow the main channel generally south for 14.68 miles.

15.5   On the east side of the river, reach a fork in the river marked by a tan island with a sign on top; turn left, heading east then south for 0.54 mile toward the Castle Rock Bay inlet.

16.04   Reach a 6-foot-wide inlet on the southwestern corner of Castle Rock Bay; head east into the bay for 0.2 mile.

16.24   Come out of the reeds and head straight east for 0.21 mile toward the shoreline under Castle Rock.

16.45   Arrive at Castle Rock Bay. Portage your watercraft 730 feet northeast to the Castle Rock Bay parking lot to complete your adventure.

Thousands of stars silhouette the elegant
granite dells of Watson Lake near Prescott.

GLOSSARY

Aperture: A dilating hole inside of a lens that controls how much light passes through the lens into a camera; denoted by an "f-stop" number such as f/2.8.

Artificial light: Light that is created, directed, or used by humans for any purpose.

Asterism: A pattern of stars that is not a constellation itself. Asterisms can be a piece of a constellation or connect multiple constellations. Examples include the Big Dipper and the Sagittarius Teapot.

Comet: An icy object in space that develops a long tail of ionized material and dust when passing near the sun.

Constellation: A group of stars that form a particular shape and often has roots in a particular culture's mythology. Constellation patterns differ among cultures.

Dark skies: Night skies free, or at least relatively free, of light pollution.

Galaxy: A very large group of stars in the universe containing millions to trillions of stars, such as the Andromeda galaxy or Earth's own Milky Way.

Globular star cluster: Clusters of tens of thousands to millions of stars that are tightly bound by their own collective gravity. Globular clusters are found in all types of galaxies and typically contain older, redder stars.

International Dark-Sky Association (IDA): Headquartered in Tucson, the International Dark-Sky Association advocates for dark skies by certifying International Dark Sky Parks and Communities. The IDA also provides tools and guidance to the world on how to limit or eliminate harmful light pollution.

International Dark Sky Communities: Legally organized cities and towns that adopt quality outdoor lighting ordinances and engage in public outreach programs to teach citizens about the night sky.

International Dark Sky Parks: Publicly or privately owned spaces protected for natural conservation that implement good outdoor lighting and provide visitors with dark sky programs.

International Dark Sky Places Conservation Program (IDSP): An IDA program founded in 2001 that recognizes and promotes excellent stewardship of the night sky.

International Dark Sky Reserves: Dark Sky Reserves are made up of a dark "core" zone surrounded by populated areas that have enacted policy controls to protect the darkness of the core region.

International Dark Sky Sanctuaries: The darkest and most remote places in the world that have a fragile conservation state.

ISO: A camera sensor's sensitivity to light. Higher ISO numbers indicate higher sensitivities to light.

Light pollution: Any adverse effect or impact attributable to artificial light at night.

Light-year: The distance light travels through space in one year at a constant speed of 186,000 miles per second.

Lunar eclipse: When the moon passes into the Earth's shadow, known as the umbra, and dims. Lunar eclipses can be partial or total in nature. A total lunar eclipse, also known as a "blood moon," occurs when the moon totally passes into the Earth's shadow, causing a red glow on the moon's surface. A partial lunar eclipse occurs when the moon passes through the Earth's lighter shadow, known as the penumbra.

Meteor: A piece of rock or debris that burns brightly in the sky as it falls into Earth's atmosphere from space.

Nebula: A space cloud of dust or gas, such as the Orion Nebula.

Open star cluster: Loosely bound groups of tens to hundreds of stars that are found in spiral and irregular galaxies.

Penumbra: A lighter shadow projected into space from Earth. Partial lunar eclipses occur when the moon crosses through the penumbra.

Shutter speed: The speed that a camera captures a photo. Shorter shutter speeds like 1/400th of a second let less light into the camera than longer shutter speeds, such as 4 seconds.

Umbra: The Earth's shadow that extends from the dark side of the Earth into space like a cone. The umbra can be seen as a round shadow moving across the moon during a lunar eclipse.

Urban Night Sky Places: Sites near, or surrounded by, large urban areas whose planning and design promote authentic nighttime experiences despite significant light pollution and that otherwise do not qualify for designation within any other IDSP category.

Waning moon: A moon that gets progressively dimmer every night in a lunar cycle after the full moon.

Waxing moon: A moon that gets progressively brighter every night in the lunar cycle before the full moon.

Zenith: The highest point in the sky vertically above the observer.

Zodiacal light: A band of light in the night sky; thought to be reflected sunlight from leftover interstellar dust in the solar system. Zodiacal light is best observed in fall and spring after sunset or before sunrise.

REFERENCES

"10 Crazy Facts You Didn't Know about Space." Arizona State University, November 25, 2020. childwellbeing.asu.edu/SpaceFacts.

"13 Things You Didn't Know about Grand Canyon National Park." US Department of the Interior, September 29, 2021. https://www.doi.gov/blog/13-things-you-didnt-know-about-grand-canyon-national-park.

"About Dark Skies." Oracle State Park. Arizona State Parks. Accessed February 14, 2022. https://azstateparks.com/oracle/dark-skies/about-dark-skies.

"About the Hualapai Tribe." The Hualapai Tribe Website. Accessed September 12, 2022. https://hualapai-nsn.gov/about-2/.

"About Tohono O'odham Nation." Tohono O'odham Nation, October 31, 2016. http://www.tonation-nsn.gov/about-tohono-oodham-nation/.

"Alamo Lake State Park." Wikipedia, January 29, 2022. https://en.wikipedia.org/wiki/Alamo_Lake_State_Park.

Alma de Sedona Inn. "Sedona's Significance to the Native Peoples of Arizona," February 25, 2019. https://www.almadesedona.com/blog/sedonas-significance-to-the-native-peoples-of-arizona.

"The Ancestral Sonoran Desert People." National Park Service. US Department of the Interior, February 10, 2021. https://www.nps.gov/cagr/learn/historyculture/the-ancestral-sonoran-desert-people.htm.

"Andromeda—Milky Way Collision." Wikipedia, October 7, 2014. https://en.wikipedia.org/wiki/Andromeda%E2%80%93Milky_Way_collision.

"Antares." Wikipedia, May 22, 2016. https://en.wikipedia.org/wiki/Antares.

"Apache-Sitgreaves National Forests—Special Places." Accessed September 6, 2022. https://www.fs.usda.gov/attmain/asnf/specialplaces.

"Arizona Hot Spring Trail." National Park Service. US Department of the Interior, September 2, 2020. https://www.nps.gov/lake/planyourvisit/arizona-hot-spring-trail.htm.

"Arizona Parks." National Park Service. US Department of the Interior. Accessed November 30, 2021. https://www.nps.gov/orgs/1758/arizona-parks.htm.

Arizona—Sonora Desert Museum. "Sonoran Desert—Sonoran Desert Region." Accessed October 1, 2022. https://www.desertmuseum.org/desert/sonora.php.

"Asterism." *Encyclopedia Britannica*. Accessed October 3, 2022. https://www.britannica.com/science/asterism-astronomy.

"Background Facts on Meteors and Meteor Showers." NASA. Accessed January 26, 2022. https://leonid.arc.nasa.gov/meteor.html.

Barker, Josh. "How Many Man-made Satellites Can You See with the Naked Eye?" Space Answers. Future Publishing Limited Quay House, February 12, 2014. https://www.spaceanswers.com/solar-system/would-i-be-weightless-at-the-earths-centre/.

Barth, Beth. "Spider Rock: Home of Spider Woman." Nizhoni Ranch Gallery, June 26, 2019. https://www.navajorug.com/blogs/news/spider-rock-center-of-the-navajo-nation.

"Beaver—Habitat, Size, & Facts." *Encyclopedia Britannica.* Accessed September 15, 2022. https://www.britannica.com/animal/beaver.

"Become a Tucson Foodie: City of Gastronomy: Visit Tucson." Tucson Convention and Visitors Bureau, 2021. https://www.visittucson.org/restaurants-and-nightlife/city-of-gastronomy/.

"Bellatrix (γ Orionis): Facts, Information, History, & Definition." The Nine Planets, January 20, 2020. https://nineplanets.org/bellatrix-%CE%B3-orionis/#:~:text=Bellatrix%20is%20a%20massive%20star,stars%20used%20in%20celestial%20navigation.

"Betelgeuse." *Encyclopædia Britannica.* Encyclopædia Britannica, Inc. Accessed April 2, 2022. https://www.britannica.com/place/Betelgeuse-star.

Bikos, Konstantin. "What Is the Penumbra?" Accessed October 3, 2022. https://www.timeanddate.com/eclipse/penumbra-shadow.html.

Britannica Dictionary. "Comet Definition & Meaning." Accessed October 4, 2022. https://www.britannica.com/dictionary/comet.

Britannica Dictionary. "Constellation." Accessed October 3, 2022. https://www.britannica.com/dictionary/constellation.

Britannica Dictionary. "Galaxy Definition & Meaning." Accessed October 4, 2022. https://www.britannica.com/dictionary/galaxy.

Britannica Dictionary. "Meteor Definition & Meaning." Accessed October 3, 2022. https://www.britannica.com/dictionary/meteor.

Britannica Dictionary. "Nebula Definition & Meaning." Accessed October 4, 2022. https://www.britannica.com/dictionary/nebula.

Cain, F. "What Part of the Milky Way Can We See?" *Universe Today*, October 10, 2014. https://www.universetoday.com/115203/what-part-of-the-milky-way-can-we-see/.

"Calculate the Value of Bats," n.d. https://www.fs.usda.gov/Internet/FSE_DOCUMENTS/fseprd476773.pdf.

"Cancer the Crab Zodiac Constellation." Learn the Sky, LLC, March 1, 2018. https://www.learnthesky.com/blog/cancer-the-crab-zodiac-constellation.

Canyon de Chelly National Monument. "History & Culture." Accessed September 28, 2022. https://www.nps.gov/cach/learn/historyculture/index.htm.

"Chiricahua National Monument." National Park Service. US Department of the Interior. Accessed April 2, 2022. https://www.nps.gov/chir/index.htm.

"Cochise." *Encyclopædia Britannica.* Encyclopædia Britannica, Inc. Accessed March 24, 2022. https://www.britannica.com/biography/Cochise-Apache-chief.

"Coconino National Forest—Lava River Cave." USDA Forest Service. Accessed August 12, 2022. https://www.fs.usda.gov/recarea/coconino/recarea/?recid=55122.

"Coconino National Forest—Red Rock–Secret Mountain Wilderness." USDA Forest Service. Accessed July 20, 2022. https://www.fs.usda.gov/recarea/coconino/recarea/?recid=74365.

"Coma Berenices." Wikipedia, February 27, 2014. https://en.wikipedia.org/wiki/Coma_Berenices.

"Coronado National Forest—Hospital Flat Campground." Coronado National Forest. Accessed September 26, 2022. https://www.fs.usda.gov/recarea/coronado/recarea/?recid=25580.

"Coronado National Forest—Treasure Park Group Use Areas." Coronado National Forest. Accessed September 26, 2022. https://www.fs.usda.gov/recarea/coronado/recarea/?recid=80170.

"Culture History of Southern Arizona: American Era." Arizona State Museum. The University of Arizona. Accessed December 1, 2021. https://statemuseum.arizona.edu/online-exhibit/culture-history-southern-arizona/american.

"Culture History of Southern Arizona: Europeans Arrive." Arizona State Museum. The University of Arizona. Accessed December 1, 2021. https://statemuseum.arizona.edu/online-exhibit/culture-history-southern-arizona/europeans.

"Culture History of Southern Arizona: Mexican Era." Arizona State Museum. The University of Arizona. Accessed December 1, 2021. https://statemuseum.arizona.edu/online-exhibit/culture-history-southern-arizona/mexican.

Deziel, Chris. "Native Americans Myths of Ursa Major." Classroom. Leaf Group, June 5, 2020. https://classroom.synonym.com/native-americans-myths-ursa-major-21318.html.

Dictionary.com. "Zenith." Accessed October 4, 2022. https://www.dictionary.com/browse/zenith.

Dobrijevic, Daisy. "Meteor Showers and Shooting Stars: Formation and History." Space, August 11, 2022. https://www.space.com/meteor-showers-shooting-stars.html.

Donahue, Michelle. "80 Percent of Americans Can't See the Milky Way Anymore." National Geographic, June 10, 2016. https://www.nationalgeographic.com/science/article/milky-way-space-science.

Dunbar, Brian. "Interesting Fact of the Month." www.nasa.gov, July 15, 2022. https://www.nasa.gov/ames/spacescience-and-astrobiology/interesting-fact-of-the-month/.

"Earth's Moon." NASA Solar System Exploration, July 2022. https://solarsystem.nasa.gov/moons/earths-moon/overview/#:~:text=Lunar%20Facts-,Facts%20About%20The%20Moon,thin%20atmosphere%20called%20an%20exosphere.

Editors. History.com. "Arizona." HISTORY, August 12, 2022. https://www.history.com/topics/us-states/arizona#:~:text=young%20little%20spring.%E2%80%9D-,Arizona's%20Native%20American%20History,Pueblo%20of%20Zuni%2C%20among%20others.

"Environmental Factors—Glen Canyon National Recreation Area (US National Park Service)." www.nps.gov, February 24, 2020. https://www.nps.gov/glca/learn/nature/environmentalfactors.htm.

ESA/Hubble. "Globular Cluster." Accessed October 4, 2022. https://esahubble.org/wordbank/globular-cluster/.

ESA/Hubble. "Open Cluster." Accessed October 4, 2022. https://esahubble.org/wordbank/open-cluster/.

"Five Things to Know about the Moon—NASA Solar System Exploration." NASA, July 28, 2021. https://solarsystem.nasa.gov/news/1946/five-things-to-know-about-the-moon/.

Garner, Rob. "Messier 4." NASA, October 6, 2017. https://www.nasa.gov/feature/goddard/2017/messier-4.

Gerke, Sarah. "Yavapai Apache." Nature, Culture, and History at the Grand Canyon. Accessed September 30, 2022. https://grcahistory.org/history/native-cultures/yavapai-apache/.

"Golden Gate of the Ecliptic." Wikipedia, August 29, 2021. https://en.wikipedia.org/wiki/Golden_Gate_of_the_Ecliptic.

Gordon, Jonathan, Tim Sharp, and Nola Taylor Tillman. "What Is the Temperature of Mars?" Space.com, January 31, 2022. https://www.space.com/16907-what-is-the-temperature-of-mars.html#:~:text=Meanwhile%2C%20the%20highest%20temperature%20on,Inyo%20County%2C%20California%2C%20USA.

"Grand Canyon National Park." Wikipedia, February 26, 2019. https://en.wikipedia.org/wiki/Grand_Canyon_National_Park.

Gregersen, Erik. "Altair." *Encyclopedia Britannica*. Accessed September 23, 2022. https://www.britannica.com/place/Altair-star.

Hall, Nancy. "The Atmosphere." May 2021. https://www.grc.nasa.gov/www/k-12/airplane/atmosphere.html#:~:text=The%20Earth's%20atmosphere%20is%20an,atmosphere%20is%20about%2060%20miles.

"Historical Timeline Lowell Observatory." lowell.edu, October 18, 2021. https://lowell.edu/discover/historical-timeline/.

"History of Sedona § (2018)." City of Sedona. Accessed September 22, 2022. https://www.sedonaaz.gov/home/showdocument?id=34040.

Howell, Elizabeth, and Scott Dutfield. "Arcturus: Facts about the Bright Red Giant Star." Space.com. Space, February 11, 2022. https://www.space.com/22842-arcturus.html.

"Hualapai Mountains." Wikipedia, July 1, 2006. https://en.wikipedia.org/wiki/Hualapai_Mountains.

"Hualapai Mountain Park History." Accessed September 12, 2022. https://parks.mohave.gov/parks/hualapai-mountain-park/history/.

"Imagine the Universe!" NASA, September 23, 2021. https://imagine.gsfc.nasa.gov/science/objects/stars1.html#:~:text=A%20star%20is%20a%20sphere,be%20applied%20to%20other%20stars.&text=A%20star's%20life%20is%20a%20constant%20struggle%20against%20the%20force%20of%20gravity.

"In Depth—Beyond Our Solar System." NASA Solar System Exploration." solarsystem.nasa.gov. Accessed July 12, 2022. https://solarsystem.nasa.gov/solar-system/beyond/in-depth/#:~:text=The%20Milky%20Way%20zips%20along,revolution%20around%20the%20galactic%20center.

"In Depth—Mars." NASA Solar System Exploration, July 2021. https://solarsystem.nasa.gov/planets/mars/in-depth/.

"In Depth—Jupiter." NASA Solar System Exploration. Accessed September 22, 2022. https://solarsystem.nasa.gov/planets/jupiter/in-depth/.

International Dark-Sky Association. "Human Health," July 2, 2021. https://www.darksky.org/light-pollution/human-health/.

International Dark-Sky Association. "International Dark Sky Places—International Dark-Sky Association," January 14, 2022. https://www.darksky.org/our-work/conservation/idsp/.

International Dark-Sky Association. "Kartchner Caverns State Park (US)," August 18, 2022. https://www.darksky.org/our-work/conservation/idsp/parks/kartchnercaverns/.

"Ironwood Forest National Monument." Bureau of Land Management. US Department of the Interior. Accessed January 25, 2022. https://www.blm.gov/national-conservation-lands/arizona/ironwood.

Kartchner Caverns State Park. "History of Kartchner Caverns State Park." Accessed September 26, 2022. https://azstateparks.com/kartchner/explore/park-history.

Kartchner Caverns State Park. "Science." Accessed September 26, 2022. https://azstate parks.com/kartchner/explore/science.

Klesman, Alison. "In Which Direction Does the Sun Move through the Milky Way?" Astronomy.com, July 2020. https://astronomy.com/magazine/ask-astro/2020/07/in -which-direction-does-the-sun-move-through-the-milky-way.

Lakritz, Talia. "Facts About Outer Space That Will Blow Your Mind." Business Insider, July 2022. https://www.businessinsider.com/things-never-knew-space-facts-2018-4# theres-a-fascinating-reason-why-space-appears-black-12.

"Large Sagittarius Star Cloud." Wikipedia, September 22, 2020. https://en.wikipedia .org/wiki/Large_Sagittarius_Star_Cloud.

"Learn About the Park—Petrified Forest National Park (US National Park Service)." www.nps.gov. Accessed June 28, 2022. https://www.nps.gov/pefo/learn/index.htm.

"'Light Pollution'—The Only Pollution that Costs More to Perpetuate Than to Elimi-nate!" Southern Arizona Chapter of the International Dark-Sky Association, April 8, 2021. https://sa-ida.org.

"Local Astronomy." Tucson Amateur Astronomy Association. Accessed November 30, 2021. http://tucsonastronomy.org/local-astronomy/.

"Local Group." Wikipedia, May 5, 2015. https://en.wikipedia.org/wiki/Local_Group.

"Lunar Mare." Wikipedia, November 1, 2013. https://en.wikipedia.org/wiki/Lunar _mare.

Mann, Adam. "Pleiades: The Seven Sisters Star Cluster." *Space*. Space.com, October 8, 2019. https://www.space.com/pleiades.html#:~:text=The%20Pleiades%20are%20a% 20group,Earth%20in%20the%20constellation%20Taurus.

"Mars Facts | All About Mars—NASA Mars Exploration." Accessed September 12, 2022. https://mars.nasa.gov/all-about-mars/facts/.

Maryboy, Nancy C. "A Collection of Curricula for the STARLAB Navajo Skies Cylin-der." Buffalo, NY: Science First/STARLAB, 0 0, 2008.

"Mary Colter's Desert View Watchtower." National Park Service. US Department of the Interior, September 21, 2019. https://www.nps.gov/grca/learn/photosmultimedia/ Mary-Colter---Indian-Watchtower.htm.

"Messier Object." Wikipedia, January 17, 2019. https://en.wikipedia.org/wiki/Messier _object.

"Mission San José De Tumacácori." National Park Service. US Department of the Interior. Accessed December 1, 2021. https://www.nps.gov/subjects/travelspanish missions/mission-san-jose-de-tumacacori.htm.

"Mount Graham." Wikipedia, February 7, 2014. https://en.wikipedia.org/wiki/Mount _Graham.

"Mount Lemmon Air Force Station." Wikipedia, December 1, 2012. https://en.wiki pedia.org/wiki/Mount_Lemmon_Air_Force_Station.

"National Natural Landmarks (US National Park Service)." National Park Service. US Department of the Interior, October 6, 2021. https://www.nps.gov/subjects/nnland marks/index.htm.

"National Natural Landmarks Grapevine Mesa Joshua Trees." National Park Service. US Department of the Interior. Accessed January 20, 2022. https://www.nps.gov/ subjects/nnlandmarks/site.htm?Site=GRME-AZ.

National Science Foundation. "The Milky Way Has 'Arms' and You've Probably Never Even Seen Them!" Accessed September 6, 2022. https://www.nsf.gov/mps/ast/out reach/MilkyWayLEDCraft2019.pdf.

"Native Constellations." Western Washington University, March 2, 2022. https://www .wwu.edu/astro101/indiansky.shtml.

"Nature—Grand Canyon National Park (US National Park Service)." www.nps.gov, July 16, 2018. https://www.nps.gov/grca/learn/nature/index.htm.

"Navajo." Wikipedia, August 1, 2016. https://en.wikipedia.org/wiki/Navajo.

"Northern Arizona." Wikipedia, December 1, 2009. https://en.wikipedia.org/wiki/ Northern_Arizona.

"Observatories in Arizona." 2021 List. *Go Astronomy*. Blue Moose Design, LLC, 2021. https://www.go-astronomy.com/observatories-state.php?State=AZ.

"Organ Pipe Cactus International Biosphere Reserve." National Park Service. US Department of the Interior, September 6, 2016. https://www.nps.gov/orpi/learn/ nature/biosphere.htm.

"Overview of Lake Mohave—Lake Mead National Recreation Area (US National Park Service)." Accessed September 11, 2022. https://www.nps.gov/lake/learn/nature/ overview-of-lake-mohave.htm.

"Painted Rock Petroglyph Campground." Bureau of Land Management. US Department of the Interior. Accessed January 27, 2022. https://www.blm.gov/visit/painted -rock-petroglyph-campground.

"Painted Rock Petroglyph Site." Wikipedia, March 30, 2021. https://en.wikipedia.org/ wiki/Painted_Rock_Petroglyph_Site.

Plotner, T. "Messier 8 (M8)—The Lagoon Nebula." Universe Today, March 21, 2016. https://www.universetoday.com/31235/messier-8/.

"Polaris." *Encyclopedia Britannica*. Accessed September 28, 2022. https://www.britannica .com/place/Polaris-star.

"Ponderosa Pine (*Pinus ponderosa*)—Forest Research and Outreach." ucanr.edu. Accessed July 28, 2022. https://ucanr.edu/sites/forestry/California_forests/http___ ucanrorg_sites_forestry_California_forests_Tree_Identification_/Ponderosa_Pine _Pinus_ponderosa/.

Priest, Susan S., et al. "The San Francisco Volcanic Field, Arizona." USGS Fact Sheet 017 -01. pubs.usgs.gov, April 16, 2001. https://pubs.usgs.gov/fs/2001/fs017-01/.

"Programs: National Conservation Lands: Arizona: Gila Box Riparian: Bureau of Land Management." Gila Box Riparian NCA. Bureau of Land Management. US Department of the Interior. Accessed April 30, 2022. https://www.blm.gov/national -conservation-lands/arizona/gilabox.

"Rho Ophiuchi Cloud Complex." Wikipedia, January 13, 2022. https://en.wikipedia .org/wiki/Rho_Ophiuchi_cloud_complex.

Rymer, Cathy. "The Ironwood: Stately Sanctuary in the Sonoran Desert." The Master Gardener Journal. University of Arizona Cooperative Extension, July 2003. https://cals .arizona.edu/maricopa/garden/html/pubs/0803/ironwood.html#:~:text=The%20 ironwood%20is%20one%20of,as%20long%20as%201%2C500%20years.

Sabino Canyon Crawler. Regional Partnering Center, May 5, 2021. https://sabino canyoncrawler.com/.

"Sabino Canyon Recreation Area." Coronado National Forest—Sabino Canyon Recreation Area. USDA Forest Service. Accessed December 2, 2021. https://www.fs.usda .gov/recarea/coronado/recarea/?recid=75425.

"Sabino Canyon Recreation Area." Coronado National Forest—Sabino Canyon Recreation Area. USDA Forest Service. Accessed December 2, 2021. https://www.fs.usda .gov/recarea/coronado/recarea/?recid=80532.

"Sabino Canyon." Visit Arizona. Accessed December 2, 2021. https://www.visitarizona .com/places/parks-monuments/sabino-canyon/.

"Saguaro National Park (US National Park Service)." National Park Service. US Department of the Interior. Accessed January 4, 2022. https://www.nps.gov/sagu/index.htm.

"Saguaro National Park." Wikipedia, December 29, 2021. https://en.wikipedia.org/ wiki/Saguaro_National_Park.

"Salt River (Arizona)." Wikipedia, January 21, 2022. https://en.wikipedia.org/wiki/ Salt_River_(Arizona).

"San Francisco Peaks." Wikipedia, February 5, 2021. https://en.wikipedia.org/wiki/ San_Francisco_Peaks.

Sessions, Larry. "Top 10 Cool Things about Stars." EarthSky, May 24, 2016. https:// earthsky.org/space/ten-things-you-may-not-know-about-stars/#millions.

"Southern Arizona." Wikipedia, September 14, 2021. https://en.wikipedia.org/wiki/ Southern_Arizona.

"Stargazing in Arizona Dark Skies." Visit Arizona. Accessed December 1, 2021. https:// www.visitarizona.com/places/dark-skies/.

Stein, Vicky. "What Is the Speed of Light?" Space.com, January 21, 2022. https://www .space.com/15830-light-speed.html.

"The Meadow (US National Park Service)," September 2021. https://www.nps.gov/ places/000/the-meadow.htm.

Town of Gilbert, Arizona. "Rotary Centennial Observatory." Accessed September 30, 2022. https://www.gilbertaz.gov/departments/parks-and-recreation/riparian-preserve -at-water-ranch/public-programs/rotary-centennial-observatory.

Tran, Lina. "Why NASA Watches Airglow, the Colors of the (Upper Atmospheric) Wind." NASA, October 2018. https://www.nasa.gov/feature/goddard/2018/why -nasa-watches-airglow-the-colors-of-the-upper-atmospheric-wind.

"University of Arizona Telescopes." UArizona Research, Innovation, and Impact. University of Arizona, September 30, 2020. https://research.arizona.edu/facilities/telescopes.

US Census Bureau. "US Census Bureau QuickFacts: Arizona." Accessed October 1, 2022. https://www.census.gov/quickfacts/AZ.

US National Park Service. "Hohokam Culture," August 2017. https://www.nps.gov/ articles/hohokam-culture.htm.

US National Park Service. "Leave No Trace Seven Principles." Accessed October 1, 2022. https://www.nps.gov/articles/leave-no-trace-seven-principles.htm.

"US Naval Observatory Flagstaff Station." Wikipedia, February 18, 2016. https://en .wikipedia.org/wiki/United_States_Naval_Observatory_Flagstaff_Station.

"Vermilion Cliffs National Monument." Bureau of Land Management. www.blm.gov. Accessed August 22, 2022. https://www.blm.gov/national-conservation-lands/arizona/ vermilion-cliffs.

"Virgo Supercluster." Wikipedia, March 17, 2012. https://en.wikipedia.org/wiki/Virgo _Supercluster.

"Visit the SkyCenter." SkyCenter. Accessed September 2, 2022. https://skycenter
.arizona.edu/content/visit-skycenter.

"Visualize the Sun's Path through Milky Way." Sky Archive. EarthSky, January 20, 2017.
https://earthsky.org/sky-archive/two-stars-flag-suns-path-in-milky-way/#:~:text
=The%20sun%20in%20its%20orbit,through%20the%20Milky%20Way%20 galaxy.

"Weaver's Needle, Superstition Mountains, Central Arizona." University of Arizona Science Arizona Geological Survey. University of Arizona, September 27, 2018. https://
azgs.arizona.edu/photo/weavers-needle-superstition-mountains-central-arizona.

"What Are Sky Islands?" USDA Forest Service. United States Department of Agriculture. Accessed November 29, 2021. https://www.fs.usda.gov/wildflowers/beauty/
Sky_Islands/whatare.shtml.

"Why You Should Experience the Painted Rock Petroglyph Site." YouTube. *Archaeology
Southwest*, October 11, 2019. https://www.youtube.com/watch?v=C8Myf6y6p4o.

"Woods Canyon Lake." Wikipedia, May 17, 2008. https://en.wikipedia.org/wiki/Woods
_Canyon_Lake.

Zawacki, Emily. "Why Are the Rocks of Sedona, Arizona, Red?" YouTube, August 8,
2017. https://www.youtube.com/watch?v=aK7Hzz2kmrw.

"Zodiacal Light." *Encyclopedia Britannica*. Accessed October 4, 2022. https://www
.britannica.com/science/zodiacal-light.